D1272861

FLORIDA STATE
UNIVERSITY LIBRARIES

MAY 3 0 2001

TALLAHASSEE, FLORIDA

ROMANTICISM IN PERSPECTIVE:
TEXTS, CULTURES, HISTORIES

General Editors:
Marilyn Gaull, *Professor of English,
Temple University/New York University*
Stephen Prickett, *Regius Professor of English Language and Literature,
University of Glasgow*

This series aims to offer a fresh assessment of Romanticism by looking at it from a wide variety of perspectives. Both comparative and interdisciplinary, it will bring together cognate themes from architecture, art history, landscape gardening, linguistics, literature, philosophy, politics, science, social and political history and theology to deal with original, contentious or as yet unexplored aspects of Romanticism as a Europe-wide phenomenon.

Titles include

Richard Cronin (*editor*)
1798: THE YEAR OF THE *LYRICAL BALLADS*

Péter Dávidházi
THE ROMANTIC CULT OF SHAKESPEARE: Literary
Reception in Anthropological Perspective

David Jasper
THE SACRED AND SECULAR CANON IN ROMANTICISM
Preserving the Sacred Truths

Malcolm Kelsall
JEFFERSON AND THE ICONOGRAPHY OF ROMANTICISM
Folk, Land, Culture and the Romantic Nation

Andrew McCann
CULTURAL POLITICS IN THE 1790s: Literature, Radicalism
and the Public Sphere

The Romantic Cult
of Shakespeare

Literary Reception in
Anthropological Perspective

Péter Dávidházi

First published in Great Britain 1998 by
MACMILLAN PRESS LTD
Houndmills, Basingstoke, Hampshire RG21 6XS and London
Companies and representatives throughout the world

A catalogue record for this book is available from the British Library.

ISBN 0–333–69827–4

First published in the United States of America 1998 by
ST. MARTIN'S PRESS, INC.,
Scholarly and Reference Division,
175 Fifth Avenue, New York, N.Y. 10010

ISBN 0–312–21287–9

Library of Congress Cataloging-in-Publication Data
Dávidházi, Péter.
The Romantic cult of Shakespeare : literary reception in
anthropological perspective / Péter Dávidházi.
p.   cm. — (Romanticism in perspective)
Includes bibliographical references and index.
ISBN 0–312–21287–9 (cloth)
1. Shakespeare, William, 1564–1616—Appreciation—Hungary.
2. Shakespeare, William, 1564–1616—Criticism and interpretation-
-History.   3. Shakespeare, William, 1564–1616—Appreciation-
-England.   4. Criticism—Hungary—History—19th century.
5. Literature and anthropology.   6. Romanticism—Hungary.
7. Romanticism—England.   8. Romanticism—Europe.   I. Title.
II. Series.
PR2979.H8D38   1998
822.3'3—dc21   97–42323
                                                                      CIP

© Péter Dávidházi 1998

All rights reserved. No reproduction, copy or transmission of this publication may be made
without written permission.

No paragraph of this publication may be reproduced, copied or transmitted save with
written permission or in accordance with the provisions of the Copyright, Designs and
Patents Act 1988, or under the terms of any licence permitting limited copying issued by
the Copyright Licensing Agency, 90 Tottenham Court Road, London W1P 9HE.

Any person who does any unauthorised act in relation to this publication may be liable to
criminal prosecution and civil claims for damages.

The author has asserted his right to be identified as the author of this work in accordance
with the Copyright, Designs and Patents Act 1988.

This book is printed on paper suitable for recycling and made from fully managed and
sustained forest sources.

10   9   8   7   6   5   4   3
07   06   05   04   03   02   01   00

Printed and bound in Great Britain by
Antony Rowe Ltd, Chippenham, Wiltshire

In memory
of my parents

Contents

Preface

'With us islanders *Shakespeare* is a kind of established religion in poetry.' The sentence is from an essay published in 1753 by Arthur Murphy to justify the ways of Shakespeare to Voltaire. Comparing the British reverence for the Bard to some kind of religion could have no pejorative overtones in this context. The metaphor was meant to be affirmative, though it was no more than a casual association, left unexamined and undeveloped in the subsequent text, in spite of occasional references to 'our immortal bard' whose amazing imagination explored 'undiscovered regions of eternity'.[1] The metaphor of religion or cult haunted the commentators of Shakespeare's afterlife in the centuries to come, but usually it expressed less sympathy for the phenomena in question, and was often used in a derisive or condescending manner, accentuated by a subversive tone of playful irony.

With no intention either to vindicate or to discredit, in this book I am trying to investigate what happens when we take the metaphor seriously. (If taking the ironical at its face value is a sign of *heroische Borniertheit* or a simplistic mind, the book may be used as sufficient evidence against its author.) Its underlying assumption is that the reception of Shakespeare in several European countries over the last two centuries can be viewed as the dissemination of a secular cult whose psychology, ritual and rhetoric reveal latent religious patterns. I cannot promise to give a full explanation of *why* this quasi-religious behaviour was adopted, and I confess to have but vague, tentative, unverified and (despite some evidence) probably unverifiable ideas about connections between (say) the birth of this literary cult and the crises of traditional religious authority in eighteenth-century England,[2] or between the Victorian transformation of Shakespeare festivals and a need for quasi-transcendental legitimations of the national ethos and its implied social hierarchy. Books have always been written at least as much by the ignorance as by the knowledge of their authors: it is the limits of our understanding that make the treatment of a topic possible at all, and with a subject as intricate as mine one has to be especially aware of the many questions left unanswered. My ambition is merely to reveal something of *how* this literary cult emerged, how it made use of some important Romantic notions (genius, originality, imagination, transcendental analogies of artistic creation), how differently it appeared in some other countries (like Hungary), and how its overall cultural significance can be evaluated without premature hostilities. There is always hope that the very rudimentariness of an account may instigate others to provide a more refined and complete version.

Yet even this modest aim requires a combination of literary scholarship and cultural anthropology. Literary historians used to be engaged in analysing the dramas themselves, whatever that may mean, or the history of Shakespeare criticism as a sequence of ideas and judgements, and only recently have they tackled the wider cultural history of the appropriation of Shakespeare. Cultural anthropologists, on the other hand, traditionally studied the ritual of African tribes, and more recently the new sects and cults of the United States, or (as in the inspiring work of Victor Turner) more familiar yet hitherto rarely examined forms of symbolic actions ranging from Christian pilgrimage to the carnival in Rio. As was pointed out recently, 'few cultural anthropologists would dispute' the aptness of the simile implied by the phrase 'bardolatry', namely 'that the author-cult of Shakespeare has functioned, and continues to function, as a kind of religion';[3] yet cultural anthropologists have avoided this terrain, and it was a long time before literary scholars discovered its importance for their own discipline. If and when the Shakespeare cult in its own right *as* a literary cult was granted sustained treatment at all, it was viewed as a conglomerate of curious anecdotes and amusing oddities not worth the serious attention of the scholar.

This can explain the great distance, indeed a barren no man's land, that used to separate scholarly and popular works on our subject, a separation so detrimental to both sides. While one should acknowledge one's indebtedness to the authors of both higher and lower scholarly prestige, their differences cannot be overlooked. R. W. Babcock's monograph (1931) on the history of English Shakespeare criticism in the late eighteenth century (*The Genesis of Shakespeare Idolatry 1766–1799*) was and forever remains a fine piece of positivist scholarship, even if it ignores all manifestations of idolatry except those surfacing in critical opinion. Books that did pay attention to non-verbal phenomena of the cult used to be lacking in a consistent point of view. Ivor Brown and George Fearon's *Amazing Monument* (1939) is a short, witty but somewhat superficial history of what the authors called the Shakespeare 'industry'; F. E. Halliday's book has a promising title, *The Cult of Shakespeare* (1957), but its author did not take its central metaphor seriously enough to explore its workings in a unified way. Louis Marder's *His Exits and His Entrances* (1963) surveyed the history of Shakespeare's reputation, including cultic phenomena as well, but they appear sporadically and in miscellaneous company. Although there was much to learn from these somewhat kaleidoscopic works, I have more to thank in pioneering monographs focusing on single Shakespeare anniversaries, like those of Christian Deelman, Martha Winburn England and Johanne M. Stochholm on the 1769 Garrick Jubilee (all published in 1964) or that of Richard Foulkes (1984) on the tercentenary festivals of Stratford and London, even if these works are not looking for connections between these celebrations and the history of Shakespeare criticism. Nearer to synthesizing is Samuel Schoenbaum's monumental *Shakespeare's Lives*, especially in its revised and updated 1991 edition; though its aim was to detect the myth-making processes in the biographies written on Shakespeare, it often traces those processes, luckily, beyond the verbal domain. Even more comprehensive is Gary Taylor's *Reinventing Shakespeare* (1989), immensely thought-provoking even when one is tempted to disagree, yet its self-confessed striving for the 'whole story' and the 'total' social structure was bound to leave something to be gleaned by a narrower, anthropologically oriented method. Though less panoramic, very instructive are some excellent recent works on Shakespeare's appropriation, like Jonathan Bate's *Shakespeare and the English Romantic Imagination* (1986) and *Shakespearean Constitutions* (1989), Margreta de Grazia's *Shakespeare Verbatim* (1991), Michael Dobson's *The Making of the National Poet* (1992), Jean Marsden's *The Re-Imagined Text* (1995) and Simon Jarvis's *Scholars and Gentlemen* (1995). Reading them it was no little relief to realize that their approaches to Shakespeare's reception are different from mine: whether they explain it in terms of cultural history, textual scholarship, theatrical adaptations, literary influences or political uses, they do not render superfluous (though sometimes they overlap with) an examination of the role played by the quasi-religious. Trying to keep a consistent, though not exclusive, focus on the religious psychology of cult formation is also different from the dominantly political interest of the authors who contributed to *The Shakespeare Myth* (edited by Graham Holderness) and from other works by the adherents of cultural materialism. Neither do I share the belief in the overwhelming importance of social aims, whether subversive or otherwise, in scholarship. Among books published outside of Britain or the United States two proved to be especially relevant: Michèle Willems's *La Genèse du mythe Shakespearien 1660–1780* (1979) and, though not on a Shakespearean topic, Balz Engler's *Poetry and Community* (1990). Reading the latter and getting to know its author in 1995 was like being reassured of long-cherished convictions that otherwise might have seemed idiosyncratic or even hallucinatory.

My indebtedness for the inspiration received from persons and for the hospitality of institutions is greater than I can express. All through the five years (from 1968 to 1973) of my studies at Eötvös Loránd University, Budapest, I had the privilege of being taught by Kálmán Ruttkay, a fine Shakespeare scholar with a contagious passion for eighteenth-century English literature, who incited his students to think for themselves in scholarship as well as in politics in an age of official blinkers. To the year I spent at the University of Sussex (1977–8) I owe the perspective learned from its 'core and context' scheme of studies: probably it was the Sussex ideal of interdisciplinary cross-fertilization that encouraged me (almost a decade later) to couple the history of literary criticism with cultural anthropology; and it was one of my Sussex professors, Stephen Prickett, who subsequently helped me all through the long road that led to this book. In the academic year 1985–6 I was invited to join the Program of Critical Theory directed by Murray Krieger at the University of California, Irvine, and to see René Wellek's library. (Receiving benevolent letters, offprints and books from Wellek himself in the 1980s endowed my peripheral existence with sustaining, if undeserved, dignity.) In Irvine it was possible to do research for nine months in more carefree circumstances than ever before, to benefit from the postgraduate seminars of Wolfgang Iser, and to learn from Myron Simon who was ever ready to discuss with me any problems, whether theoretical, historical, or personal. Returning home I worked at the Institute for Literary Studies, Budapest, and it was here that I finished a book, *'Isten másodszülöttje': A magyar Shakespeare-kultusz természetrajza* ('God's Second Born': Anatomy of the Hungarian Cult of Shake-

speare), surveying the history of Shakespeare's Hungarian afterlife from its late eighteenth-century beginnings to our own day.
Two of my colleagues from the English Department of Eötvös
Loránd University, Ádám Nádasdy and Ferenc Takács, were helping
me with advice and criticism as that book took shape. Before it
was published at the end of 1989 I was able to spend three months
as a Folger-Soros Fellow in the Folger Shakespeare Library; as an
outsider I gratefully remember the encouragement received there
from Gary Taylor; also the advice of Barbara Mowat, though I
could not take it at the time, that I should write a comparative
study on the subject. For two months in the summers of 1993
and 1995 British Academy scholarships made it possible for me
to do research in the hospitable library of the Institute of Germanic
Studies (belonging to the University of London); in 1995 that was
complemented by a month in Trinity College, Cambridge, in the
inspiring company of Anne Barton, Jeremy Maule and Roger
Paulin. Finally it was there, in the college of such admired authors
of my youth as Frazer, Whitehead, Russell and Wittgenstein, that
I realized the utter hopelessness, yet the unquestionable obligation,
of trying to repay at least a fraction of what we receive.

Acknowledgements

Two brief sections of Chapter 3 have been previously published, albeit in a different and less developed form, in the essays I contributed respectively to *European Shakespeares: Translating Shakespeare in the Romantic Age* (eds Dirk Delabastita and Lieven D'hulst, Amsterdam: John Benjamins, 1993) and to *Shakespeare and Hungary* (Shakespeare Yearbook vol. 7, eds Holger Klein and Péter Dávidházi, Lewiston, Queenston, Lampeter: The Edwin Mellen Press, 1996). I thank both publishers for kindly allowing me to modify and incorporate material whose copyright they possess.

1

The Exploration of a Literary Cult: Theoretical Assumptions and Methodological Problems

'Shakespeare's recognition is part and parcel of civilization. It is a kind of *cult* testifying *culture*.' It was with these solemn words that the Hungarian Mór Jókai (whose exuberantly romantic novels were widely read in nineteenth-century Europe and enjoyed by Queen Victoria herself)[1] began his account of the 1864 production of *A Midsummer-Night's Dream*, a lavish tercentenary performance of the National Theatre followed by an afterpiece enacting the apotheosis of the Bard. His observation that our reverence for Shakespeare is a kind of cult could have survived as the fascinating starting point of closer scrutiny but it was ignored because it sounded deceptively like a commonplace aphoristic equation, a claim to possess some clear-cut, ultimate and *final* wisdom, evoking a self-deluding sense of knowing all there is to know (or at least worth knowing) about the subject. Similarly, the contention that this cult is an indication of culture, and that the former is (always and of necessity) evidence of the latter, sounded like a merely rhetorical embellishment of a tercentenary article, not to be taken seriously as a challenging thesis that would be worth testing, verifying or falsifying by empirical means. And this situation has not changed substantially since then; the facile acceptance of unexamined metaphors and all-too-familiar rhetorical statements tends to preclude critical analysis. The phrase 'Shakespeare cult' is one of those terminological counters we play with far too thoughtlessly both in the technical discourse of our discipline and in the more casual language games of the educated layman. A counter assumed to be convertible into practically every currency, it is hardly ever considered worth defining, and even

1

less do we take it seriously as a possible object of systematic research. The juxtaposition of 'Shakespeare' and 'cult' looks so disarmingly simple that we immediately accept it as a solution and thereby lose sight of the problem. We tend to forget that when yoked together, the name of a writer and that of a religious phenomenon suggest a daring hypothesis, assuming the existence of a latent analogy between literary life and religious practice. Nor does it occur to us that a patient exploration of that analogy and its amply documented historical variants could enhance our knowledge about the anatomy of literary cults in general and maybe, to a lesser extent, that of other quasi-religious secular cults as well. To achieve this, the analogy should be allowed to reorient our research: the traditionally central problems of Shakespeare's reception (aesthetic norms, translation, etc.) will be taken out of their usual context of literary criticism, linguistics, history of ideas or translation studies, to be treated within an interdisciplinary framework constituted by the anthropology of literature.

The methodological consequences of turning a casual metaphor like the Shakespeare cult into a heuristic technical term and taking it seriously enough to let it serve as the organizing principle of research are enormous and not without certain risks. The results of any scholar's approach to the afterlife of Shakespeare and his works will always and of necessity reflect the theoretical and methodological assumptions the research started with. Having given up the positivist dream of collecting the corpus of the so-called basic facts before subjecting them to subsequent interpretation, it is only fair to admit the ineluctably self-serving tendency of the underlying assumption which determines the selection and combination, indeed the very construction, of facts in one's account of Shakespeare's reception as the workings of a literary cult. Whether classified as psychological, ritual or rhetorical phenomena, neither the latent meaning of countless examples nor their remarkable coherence can be grasped *unless* we assume the presence of an underlying religious pattern, but then the assumption itself is greatly responsible for the conclusions drawn from the material it helped to select. Our conclusions are governed by a terminology suggested by a hypothetical system of correspondences between literary and cultic phenomena: once the central analogy is accepted, the apologetic strategies of criticism will resemble the arguments of *theodicy*, devout journeys to Stratford will recall *pilgrimages*, the enthusiastic acquisition of little objects that used to belong to Shakespeare will remind us of *relic worship*, people's behaviour at some anniversary celebrations of the poet's birth will look like participation in a quasi-religious *ritual*. We may (and should) use strict criteria before actually accepting something as analogous with theodicy, pilgrimage, relic worship or ritual, but a residual element of fictitiousness will be omnipresent in the findings of our research. The same applies to naming the historical epochs of Shakespeare's Hungarian reception according to their respective cultic functions (the ages of 'initiation', 'myth-making', 'institutionalization', 'iconoclasm', 'secularization and revival'); no matter how apt such terms may seem within our chosen perspective, they will inevitably reduce and to some extent recreate the phenomena we are dealing with, leaving us no other consolation than the thought that this would not be otherwise with *any* terminology, and the degree of adequacy can always be tested by searching for exceptions or demonstrating the (inevitable) need for complementary explanations.

Although one can fully agree with the observation that 'cult' as a term 'can never be more than the modern researcher's collective label for a set of phenomena', that highlighting merely the cultic function of (say) translating Shakespeare is not 'the whole answer', and that in this maximalist sense of course 'it does not add up to an explanation' or 'account for' 'what happened',[2] as a critique this is not as devastating as it looks, and it could be levelled with more or less justification against practically any other method as well. Causal explanations are bound to be somewhat inconclusive and deficient if only because 'in an ultimate sense' (as René Wellek persuasively argued) they are 'impossible in matters of mind; cause and effect are incommensurable, the effect of specific causes unpredictable'; the social situation determines whether something is possible (as opposed to its being actually realized) in the realm of art, and nobody 'has yet succeeded in proving that because of certain events either in history or in literature there must have followed another specific event'.[3] Furthermore, the objection that the cultic pattern can never pass for a pure and uncontaminated explanation of the phenomena themselves relies far too heavily on old positivist assumptions no longer tenable: that we could get direct access to 'what happened', that we could see events in themselves and not *as* something, not *as* (partly at least) something *else*, and that we could 'adequately describe' and fully explain them without any kind of retrospective addition. However, even the above-quoted adversary of this approach was ready to assume that there may be something to be gained from describing the reception of Shakespeare in terms of a literary cult, and to me this gain seems to be considerable, making it worth trying, if only as a complement to more traditional methods. By no means offered as the ultimate explanation or a comprehensive description of the means by which European culture assimilated Shakespeare's heritage, the heuristic assumption of a cultic analogy may help us to make sense of data otherwise disconnected, underrated or ignored, even if this sense is partly made by the assumption itself.

THREE ASPECTS OF A LITERARY CULT

To explore the reception of Shakespeare as the manifestation of a cult can, at the very least, complement the work of literary historians or historians of criticism who often deplore (and ignore) some critical responses to Shakespeare as conceptually empty outbursts of enthusiasm. Especially when the scholar's reflexes have been conditioned by the neopositivist mistrust in the meaningfulness of emotive language and aesthetic judgements[4] or (say) by the anti-rhetorical essentialism of British empirical philosophy, most eulogistic references to Shakespeare will sound meaningless and irrelevant verbiage. For the historian of a literary cult, however, even the unargued and soaring praise is worth studying because its allusions and rhetorical devices may reveal the psychology of cult formation. The literary historian may be right, from his point of view, when dismissing an 1834 account in the Hungarian press about the 1769 Stratford Jubilee as an article that offered to the contemporary reader nothing but a bunch of shallow commonplaces about Shakespeare,[5] yet to the historian of the cult the same article is a precious document because it let the contemporary reader know how the civilized English nation revered little objects as relics just because they were made of Shakespeare's mulberry tree, and implied that a writer (what is more, one of humble origin) can be considered worthy of quasi-religious adoration. The article tells little, if anything, about the literary characteristics of Shakespeare's *oeuvre*, but it initiates the reader into his cult. The last sentence, exhorting Hungarians to erect a similar memorial statue for Károly Kisfaludy, an early Romantic poet, playwright, writer and editor, one of the fathers of modern Hungarian literature, tells nothing whatsoever about Shakespeare, but makes the implied approbation of a cultural transfer explicit: it endorses the transplantation of a set of reverential customs and ritual into the realm of secular literature.[6] The historian of cultic behaviour must be grateful for the generic diversity and generous comprehensiveness of anthologies like Brian Vickers' six-volume *Shakespeare: The Critical Heritage* or the bulky *Magyar Shakespeare-tükör* (*Hungarian Shakespeare Mirror*) compiled by Kálmán Ruttkay and Sándor Maller; had their editors excluded everything but cogently argued critical works, these collections could not have preserved so many valuable documents of cult-formation and would have been much less useful for our purposes. A reviewer of the latter anthology reproached its editors for having included texts teeming with irrelevant commonplaces about Shakespeare; however, these very documents may be analysed as indirect evidence telling us more about the anatomy of a literary cult than many a critical masterpiece would do. The cultic significance of a text may be entirely independent of its referential worth as a statement about its professed object.

But to re-evaluate documents first we have to define the cultic. Just as the loose, elusive and irresponsible use of the concept of 'myth' exasperates those longing for a clear-cut terminology,[7] it would be well-nigh impossible to use the word 'cult' as a technical term without first trying to mark out the limits of its conceptual realm. Yet ever since Ben Jonson's famous contention that he loved Shakespeare and did honour his memory 'on this side idolatry',[8] those innocent enough to believe in the neat separability of the two sides had to realize how difficult it is to tell where exactly the non-cultic ends or the cultic begins, in texts, in other people and not least in ourselves. When trying to identify the 'mark of idolatry' Alfred Harbage (in an essay ironically heading the 1964 quatercentenary number of the *Shakespeare Quarterly*) confidently thought it to be 'not excessive enthusiasm, a rapturous tone, the use of superlatives, the invention of new terms of praise in ecstatic prose or verse' like Ben Jonson's comparing Shakespeare to gods ('like Apollo . . . like a Mercury'), but the substitution of the plays' artistic excellence with the myth of their supposed universal perfection, the turning of human artefacts into absolute standards of all kinds of human achievement, be it scientific, ethical, historical or philosophical, the 'idolatrous transformation' of a play 'into something it is *not*', robbing us 'of the wonderful thing which, in parts, it really *is*'.[9] Such strictures against the 'transmutation'[10] of Shakespeare rely on the tacit positivist or objectivist assumption that there is a *real* Shakespeare (Harbage actually makes this assumption explicit) and that we can get to know him through the right kind of knowledge; this stance is not only unduly hostile to bardolatry, condemning it without noticing its positive contributions to culture, but its wholesale condemnation seems to rely on a naive epistemological realism that can hardly be justified. When he maintained that 'faith should begin where we reach the limits of knowledge' and committed himself in general to the down-to-earth 'sons of Martha', the biographers, the textual scholar, the literary historian, the 'rational' critic, all 'this side idolatry', he meant not only to warn against an undue supplementation (or contamination) of positive and self-contained knowledge with mere belief, but he was also firmly convinced that no residue of such contamination was unavoidable. Yet Harbage had to realize that in actual cases the purely non-cultic is hard to find: when trying to defend Coleridge from the usual accusation of idolatry, he acknowledged that he could only partly do so, and he discovered traces of the cultic in himself as well. He confessed that he was 'devoted to primitive Shakespeareanity' and realized that nobody 'can claim total immunity from the effects of the myth of perfection', much as we all 'should combat it, in others and ourselves'.[11] (The phrase 'Shakespeareanity', most probably coined on the analogy of 'Christianity', had already been used with a more transparently analogous spelling by Douglas Jerrold in 1842, who made one of his protagonists call the strolling players 'the humble, much-enduring missionaries for the diffusion of Shakespearianity', combining the roles of 'the merry preacher' and 'the poet's pilgrim'.[12])

In recent decades many a scholar has likewise found that to stay this side idolatry is not simply a matter of determination. Kenneth Muir's essay, despite its programmatic title *This Side Idolatry* and its proclaimed aim of surveying the flaws in Shakespeare's plays and the modern critical strategies used for explaining them away, leads to the author's recognition that much as he came to bury Shakespeare, not to praise him, he uses the same apologetic devices himself.[13] Even as resolutely irreverent a historian of Shakespeare's reputation as Gary Taylor feels obliged to confess that he sometimes followed the common apologetic practice of modern criticism in not only excusing but actually praising Shakespeare for the very incoherence of temporal sequence that Thomas Rymer had reprobated.[14] The search for an argument by which a critic can applaud Shakespeare for the very thing he used to be reprimanded for is not uncommon in connection with other types of incongruence either; long gone are the days when the inexorable Malone, spotting that Shakespeare quoted the same document the second time with slight textual differences, attributed such 'inaccuracies' simply to the playwright's 'negligence', insisting on a regulative distinction between what the works would (and should) have been without the intervention of human frailty and the erratic actual versions.[15] Dr Johnson thought the critic should point out Shakespeare's faults in order to authenticate his praises; the modern scholar, the other way round, feels obliged to praise so as to authenticate his critical observations. Not even an author of major books on Shakespeare's 'unconformities' and their subsequent interpretative suppression can be completely exempt from this sense of obligation: Kristian Smidt's recent study '"Shakespeare can do no wrong": bardolatry and scholarship' (1994) ends with a somewhat apologetic remark, emphasizing the scholar's distance from 'iconoclasm *per se*', spelling out his admiration for Shakespeare (if only in the sober Jonsonian 'this side idolatry' sense), and characterizing his this-worldly approach as the indirect acknowledgement of a greatness verging on the transcendental. 'And I am sure one may be all the more impressed by his seemingly superhuman victories if one sees that they were won in constant battle with the limitations of common mortality.'[16] Yet all our failures to remain absolutely immune to the allurement of the *other side* cannot dishearten our attempts to draw a new dividing line and to observe the consequences of the inevitable trespasses and transfers.

To clarify our concept of 'cult' we do not need to find a universal and ultimate definition that claims to capture some kind of Platonic essence that all cults past, present and future are bound to approximate. Let it suffice to give a tentative definition of 'cult' merely for heuristic purposes, self-serving to some extent as all definitions inevitably are, and providing an instrument whereby to select relevant data out of the embarrassing richness history provides. Without such a criterion even a historical survey of Shakespeare's changing reputation is hardly possible; the problems of such attempts could be characterized by what Louis Marder says in defence of his inevitable omissions: 'Since everything with Shakespeare's name on it was considered as contributing to his reputation, the amount of material was unlimited.'[17] But the number of a scholar's days are limited, as is that of the pages at our disposal; to achieve the right kind of thematic limitation a clear concept of the literary cult is indispensable. No less important is a negative criterion: before a relatively late stage of research our definition should not impose an overall value judgement on the phenomena it tries to encapsulate; in other words, it should be as unbiased and uncommitted as possible. To meet these basic requirements we should bear in mind the common etymological root and subsequent divergence of 'cult' and 'culture': in Latin both *cultus* and *cultura* were derived from *colere* (*colo, colere, colui, cultus*) which meant 'to cultivate something' as well as 'to show respect for something'; almost the same symbiosis and latent dichotomy of the agricultural and the religious survived in *cultus* ('the cultivation of something; respect or adoration for something'), whereas *cultura* contained more uniformly down-to-earth meanings ('cultivation; richness; intellectual education') with no trace of the transcendental. Considering these antecedents I propose three-fold definitions to distinguish cult and culture in terms of their specific *attitudes*, their different *ritual* and their respective ways of using *language*. More precisely I call the reception of an author cultic if its manifestations correspond to three criteria: (a) an attitude of unconditional reverence (a priori apologetic explanations analogous with religious theodicy; an aversion to material representations analogous with religious iconophobia); (b) a ritual both verbal (hymnic praise, recital of laudatory verses) and behavioural (pilgrimage, relic worship, jubilees and other festivities with quasi-religious rites); and (c) a special use of language characterized by religious metaphors and similes as well as transcendental statements with no claim to (empirical) verifiability. As regards the conceptual domain of culture, it is wide enough to include the cultic but it also contains distinctive elements: (a) an attitude of conditional and qualified reverence, a principled denial of total self-submission, an insistence on critical analysis, on applying measures, on ascertaining degrees, on relative authority; (b) a dominantly secular ritual meant to regulate the understanding, evaluation and spread of cultural goods; (c) a use of language that prefers down-to-earth statements and is (at least virtually) amenable to empirical verifiability or falsifiability. This simplistic scheme is but a provisional heuristic device and does not correspond to the complexity of phenomena; nevertheless using, carefully and flexibly, these sets of criteria in order to decide which of the data are relevant for our purposes is not necessarily falling into the trap of formalism, or if it is, all sustained scholarship is formalistic. These three manifestations of any given cult are not independent of each other; indeed they may overlap so much that they turn out to be different aspects of the same thing. Cults may also differ in the relative dominance and changing proportions of these features, though usually they show a remarkably even distribution of all three properties.

Unconditional reverence

Interrelated as they are, the three main aspects of the Shakespeare cult should be separated for closer preliminary inspection. As regards its attitude of unconditional reverence, a commitment so total and devoted, so final and absolute that it precludes every conceivable criticism of its object, turns criticism into apology, and comes to the rescue whenever some artistic flaw of the plays needs explaining away, it survived its great Romantic heyday in the late eighteenth and early nineteenth centuries and is still with us, even though its latent transcendental premises have been exposed and refuted over and over again. In retrospect it sounds more an example of wishful thinking than a descriptive statement that in 1907 Walter Raleigh considered the great hyperbole of Shakespeare as the Creator already bereft of its former ceremonious function and thus irrevocably *passé*. Idolatrous attitudes die hard, and although Raleigh declared that it was high time to treat the playwright as a mere human being, a craftsman producing disputable dramatic personae and not flesh-and-blood people,[18] his admonition was often forgotten in the century to come. It was highly symptomatic that more than half a century later, in his quatercentenary lecture (in 1964) Frank Kermode still found it necessary to make the semi-serious statement that he assumed Shakespeare to have been a human being, not God, not an angel or saint, and that neither the playwright nor his *oeuvre* was incomparable and *sui generis*.[19] In the same year another commentator resented the overwhelming 'tyranny' of Shakespeare, lamenting that 'the spectacle afforded by modern criticism is the shadow boxing of rival bardolaters',[20] and as late as in 1972 a scholar analysing the relation between Shakespeare and his critics came to the conclusion that this author was still mostly beyond criticism, his plays had to be considered flawless, and teachers, critics, students and all kinds of readers were compelled to justify this indubitable perfection.[21] In 1977 a monograph still had to refute the myth of Shakespeare's unlettered genius, decades after T. W. Baldwin's painstaking analysis of Shakespeare's considerable learning (1944), because the miraculous version suited the English national mythology better than its more pedestrian rival would have done.[22] The imprint of this highly Romantic notion is still with us, as it was epitomized in Arnold's early sonnet *Shakespeare* (1844), a poet enigmatically 'Out-topping knowledge' yet 'Self-school'd, self-scann'd, self-honour'd, self-secure', an inscrutable, mountain-like giant of majestic heights and transcendental loneliness, 'Making the heaven of heavens his dwelling place' and sparing only 'the cloudy border of his base / To the foil'd searching of mortality'. In an age when greatness is cut to a reasonable size by psychological or historical contextualization, we are still prone to make an exception for Shakespeare, assuming him to be unfathomable and superhuman, and granting his work the privilege of a priori apologetic treatment.

In Hungary the apologetic techniques of Shakespeare criticism had been described (approvingly, though tongue-in-cheek) in a Latin treatise[23] by a university professor as early as 1784, and it came to be mastered and applied so skilfully that in retrospect its quasi-religious arguments and terminology look like the hallmarks of the Romantic age and constitute a characteristic part of its legacy. 'He is a genius of inexplicable perfection!'[24] The rapturous exclamation of Emil Buczy in 1817 relied not only on the Romantic notion of genius but also on the common quasi-transcendental assumption of the apologetic tradition: the critic should accept as perfect even what he cannot explain; moreover, inexplicability is an attribute, almost an indication, of Shakespeare's perfection. (One step further and we would be near to the logic of considering inexplicability as *evidence* of perfection, which is not far from the similarly reverential mentality of *credo quia absurdum*.) The most fully-fledged example of the Romantic manifestations of unconditional reverence is displayed in a review written by a later inheritor of this legacy. Grumbling about the shortcomings of an 1892 performance of *King John*, a Hungarian critic (publishing under the pseudonym Ignotus) made sure that his objections were not directed against Shakespeare whose winged genius he heard soaring above the poor theatrical representation. Moreover, Ignotus found the critical attitude out of place here: 'We confess timidly that we cannot ascend to the same height as the Germans who called *King John* a bad play, neither can we follow that colleague of ours who wrote an article in a newspaper to tell us what was wrong with the play.' This modesty in front of great things is subtly changing into humility in front of the sacred, the debate with others gives way to a gesture of confession, implying the common assumption of theodicy. It simply *cannot be* that the work of the Creator is flawed: 'We confess sincerely that we blame our own eyes if we see flaws in Shakespeare.' Yet the urge to defend Shakespeare against any conceivable objection searches for further apologetic arguments: 'For us all his plays are equally like a revelation, and we take off our shoes, hearing in them the eternal laws of humanity and poesy, disturbed only by a few distasteful features, confetti, and puns, for which the poet's age was responsible.' *Revelation* and *take off our shoes* and *eternal*: the vocabulary unmistakably highlights the latent analogy with the divine presence. (In the majestic scene of divine revelation, when God appeared to Moses in the burning bush, disclosing what his name was 'for ever' and revealing his will, he said 'put off thy shoes from off thy feet, for the place whereon thou standest *is* holy ground' (Exodus 3: 5; cf. Joshua 5: 15).) The latent equation of Shakespeare with God is so suggestive that it is hardly surprising to find (in Ignotus's next sentence) any earthly embodiment of his transcendental essence declared to be necessarily unworthy: 'And perhaps it is our unconditional admiration that makes us feel that there is hardly a theatre or an actor showing at least a shadow of what we cherish in Shakespeare.'[25]

This fully conscious and publicly self-confessed 'unconditional admiration' is so overwhelming that it employs two (otherwise alternative) types of apologetic strategies at the same time: the flaws spotted only seem to be flaws due to the imperfections of the critic's eyes; the flaws spotted are real but are caused by the necessary concessions even a genius had to make to the uncouth taste of his age. The logical peculiarity of this double apology is a symptomatic desire for over-security: the first argument could have sufficed, and the addition of the second causes a self-contradiction, because once the flaws are but a mere illusion, a false perception of ours, hallucinatory, deceptive and ultimately unreal, we need not (and cannot) blame them on Shakespeare's age and there are no real flaws to explain away. (This urge for over-security is probably an indication of the bad conscience caused by the sheer thought of artistic shortcomings in connection with the admired Bard; the cultic attitude is so strong that even the contemplation of unreal flaws is feared as blasphemy.) No less symptomatically, there is another latent self-contradiction in the argument as well: once we admit that compared to the direct mystical communion with the transcendental essence of divinity all communications via earthly embodiments can be but imperfect approximations, and once we apply the logic of this doctrine analogously to our relation to Shakespeare, we have no right to grumble about the shortcomings of any particular performance, nor can we be fully satisfied with any other performance. (Ignotus's last sentence shows some awareness of these logical implications of his premises.) This aversion to all man-made representations of the quasi-transcendental is psychologically related to what cultural anthropologists call *iconophobia*[26] in religious matters: the attitude that condemns as blasphemous 'any graven image, or any likeness *of any thing* that *is* in heaven above' (Exodus 20: 4), is of the same type as the one that makes somebody shudder at the thought of *any* performance of a Shakespeare play. In all these argumentative strategies we may recognize the basic manoeuvres of *theodicy*, originally a theological and philosophical genre in Christian apologetics and now transferred to literary criticism. Theodicies proper (that is, defensive theological treatises) were meant to confirm religious faith by trying to reconcile the dogma of God's perfection and omnipotence with the evils and miseries of our earthly existence; their self-confessed aim, to justify or vindicate the ways of God to man, was adopted by major didactic poems (like *Paradise Lost* or *An Essay on Man*) and philosophical works (by Leibniz, Shaftesbury and Hegel) and was adapted, consciously or otherwise, to the apologetic needs of Shakespeare criticism. Moreover, when seeking to explain away the artistic flaws discovered in the plays the same (now *quasi*-theological) defensive strategies are striving to overcome the ultimate self-contradiction familiar from religious apologetics: once we are convinced that something is inscrutable or inexplicable then it is useless to scrutinize it for a satisfactory explanation, and once something is considered unfathomable no discovery of its deepest meaning can be validated. If any Romantic was truly convinced that Shakespeare had been a genius of *inexplicable* perfection, or if any admirer of his plays truly believed in the allegorical equation of Shakespeare's work with that of God, then they had no right either to find a valid explanation or to feel superior when falsifying one proposed by somebody else. Inexplicable perfection is something to be postulated, that is to be assumed without proof to be true and subsequently to be attributed to somebody, but then the matter is closed, because our very act of providing more than a tentative and admittedly inconclusive explanation would belie the truth of our postulate or at least the seriousness of our commitment to it. The cultic attitude is logically self-consistent as long as it confines itself to worshipping the superhuman, but it cannot have a legitimate claim to rational analysis, and its pronouncements are essentially verbal rites rather than critical assertions.

The characteristic response that distinguishes the cultic attitude from the critical is the unconditional readiness to acknowledge and defend Shakespeare's unfathomable perfection even when the plays happen to show features the admirer would deplore in some (or any) other work written by somebody else. Hence the cultic attitude is too predictable not to preclude any serious critical analysis, and the inventiveness it fosters is that of finding apologetic arguments at all costs and against all odds, or of creating a quasi-religious idiom of adoration that exempts the critic from the obligation to test and argue altogether. In each case the cultic attitude implies a postulate of respectability as something taken for granted and unavailable for scrutiny; this implication seems to confirm the view that the modern notion of *prestige* may be derived from a kind of *taboo*, and that 'once tacitly adopted, taboo indicates a sealed inaccessibility, and contestation is substituted with increased emotional intensity'.[27] The interrelation of prestige and taboo is illustrated whenever we tacitly exclude the possibility that the Shakespeare play we are going to see or read can be imperfect, and whenever a critic desperately (with increased fervour) seeks for transcendental allusions or other devices of self-submission to praise the incontestable. As regards the attempts to seal the declared or implied inaccessibility of Shakespeare's perfection, the alternative to attributing transcendental qualities to his work is the critic's humble yet secularly worded admission of total self-surrender. To illustrate the latter device one should turn to post-romantic criticism, and quote a typically defeatist argument from an impressionist critic, like the Hungarian Viktor Cholnoky: whatever the critics have written about Shakespeare 'with the pretension of objective truth', it succeeded no more (at best) than those who wanted to climb Mont Blanc but managed to reach Grand Mulets only. The metaphor of mountaineering is exploited here to illustrate the uselessness of all external aids beyond a certain point: 'On this man-mountain one cannot climb higher than its waist, and we can but look up from there, with amazement and blissful adoration, to his alpine-like radiating face, throwing away the telescope, the mountaineer's stick, all the aids of our approach.' The argument unwittingly reveals how a Hungarian critic at the turn of the century (1908) used the occasion to extol Shakespeare for an indirect justification of his own impressionist methodology: illustrating the inaccessibility of Shakespeare by an extolling metaphor, the critic implicitly repudiates all analytical methods as futile procedures, and he explicitly endorses their substitution with sheer adoration and an acknowledgement of our ultimate helplessness: 'One can understand but fractions of Shakespeare via objective scrutiny, feeling the power of the whole invariably evokes in the human soul a subjective amazement, and the happy exclamation "no more research".'[28] This is not only a preference for amazement as opposed to scrutiny, but also the willing suspension of rationality in front of a quasi-transcendent being whose ways are inscrutable.

Finally it is in juxtaposition with its opposite that the cultic attitude can be summed up and the complementary descendants of *colere* can be shown to dovetail. Cultic deification and its unconditional admiration of the quasi-transcendental can be meaningfully contrasted with the entirely secular-minded perspective of those nineteenth-century critics, like the Hungarian Pál Gyulai, who insisted on a down-to-earth comparative and relativizing approach to Shakespeare even amid or after the lavish tercentenary panegyrics. As Gyulai reminded his rapturous fellow-critics in 1865, even the greatest of poets cannot always produce masterpieces but is bound to have some second-rate or third-rate works, even a genius may develop and decline like all other human beings, occasionally the formation of his work may be influenced by unfavourable circumstances, no artist can unite all sorts of excellences, and even the greatest strength is coupled with some kind of weakness or one-sidedness. 'Among the devotees of the Shake-

speare cult there are those ridiculous ones who find some pro-
fundity even in his simplest lines, idolize his very shortcomings,
and declare practically all his works equally exquisite masterpieces.'
Yet Gyulai's soberly balanced stance entails a no less resolute
condemnation of both extremes, on the one hand the snobbery
of those who frown upon the publication or staging of Shakespeare's less famous plays (theirs is 'a certain conceited rigour
and haughty derision *vis-à-vis* a great poet whom they don't care
to understand'), on the other those who forget that 'absolute
perfection can be but an ideal in art as well as in the realm of
morality; what we can truly expect is human perfection, which
is nothing else than a greater than usual share of good attributes.'[29]
Although in his more ecstatic moments, such as once in 1855,
Gyulai himself would call poetry a second revelation,[30] such
occasional forays into the quasi-transcendental do not go as far
as considering the critical evaluation of poetry illegitimate, needless
or impossible.

Ritual celebrations

The Shakespeare cult as *ritual* is a transfer of mostly religious
rites to literary life. With some of these rites the religious origin
is obvious, with others it is faded or indirect, and they can be
coupled (or merged) with symbolic actions of secular origin, but
the ensuing quasi-religious ritual is coherent enough to function
as a system and integrate even its originally disparate elements.
Some of the rites are verbal: predictably apologetic and theodicy-
like arguments serve ritual functions that descend from the glorifying intent of hymns; such arguments are but pseudo-critical,
though there is no distinct dividing line between quasi-religious
praise and criticism proper. Even more obvious is the hymnic
descent of those laudatory poems and songs which were read,
recited or sung in front of a community to celebrate the Bard:
both their quasi-liturgical function and their close-knit web of
transcendental allusions betray their cultic use. Studying literary
cults one can also find examples of barely secularized prayers,
like that of a Hungarian writer Magda Szabó who went to Yarmouth (as late as in 1962) to search for a spot of the seaside left
intact (hence still authentic) since Dickens's time, so as to be alone
there and to *thank* the writer (aloud) for the creation of *Oliver
Twist* and *David Copperfield*.[31] The non-verbal part of the ritual

system may include pilgrimages to sacred places, relic worship, the celebration of sacred times, enactments of Shakespeare's apotheosis (deification) and all sorts of communal festivities permeated by transcendental symbolism. It is no mere whim of the metaphorical imagination to associate the visit to Stratford with pilgrimages, especially to the places of birth (nativity) and death (grave, shrine) of a religious founder. Ever since the eighteenth century a growing number of people have been going to Stratford and felt the successive psychological stages of a literary pilgrimage; their pilgrim disposition is likely to make them collect or purchase mementoes of the poet revered as relics, be they little wooden objects made of the poet's mulberry tree or splinters carved off from his chair. A special subtype of relics consists of the manuscripts reputedly by Shakespeare, like the late eighteenth-century collection that inspired ecstatically devout gestures before they were discredited as forgeries. Nowadays printed souvenirs appeal to the pilgrim spirit dormant in many tourists: booklets of choice quotations from the Bard, like breviaries of old, are precious items to buy in one of the Shakespeare shrines, and many of them indicate somehow that they were issued, and indeed bought, in Stratford, that is after the spatial and (by implication) spiritual journey was duly accomplished by the new owner.

The best occasions for all these verbal and non-verbal rites are the Shakespeare festivals that descend from the long tradition of celebrating the centenaries and anniversaries of Shakespeare's birth and death. The ultimate origin of the rites and symbolic actions at such occasions is discernibly ancient and traditional, very often transparently biblical, though sometimes too far removed from its archetypal precedents to be easily identifiable. The genealogical recognizability of symbolic actions may range from the barely secularized version of the Eucharist at the 1769 Stratford Jubilee to the more elusive ceremony that took place in 1936 when a replica of the Globe theatre was opened in Dallas: lumps of earth taken from Shakespeare's garden and water from the Avon were sprinkled over the new stage. The earth was sent to America in a box made of the wood of the Stratford Memorial Theatre that was burned down in 1926, so even the box symbolized an authenticating continuity, the miraculous survival of things Shakespearean. The meaning of the ritual sprinkling must have been felt appropriate, yet the exact origin and steps of transmission of this symbolic action is difficult to ascertain, unless we are satisfied by casual associations like the parallel (drawn half-jokingly by the historians of the Shakespeare 'industry') between the function of Avon water for Shakespeareans and the magic power many Christian believers may attribute to the water of the Jordan.[32] Such jocular responses have a long tradition of their own, and Washington Irving's subtly ironical essay on his 'poetical pilgrimage' to Stratford (in 1815) is a telling example from the Romantic age,[33] but however amusing such condescendingly sceptical comments may be, to explore the ritual aspect of the Shakespeare cult first we have to take it seriously. This has often been denied, and for diverse reasons: those (like some ecclesiastical persons) committed to a religious faith condemned any Stratford ritual as spilt religion, out of place and (if taken seriously) blasphemous; others were annoyed by the relics' questionable authenticity; still others, including some scholars and critics, may have been afraid of eroding the prestige of their own profession by letting it be associated with such dubious practices. The religious psychology of the rites themselves is not only articulated by many of its participants but is also confirmed indirectly by some kinds of animosity and rejection. Just as the new religious cults are often indiscriminately and jealously opposed by some militant representatives of traditional churches for whom all new cults are but devilish plots against the true faith, the hostile reaction to the quasi-religious manifestations of the Shakespeare cult is sometimes triggered off by an anxiety similar to what sociologists once called 'cultphobia',[34] a fear that it would violate the territorial integrity of religion *proper*.

Quasi-religious uses of language

The cultic *use of language* is marked by a preference for such glorifying statements as can be neither verified nor falsified, not only because usually they are not amenable to any kind of empirical testing but also because these elusive adulatory statements were *not meant to be* empirically tested or analysed in any rigorous manner. They cannot be reformulated as syntheses of particular statements about concrete details, and although at first sight they may look like referential and descriptive representations of a factual state of affairs in the old positivist sense, they are metaphorical expressions of emotional states, mostly confirmations of a cultic attitude: the unqualified and unconditional reverence for a quasi-transcendental authority. Their hymnic tone, their vocabulary, tropes and allusions constantly transcend the boundaries of the secular. In Hungary Shakespeare has been called the second son of God, his dramas have been compared to a new revelation and his birthplace to Bethlehem, to mention but a few examples of the sacralizing and myth-making idiom that has prevailed in Shakespeare criticism from the mid-nineteenth century onwards. All this may be called the cultic use of language even if it pervades non-cultic genres like literary criticism, genres that otherwise at least intend to use a dominantly referential, descriptive and verifiable language. Of course it is difficult to separate the non-cultic and the cultic uses of language as neatly as when we contrast a statement disclosing the hidden sonnet in the famous dialogue of Romeo and Juliet with the statement of the Hungarian Romantic poet, Sándor Petőfi, claiming that Shakespeare himself is half the created world. Whereas we can easily test and verify the presence of the hidden sonnet by checking the rhyme scheme and other criteria of sonnets in the dramatic text in question, there is no empirical way to test whether Shakespeare amounts to half the created world or not. The difference is not only that between literal and metaphorical meanings, nor just a question of concrete versus vague denotations, but also one between the matter-of-fact and the ecstatically reverential.

Yet sometimes this difference is not easy to discern, and there are puzzling borderline cases in which a pseudo-descriptive cultic utterance can be mistaken for an empirically verifiable one. The occasional oscillation of a statement between the non-cultic and the cultic can be illustrated with many a centenary speech; in his 1964 essay György Lukács self-confidently reproached those who had compared Shakespeare's art to that of Mozart, Raffaello, Bach or Michelangelo, because 'no matter how true some details of these comparisons may be, essentially they ignore Shakespeare's enormous qualitative superiority'.[35] It would be difficult to tell whether to talk about Shakespeare's allegedly enormous superiority over the giants of music and painting as something empirically demonstrable is an erroneous statement in the non-cultic use of language or a cultic utterance camouflaged as description. Sometimes less ambiguous cases turn out to be similarly deceiving, hence the vain attempts to treat a more obviously cultic former utterance as if it had been a descriptive assertion. The rapturous extolling of Shakespeare in 1841 by a Hungarian Romantic poet, Mihály Vörösmarty, was to be scrutinized half a century later as if it had been amenable to empirical verification and falsification.[36] Coupled with Petőfi's above dictum and Alexandre Dumas's famous saying (that Shakespeare created more than anybody except God), Vörösmarty's claim (that Shakespeare's works equal half the worth of a great nation's entire literature) was weighed painstakingly to see just how far such utterances exaggerate and exactly what size their grain of truth is.[37] As late as 1917 a literary historian looked back on the Romantic tributes to Shakespeare only to conclude that such extreme praises would have been unjustifiable and merely rhetorical in the case of any other author but Shakespeare![38] In Shakespeare's case, the scholar implied, we are to take them seriously and test their precise referential validity. The error in such misinterpretations of the cultic use of language is counterproductive: to find a *degree* of exaggeration is misleading and tautological because such utterances look like exaggerations only when they are mistaken for referential statements, but in their own cultic usage they cannot be *to some extent* true or false.

It is a disservice to judge cultic utterances as the referential statements they are not, because we can reveal only their shortcomings and never what they are for and what they are good at. The cultic may well be erroneous by non-cultic standards, yet if it were *only* an erroneous approximation of the non-cultic, there would be no need for its existence and it would have disappeared long ago. Just as myth, to survive, must have always provided more than its Frazerian definition ('mistaken explanation of phenomena, whether of human life or of external nature'[39]) would suggest, the cultic use of language must have a saving grace of its own and should be treated accordingly. As the cultic use of language is dominated by unverifiable quasi-transcendental statements, its historical documents can be better analysed by focusing on the internal connections, psychological motivation and cultural impact of their language rather than by trying to test and contest their referential truth *vis-à-vis* their object. Just as a historian of literary criticism may draw significant conclusions from an old critical text without challenging its judgement, just by analysing its assumptions, its latent norms and its cultural consequences, the historian of a literary cult may learn a lot from studying the cultic use of similar (or the same) documents without checking the validity of their referential statements. And just as the historical significance of a critical statement or a whole review may be independent of whether its judgements would be considered right or wrong today, their cultic significance may be independent of our personal opinion about the truth-value of their pseudo-critical, a priori apologetic arguments.

If we make the characteristic attitude, ritual and language of a major literary cult the object of historical research we may contribute to the general study of cults as well, a much neglected field whose backwardness has often been lamented by representatives of other disciplines. Religious cults have received much more attention, yet in 1985 two sociologists of religion found their exploration highly unsatisfactory. 'The published literature on cults is at present as chaotic as was the material on which cultural anthropology was founded a century ago: an unsystematic collection of traveller's tales, mostly journalistic, often inaccurate, and nearly devoid of theory.'[40] The causes of this neglect in the case of new religious cults is obvious: they were short-sightedly dismissed 'as ephemeral, silly, and bad imitations of "real" religions', despite the fact that their systematic study might have revealed a lot about how even world religions begin.[41] Until recently cultic phenomena had been slighted the same way as pilgrimage and other relatively marginal social practices tended to be, at least in comparison with the attention lavished on the description of well-established and institutionalized movements and prestigious historical events.[42] Anthropologists interested in myths and ritual had disregarded modern cults and preferred to examine African tribes so as to reconstruct a highly hypothetical 'primitive mentality', implying (via Cassirer's revival of Romantic speculations about the mythopoeic and picturesque thinking of archaic man) that the so-called primitive man of the present is a living memento of what archaic man used to be like,[43] and the oral, supposedly animistic and imagistic cultures of both were basically different, except in rare moments of atavistic returns, from the highly literate and sophisticated modern cultures the anthropologist came from. Some anthropologists, however, sought the solution elsewhere and nearer to our target: giving a critical survey of the ritual theories of myth Joseph Fontenrose concluded that the further proliferation of reductionist theories about the genesis of myths would be futile and should be replaced by concrete research exploring their functions; he himself contested former accounts of myth-making around historical figures as diverse as Thomas Becket and Guy Fawkes.[44] Even more instructive have been Victor Turner's explorations of religious and secular ritual: whether focusing on Christian pilgrimages or the carnival in Rio, he thoroughly examined the symbolic meanings and social context of cultic phenomena. Yet the richly documented cult of Shakespeare may provide further clues to the anatomy of cultic behaviour in general, and its exploration may reveal the paradigm of cult formation around a secular figure at a relatively late stage of European civilization.

IN SEARCH OF A SUITABLE METHOD

Anthropological holism

The first of our methodological principles follows from the decision to examine the cult of Shakespeare as a fully-fledged paradigm also representative of less complete literary cults: to survey its three main aspects (attitude, ritual, language) a holistic approach is required whereby seemingly disconnected or hitherto neglected phenomena can be treated as parts within the same system. As it is especially between the verbal and the non-verbal that we want to postulate a connection, the method to be employed will be based on that special type of holism called *anthropological* holism, best expounded by Wittgenstein and Austin, maintaining that 'there is an internal connection between *being a symbol* and playing a role in a system of *non*linguistic conventions, practices, rituals and performances'. Perhaps to postulate this connection we need not necessarily assume that language is 'ontologically dependent' on forms of life, on 'the cultural background of beliefs, institutions, practices, conventions', but we have to admit that in a practical sense language *functions* more like a lifestyle than a collection of words or sentences, and 'that, in the long run, there is no real distinction between what is linguistic and what isn't or, ultimately, between languages and whole cultures'.[45] Similarly, we need not commit ourselves to semantic holism (the tenet that only whole languages or whole systems of beliefs have real meanings[46] and the meanings of their smaller parts are but derivative[46]), but we have to accept that the meaning of a sentence, whether in a poem dedicated to Shakespeare or in a critical essay written to come to terms with his artistic irregularities, is not independent of the other verbal and ritual forms of reverence used in the same period. Even if we accept that at an early age we began to acquire the meaning of smaller units piecemeal, we can safely assume that our learning process implied the constant comparison of verbal and ritual meanings and the recognition of their congruence or discrepancies. Abstraction, separation or isolation are also indispensable to learn, and our compartmentalized world relies on them too heavily not to make their result look deceptively natural, but it imposes on us either-ors that preclude the acknowledgement of hidden connections.

This holistic comprehensiveness differs from the traditional methods used by historians of religion and literary historians who tend to confine their attention to one aspect singled out as essential. Anthropologists complained that historians of religion had usually considered the doctrinal aspect of religion more important than its so-called external and behavioural manifestations (like ritual) or its more popular, less institutionalized, less strictly regulated, 'liminal' or 'liminoid' activities. The traditional disregard of the latter explains why anthropologists interested in pilgrimage could rely on so (relatively) scanty previous literature on the subject, and why they were wise to keep a wide focus, including the entire complex of behaviour connected with pilgrimage.[47] Whether the phenomena thus grouped together by research fall into a strictly *systemic* pattern, or whether their increased coherence is only due to their being heuristically grouped together, are questions of secondary importance compared to the new insights gained from the holistic approach. And whatever we may think about the genetic priority of myth over ritual or vice versa, a comprehensive view may highlight their functional connections without making us choose one of them and exclude the other.

The perspective that can comprehend such diverse traits may seem surprisingly uncommitted to literary scholars whose traditional discipline has always focused exclusively on the realm of letters and trained its students to expect all the important things to happen *there*. How, then, could non-verbal ritual have an equal share, let alone a place in the foreground? (One cannot but agree with the rueful observation that nowadays even 'where literature *as* ritual is considered, the almost exclusive concentration on the text and the reading process restricts the critics' field of vision'.[48]) Symptomatically, Babcock's lucid account of late eighteenth-

century Shakespeare criticism in England was confined to scrutinizing the gradual surrender of classicist norms to the idolators
of the Bard. The ensuing eulogies, however, were not viewed
and analysed as parts (i.e. verbal rites) of the cult as a whole, all
non-verbal manifestations of the cult were deliberately excluded,
and even the fascinating case of the Ireland forgeries was dismissed 'for the matter is not strictly an affair of literary criticism'.[49] By reorienting research so as to focus on all significant
manifestations of literary cults, however, an amazingly elaborate
system emerges out of phenomena that used to be taken as nothing
but incoherent, though perhaps amusing, bits and pieces from
the periphery of intellectual life. The Shakespeare cult abounds
in both verbal and non-verbal expressions of reverence that have
one thing in common: they are governed by some latent religious
archetype. If one were to reconsider Babcock's *The Genesis of Shakespeare Idolatry 1766–1799* along these lines, the first task would
be to demonstrate that the late eighteenth-century disarmament
of English Shakespeare criticism went parallel with the establishment and proliferation of non-verbal ritual in a perfect harmony
that reveals their common origin in an attitude of quasi-religious
devotion. (This common origin explains why recitals of praises,
whether in prose or verse, could be fitted in so well with other
programmes of the Shakespeare festivals.) It is no mere coincidence that whereas Babcock found idolatry in Shakespeare criticism to have prevailed by about 1766, the great Shakespeare Jubilee
took place in Stratford only a few years later, in 1769, and that
around the second centenary of Shakespeare's birth we witness
the emergence of a triumphant literary cult with all its manifestations and paraphernalia.

Tactical agnosticism

Our second methodological principle, an agnostic suspension of
judgements, including value judgements, until the final stage of
research, is more difficult to adopt, especially once we decide to
take our subject seriously. Those few authors, like Washington
Irving in 1815, who bracketed the question of truth when dealing with the myths and relics of Shakespeare, did so by way of
(and at the cost of) relegating them to a sphere where nothing
needs to be taken seriously any more. 'What is it to us, whether
these stories be true or false,' asked Irving with characteristic ease,

as long as a willing credulity gives *enjoyment*?[50] But the historian of a literary cult should bracket (and thereby postpone) the questions of truth and ultimate value in order to take the whole issue seriously. Besides, such a historian can be the most perceptive probably when he or she treats the attitudes preserved by the documents in a spirit of sympathizing detachment. Though not without a certain paradoxicality or latent self-contradiction, this carefully balanced attitude can be more fruitful than joining either the flock of zealous idolaters or their fierce opponents: as the statements of both parties are unverifiable (strictly speaking at least), and quasi-transcendental claims (like the one calling Shakespeare God's second son who was sent to Earth to illuminate the created world for us[51]) are no less unfalsifiable than transcendental ones would be, we can learn more from their psychological, structural and functional analysis than from making any attempt, doomed to failure from the start, to test or revise their descriptive purport. (One doesn't have to be an agnostic in matters of transcendence proper to be tactically or methodologically agnostic about quasi-transcendental claims.) Whereas Shakespeare's *oeuvre* can no longer be fully separated from centuries of interpretation, and all exhortations to read them *in themselves* or as if for the first time in history demand the impossible, we can still proceed the other way round: it is possible to examine the verbal or ritual appropriations of Shakespeare's work without trying to ascertain their adequacy in terms of objective referentiality. All textual documents of appropriation, whether critical interpretations of plays, personal records of journeys to Stratford or historical mementoes of anniversary celebrations, can be reinterpreted as manifestations of a literary cult, precious because they reveal quasi-religious motives and not because they are in any objective sense true. Hence we can agnostically bracket even the haunting question of whether Shakespeare *deserved* such extremely reverent treatment or not. Of course, personally one can be firmly convinced (as I am) of Shakespeare's artistic greatness, but when we are trying to explain the workings and explore the causes of his cult we need not resort to the tautological (and in itself cultic) pseudo-explanation that the cult emerged by necessity around Shakespeare because he was the greatest playwright. (Should we accept this argument we could hardly resist the almost parallel reasoning that he was called the second son of God because that's what he truly was.)

To avoid pious tautologies one resorts to a tactical agnosticism similar to Gibbon's methodological gambit when challenged by the task of explaining the early spread of Christianity. He knew, admittedly, that he could have followed the example of theologians and could have referred simply to the irresistible truth of Christian doctrine and the providence of God as the ultimate answer to the great question, yet he accepted the 'more melancholy duty' of the historian and bracketed this 'obvious but satisfactory' solution for the sake of painstaking sociological explanations. In his pivotal sentence he wrote:

> But as truth and reason seldom find so favourable a reception in the world, and as the wisdom of Providence frequently condescends to use the passions of the human heart, and the general circumstances of mankind, as instruments to execute its purpose, we may still be permitted, though with becoming submission, to ask, not indeed what were the first, but what were the secondary causes of the rapid growth of the Christian church?[52]

This fine manoeuvre is probably the best example to follow by any historian of literary cults, though of course even in Shakespeare's delicate case it is much less compelling to veil one's dissenting opinion with 'becoming submission' than in an account of direct theological importance. Yet Gibbon's understandable caution (after an admittedly 'rash' conversion to Catholicism and a somewhat uneasy return to Protestantism[53]) and his deeply ambivalent feelings about religion[54] may have been but part of the motives for choosing this subterfuge; had he been a fervently pious Christian or a stubborn atheist he might have chosen the same method to safeguard his right to examine his material with what he called here 'the great law of impartiality'.[55] The historian of a literary cult should follow suit: impartiality may have become theoretically problematic as a concept, yet it stays with us as a practical ideal to approximate, and we should protect it by evading or at least postponing the verdict on the ultimate question of the Bard's transcendent or secular origin. (Due to Voltaire's zealous theatrical activity in Lausanne, Gibbon acquired a taste for the French theatre that 'abated', as he admits in his autobiography, his 'idolatory [*sic*] for the gigantic genius of Shakespeare, which is inculcated from our infancy as the first duty of

an Englishman'.[56]) It was much debated whether Gibbon's account
of the early history of Christianity might be approved by Christian authors or he 'dexterously eluded or speciously conceded'
the crucial dogma, the divine origin of the Christian religion;[57]
such agnostic bracketing of one's judgement on (quasi-)tran-
scendent origin is similarly ambiguous when studying the cult
of Shakespeare, but this ambiguity provides a more favourable climate for patient research than would any premature
commitment.

This subterfuge of tactical agnosticism is merely *tactical* in the
sense that it is meant to avoid the undesirable consequences of
both rival positions. Whereas to assent to Shakespeare's superhuman status would easily make us indifferent to the genesis of
this claim and the mental operations that gave birth to it, to declare
him merely human (a rather safe bet, perhaps, and nothing terribly new according to most people) would compel us to deplore
the transcendental allusions of his praise either as sheer folly or
as blasphemous heresy, and to stop analysing them any further.
As opposed to jumping to such self-paralysing conclusions we
should resort to the method of tracing the genealogy of the
quasi-transcendental *as if* it were a product of the human mind,
a treatment no different from the one any divine entity ought to
be given in literary criticism even if the critic happens to be a
firm believer. (One of the most persuasive advocates of treating
God 'as a human artifact' in criticism was Northrop Frye,[58] a
minister ordained in the United Church of Canada and a literary
critic of exquisite religious sensibility, who nevertheless insisted
on keeping the standards of criticism separate from those of theology, and argued that a literary critic or a historian had no other
option but 'to treat every religion [. . .] as though it were a human
hypothesis, whatever else he may in other contexts believe it to
be'.[59]) The tactical agnostic suspends his or her final judgement
about the validity of a transcendental claim not because he or
she is necessarily a philosophical agnostic in private life as well,
but *adopts* the agnostic position for a while *in order to* be exempt
from commitments incompatible with treating the transcendental as a figment of human imagination. Thus we treat Shakespeare as if he were a god created by his idolaters, we analyse
him as a quasi-religious mental construct with a cultural history
of its own, though we suspend our judgement, grotesquely over-
pedantic as this caution may seem, regarding his ultimate

transcendental or this-worldly status. Calling this suspension *agnostic* may sound presumptuous, but it is modelled on how a convinced (not merely tactical) agnostic would approach the historical development of any views on God. The best example is a brilliant essay by the father of the term, Thomas Henry Huxley, 'The evolution of theology: an anthropological study', written in 1886, three years before he published his three major studies on agnosticism. 'From my present point of view,' Huxley writes in the opening paragraph, 'theology is regarded as a natural product of the operations of the human mind, under the conditions of its existence.' He declares that he will treat theological ideas as 'phenomena the study of which legitimately falls within the province of the anthropologist', and will abstain from taking sides as regards the ultimate question of their validity.

> With theology as a code of dogmas which are to be believed, or at any rate repeated, under penalty of present or future punishment [. . .] I have nothing to do, and, so far as it may be possible, I shall avoid the expression of any opinion as to the objective truth or falsehood of the systems of theological speculation of which I may find occasion to speak.

So far as may be possible: of course Huxley knew perfectly well that it was impossible to erase all traces of epistemological commitment, and that referring to theology (in the omitted part of the above quotation) like 'a storehouse of anaesthetics for those who find the pains of life too hard to bear' implied a judgement that many of his readers may have found insulting. It was probably due to an awareness of the hidden cutting edge of his argument that he found it necessary to warn his readers: although he did not want 'to interfere [. . .] with beliefs which anybody holds sacred', those who read beyond this first paragraph do so at their own discretion.[60] To be on the agnostic side, then, is not the same as to be on the safe side, and no attempt to suspend our final judgement can be effective and diplomatic enough to appease those firmly convinced of the sole truth of their position. This applies to Shakespeare scholarship as well: the literary historian who calmly professed that 'a god is made not born' and accordingly searched for scholarly and theatrical antecedents of the idolatrous 1769 Jubilee,[61] took a bold, even if no longer dangerous, step towards revealing the early connection between the secular processing of the works and the quasi-religious deification of their author.

Treating the verbal and ritual deifications of Shakespeare as mental constructs and suspending our final judgement about their intended referential truth-value may also help us to evade some pitfalls of interpretation. First of these problems would be the invisible myth-making between the actual historical event and the subsequent narrative account: as the myth-making interference is impossible to prevent, and its result cannot be fully separated retrospectively from the ever-receding events themselves, to analyse what was meant to be a descriptive account as if it were essentially a man-made myth exempts us from trying the impossible and directs our attention to the creative metaphorical potential of the texts in question. Nevertheless the reinterpretation of descriptive accounts as myth-making has certain hermeneutical difficulties that were tackled by philosophers of the Romantic age. As Schelling pointed out, in order to understand myths of the past one has to step out of one's habitual state of mind and adopt the mental habits of the people who created them.[62] How far this is possible remains a question, but a constant preoccupation with the truths and errors of a given text may reactivate the norms of our own mentality, and Frazer's definition of myth as a mistaken explanation of phenomena may be partly responsible for his sometimes anachronistically over-rationalized explanations of the material he accumulated. Wittgenstein was right not only when he remarked that Frazer's reductionist approach makes 'the magical and religious views of mankind [. . .] look like *errors*', or when he added that explaining away magic as faulty physics or erroneous medicine (etc.) is missing an important aspect of human nature, ignoring man as 'a ceremonial animal', and thus failing to realize that 'men also perform actions which bear a characteristic peculiar to themselves, and these could be called ritualistic actions', but also when he traced back these reductionist explanations to Frazer's inability 'to conceive of a life different from that of the England of his time'.[63] This verdict may not do justice to the achievement of the great anthropologist, yet it sums up the origin of our hermeneutical problem: insisting on correcting the notions that we assume to have been implied by cultic behaviour we are prone to replace the quasi-religious mentality of another cultural sphere of another age with the pedestrian rationality of our own place and time.

Since this replacement is spontaneous, instinctive and most often unconscious, we cannot easily prevent it. Most of us have to go a long way in self-discipline to be able to observe somebody else the way I. A. Richards proposed to scholars when confronted with the uninformed literary interpretations of others, the way a clinical psychologist would listen to the fantasizing of a patient: without arguing about the truth or falsity of obsessive arguments and focusing on their inner logic and searching for clues that would reveal their motivation.[64] Although there is nothing pathological in the mentality of those appropriating Shakespeare in a quasi-religious manner, and their human frailty is not more ridiculous or shameful than that of anybody else, the response to them is often hostile, and the irritation of critics and scholars is sometimes due to a bad conscience or a half-suppressed awareness of embarrassingly similar attitudes. When starting to do research on the cultic aspects of Shakespeare's afterlife I was talking at a Hungarian conference (in 1984) about some examples of explicitly religious behaviour of twentieth-century visitors in Stratford, only for it to be retorted, in no uncertain terms, that such ludicrously odd behaviour was far below the level at which a scholar should look for a suitable object of study. If somebody is as *aberrant* as the writer who had longed all her life to kneel down at Shakespeare's grave, the self-assured argument went, there is no point in taking her psyche seriously, hence any attempt to understand her motives is a sheer waste of time, especially because the whole affair has nothing to do with literary texts, the only legitimate objects of true scholarship. The weakness of this reasoning is the assumption that the study of literary texts or the judging of their artistic merit can be separated from any forms of their appropriation, including the cultic patterns of behaviour mentioned. The assumption that we (the normal) are intact from those *abnormal* ways of adoring the Bard goes hand in hand with the arrogant supposition that we can (and are entitled to) tell in each case whether the enthusiastic pronouncements of our predecessors or contemporaries are (in an ultimate sense) true or foolishly exaggerated. As opposed to such barren haughtiness it is better for the historian of a literary cult to choose a more modest, indeed more humble, stance, to take I. A. Richards's advice, that is to interpret his documents not only (not even primarily) as *statements* about external facts, but as *expressions*[65] of mental states not wholly different from his or her own.

Functional evaluation

The third and last methodological principle concerns the final stage of research when the postponement of a synthesizing value judgement is no longer advisable or feasible, and one has to find such criteria of evaluation that can overrule the usual biased extremes. Only an evaluation based on a candid survey of *historical functions* may protect us from the trap of premature commitment to either a wholesale condemnation or a similarly indiscriminate laudation of cultic phenomena. Of the two possible extremes of response the laudatory is less frequent, though if 'cult' is associated with mainstream religion esteemed (as by Durkheim) as one of the prime sources of anything vital in any society, then 'cult' as a blanket term for the visible manifestations of religion may be considered (especially by those with an iconophile religious sensibility) as something by definition precious. Nevertheless the connotations of the word 'cult' are more likely to evoke diverse kinds of animosity, ranging from the theological and moral indignation of the American ACM (Anti-Cult Movement) to the bitter associations of those East Europeans for whom the word has been irredeemably discredited by its dubious use in the infamous phrase 'personality cult', a euphemistic label designed to cover the totalitarian regime of the 1950s, with its haunting memories of terror, demagogy and fanaticism. (Despite its originally euphemistic intent the heuristic aptness of the phrase may be suggestive enough to instigate research on political cults: the obligatory political idolatry of the 1950s did abound in cultic rituals such as standing ovations with rhythmical applause, public avowals of errors or the ritual manslaughter of predetermined trials, in cultic requisites such as the altar-like niche with the statue or portrait of the party leader, and in cultic myth-making such as the officially disseminated legends about how human the superhuman leader can be.) In addition to such concrete historical contaminations of its meaning, the word 'cult', whether in itself or in the phrase the 'Shakespeare cult', is often used as if it were synonymous with 'idolatry', and the latter is (as, for example, Walter Raleigh pointed out) sheer superstition, in other words a manifestation of ignorance.[66] These pejorative overtones may have been strengthened by a popularized heritage of the Enlightenment, 'superstition and fanaticism being the two categories into which the *philosophes* distributed most religious phenomena',[67] a heritage that disseminated the vague yet axiomatic conviction that an enlightened mind should have nothing to do, unless condescendingly, with something as primitive as the cultic forms of worship. Sometimes it is difficult to distinguish this basically secular-minded dismissal of cults from the contemptuous use of the word by adherents of a religious orthodoxy: in the United States the latter adversaries of new religious movements use the word 'cult' so pejoratively that in 1986 a sociologist found it comparable to 'racist labels' because 'it automatically evokes prepackaged stereotypes and emotional reactions, both usually negative'.[68] A similar polarization of wholesale value judgements could be cited from other countries; in Hungary, for example, the Shakespeare cult was either assumed to be something admirable, as when a scholar applauded (in 1909) that up to 1864 Shakespeare found in that country adorers whose choir of hymnic praise was disturbed by just one single dissenting voice,[69] or it was denied any saving grace, as when (in 1923) a writer (incited by Tolstoy's anti-Shakespearean wrath) condemned it as a formidable tool of cultural oppression, a devastating weapon wielded by a snobbish and reactionary bourgeoisie which used Shakespeare in an insidious plot to intimidate the exploited classes and divert them from the kind of literature that could reveal social injustices.[70]

Such diatribes against the Shakespeare cult rarely contain more than a tiny grain of social truth and are usually too impatient to perceive any evidence beyond their bias. The more promising method of functional evaluation to employ here is utilizing the insight of the cultural anthropologists who discovered the indirect cultural productivity of diverse cultic activities. A good example is the observation that the routes of pilgrimage from Germany or the Netherlands via France to the Northern Spanish Santiago de Compostela helped to disseminate the Roman style in architecture and the mental prerequisites of its appreciation. In the Middle Ages the roads leading to the main places of pilgrimage began to flourish in economic terms as well: not only were chapels, abbeys and shrines built along the way, but also the infrastructure of asylums, hospitals, inns, markets and taverns. We can safely accept the conclusion of an analysis of various pilgrimages as social processes (and that of a thorough study on Christian pilgrimage) that this religious institution contributed to the spread of roads and to the expansion of commerce and urbanization in general at least as much as the more directly economic and political factors did.[71] The development of Chartres, Canterbury, Toledo and Compostela owes a lot to the thousands of pilgrims who visited them; a historian of Gothic architecture justly pointed to these examples as illustrations of the general thesis that the transformation of the otherwise static structure of the medieval economy was triggered off by religious customs and experiences.[72] It is no exaggeration that the pilgrimage had been the prime source of mobility within the bondage of feudal serfdom,[73] and it paved the way for later means and forms of mobility. Moreover, there is much truth in the view that the Protestant ethics Max Weber considered a necessary (though not sufficient) condition of capitalism had to be complemented with a 'pilgrim ethics' that helped to create the network of communication needed to make the international system of capitalist commerce and industry efficient.[74] Now confronting these additional effects with the original aim of the pilgrimage it is clear that the cultural values fostered by a religious practice may be accidental yet considerable. The pilgrimage as a religious custom had never been prompted by a desire to disseminate architectural styles or to build hospitals, and such worldly benefits could never do justice to its spiritual significance, yet these side effects illustrate how a cultic activity may indirectly, indeed unwittingly, yet organically instigate economic growth and nourish cultural development.

This approach may have shortcomings of its own, like its search for the saving grace of any social practice beyond its self-declared purposes, but it may serve as an encouraging example of how we should weigh the many additional functions and indirect effects of the Romantic cult of Shakespeare before passing judgement on its overall cultural value. An examination of the main interrelated issues such as the manifestations of an a priori reverential attitude, the acquisition of a quasi-religious ritual and the use of sacralizing and unfalsifiable language should be followed sooner or later by at least tentative answers to such bracketed problems of evaluation like the influence of that attitude on the diverse genres of Shakespeare scholarship and criticism, the role of that ritual in the institutional structure of a country, or the mental habits fostered by the implications of that language. It is unnecessary to postpone the tackling of all these problems till the last chapter, and as they are impossible to suppress altogether, they will obviously lurk behind such historical analyses of the cult as (say) the chapter on the nineteenth-century aftermath of Garrick's Jubilee and the political appropriations of Shakespeare's anniversaries. Yet *trying* to defer our final judgement till the end is a safeguard against the urge to sneer at the ecstatic ways people of past ages expressed their veneration for a playwright. 'Debunking', as A. N. Whitehead memorably remarked when talking about the characteristic aim of eighteenth-century rationalists and his preference for the seventeenth-century interest in religion, 'is a good thing to have done, but is comparatively shoal water.'[75] This comment may fail to do justice to the eighteenth century but is good to bear in mind when watching our predecessors as they treasure splinters carved from Shakespeare's chair.

2

The Genesis of a Ritual: The Shakespeare Cult in English Romanticism

FROM CELEBRATION TO WORSHIP: BIBLICAL ALLUSIONS IN THE 1769 SHAKESPEARE JUBILEE

The Stratford 'Jubilee', organized in 1769 by David Garrick, provided a ritual pattern for many subsequent celebrations of Shakespeare. In 1770 the jubilee of the previous year was labelled 'theatrical idolatry'[1] by Francis Gentleman, the actor, playwright and critic. If purged of its strongly pejorative connotations the expression would be suitable for describing the attitude that brought about a whole new paradigm in dealing with Shakespeare and his works. This attitude applies not only to such overtly idolatrous ritual manifestations of respect as the ceremonial adoration of Shakespeare's statue in the theatre or the enactment of his apotheosis, but also to the verbal system of myth-making requisites around the much repeated analogy between the Bard and the Creator. The resistance to the new paradigm was sporadic, feeble and occasionally half-hearted; as was pointed out, even the satirical portrayal of Garrick as the saint of a new religion indicated 'a sort of shamefaced approbation'.[2] The charismatic actor was endowed with the psychological shrewdness and dramaturgical skills required for organizing spectacular events into a rhythmical and meaningful sequence. By selecting mostly well-known symbols he could elicit the associations and emotions he thought proper for the occasion, yet all those familiar elements made up a symbolic system that was felt to be both new and authentic. As if to prove the later thesis that tradition can be invented,[3] Garrick seems to have invented one of the ritual archetypes of literary cults. Although he incorporated (and thus sanctified) some forms of reverence that were already practised

34

in connection with Shakespeare, and he improvised some new ones, the most striking of his innovations is, paradoxically, that he adopted and adapted some of the venerable symbolism known from ancient religious ritual. Though one cannot but accept that for the sophisticated contemporaries of Garrick the requisites and procedures (the mulberry tree, the statue-worship, the Shakespearean procession) were 'stale' and 'trite', or even 'tired old clichés',[4] even these elements were transmuted when mixed with liturgical or ritual allusions to the hallowed solemnity of religious worship. 'For Garrick was a worshipper himself', as William Cowper characterized him succinctly in *The Task* (1785), 'He drew the liturgy, and form'd the rites / And solemn ceremonial of the day, / And call'd the world to worship on the banks / Of Avon'.

The liturgy he drew and the rites he formed, however, were not just solemn, but were taken from heterogeneous sources not necessarily all religious in origin; they ranged from the high seriousness of transcendental devotion to the carefree playfulness of secular vivacity. As chief organizer and official steward of the Jubilee, Garrick intuitively knew the psychic needs of his audience; and he seems to have possessed a rare feeling for the religious cult in its more archaic form when the sense of the transcendental had been strong enough to allow a blend of both solemn and ludic elements without any fear of incongruity.[5] By now literary cults have been firmly planted in the secular realm of social practices; therefore in retrospect we may be deceived into seeing the familiar spectacle of the Jubilee as nothing but an early English instance of a thoroughly secular literary cult. Its genesis and anatomy reveal, however, that it owed its existence to a fine religious sensibility well aware (consciously or otherwise) of the interdependence between secularization and religious revival, and always ready to renegotiate the intricate relation of the sacred and the profane.

The name of the event, given by Garrick himself, was inspired by an ancient religious idea the transmutations of which pervaded the entire history of Christianity and subsequently became, through a further metamorphosis, one of the implicit organizing principles of some major literary cults. The Hebrew ancestor of the word 'Jubilee', *yobel*, originally meant a ram's horn and then the trumpet made of it. This trumpet heralded the beginning of legal and spiritual restoration in every fiftieth year (after seven times seven years) on the tenth day of the seventh month, the day of atonement for the sins of the people. Thus the King James

Bible, the Authorized Version (1611) used by Garrick and his contemporaries, names the trumpet signalling the fiftieth year 'the trumpet of the jubile', the whole event of that year 'a jubile' or 'the jubile', and the year itself 'the year of this jubile' (Lev. 25). Sowing and reaping were then forbidden, as in every seventh (sabbatical) year; moreover, according to the tradition recorded in the Old Testament the Lord instructed Moses that in this year all former debts should be released, all servants, slaves or captives should be emancipated and sent home, and any land purchased since the last jubilee should be returned to its former owner: 'And ye shall hallow the fiftieth Year, and proclaim liberty throughout *all* the land unto all the inhabitants thereof: it shall be a jubile unto you; and ye shall return every man unto his possession, and ye shall return every man unto his family' (Lev. 25: 10). The practical need for this law may have been due to diverse economic and political considerations, but spiritually it was meant to remind people of the secondary nature of worldly possessions and social inequalities compared to the equality before God's ultimate authority. This underlying message is suggested by the rule that all through that year the natural produce of the uncultivated land was considered common property (everybody was allowed to eat it but hoarding a personal stock was forbidden); the same idea is revealed in the solemn explanation given for the obligation to return real estates to their former owners: 'The land shall not be sold for ever: for the land is mine; for ye *are* strangers and sojourners with me' (Lev. 25: 23). As the religious essence of this civil institution is the *release* of obligations, the *liberation* from bondage and the *restoration* of a former (original) state of affairs, it contained the germ of later reinterpretations: in the tradition of the Roman Catholic church *jubilaeum* or *jubilaeus annus* meant a year that offered remission from the punishment for former sinful behaviour. Though *jubilaeum* is a late Latin word etymologically independent of *yobel*, the striking similarity of these words accentuates a common semantic element that was to survive, with modifications, in many ritual and verbal manifestations of the Shakespeare cult as well: the abolition of the temporary differences of a worldly hierarchy for the sake of restoring the ultimate unity of an other-worldly order.

The name of the event revived this ancient religious idea as well as more recent notions, and Garrick's contemporaries probably understood and accepted its complexity. In May 1769 a newspaper published the official letter in which the mayor, aldermen and burgesses of Stratford transmitted to the actor the freedom of the borough: the document was released with the comment that 'a jubile in honour and to the memory of Shakespeare will be appointed at Stratford the beginning of September next, to be kept up every seventh year' and at 'the first jubile' a large building will be dedicated to Shakespeare.[6] Both the spelling of the word and the plan to repeat the event in every *seventh* year must have been familiar to contemporary readers. Although subsequent organizers gave up this hallowed number of years in favour of more or (later) less frequent celebrations, the original intention was redolent with biblical connotations. These were indirectly acknowledged even by some satirical or ironical comments subverting yet preserving the religious vocabulary and logic: shortly after the event, in September 1769 the *Town and Country Magazine* reported that some people considered the rains (that prevented the procession) 'as a judgment on the poetical idolatry of the jubilites'.[7] (Probably the word 'jubilites' itself, coined for the occasion to designate the participants,[8] evoked vaguely biblical associations, both because of the stem 'jubile' and the suffix '-ites'.) But for mid-eighteenth century Londoners the word *jubilee* also meant the exuberant festive celebration of a military victory or some other happy occasion, a form of popular entertainment in one of the parks, with a masquerade, lively music, dancing and finally perhaps a spectacular display of fireworks. In addition to these well-known meanings the word may have elicited some vague and dubious associations: the inhabitants of Warwickshire may have been reminded of cunning papist plottings (in 1605 Stratford was indirectly involved in the Catholic gunpowder plot), and there was the striking phonic similarity with a controversial legislative device introduced in the previous decade as the 'Jew Bill'.[9] All in all, the word, whether spelt *jubile* or *jubilee*, once connected with the name of Shakespeare must have sounded familiar yet enigmatic enough to trigger off a series of subliminal notions and puzzling expectations of something both sacred and profane, solemn and joyous, traditional and exceptional.

The story of the Jubilee is well-known, and several book-length studies[10] have tried to reconstruct the sequence of its events, yet it must be recapitulated because there has been little recognition of its essentially cultic symbolism and consequently the importance of some details have been unduly slighted or altogether ignored. The idea of the festival came too late to commemorate the bicentenary of the poet's birth in 1764; the prehistory of the

Jubilee started as late as 1767 when Stratford wanted to build a new town hall and its magistrate decided to erect a statue of Shakespeare in a niche to adorn the northern facade. The English cult of Shakespeare owes a lot to this humble fact of provincial life: a statue was needed for a new building. With admirable psychological shrewdness the magistrate asked Garrick to order both a statue of the Bard and a portrait of himself so as to commemorate their joint fames together. The request was too flattering to resist, and it inspired the actor to propose a festival to the memory of Shakespeare, to plan its scenario, and to cover its expenses. In May 1769 Garrick received an official letter announcing that the 'town, that glories in giving birth to the immortal Shakespeare' elected him an honorary burgess and would give him the freedom of the borough document 'in a box made from a Mulberry-tree undoubtedly planted by Shakespeare's own hand'.[11] This mode of symbolic authorization is remarkable because of the magical logic inherent in the idea of receiving authority by touching a part of a tree planted by Shakespeare himself. (In addition to this quasi-sacred authenticity of the wood itself, the carving of the box enriched its symbolic significance. On its front, Fame is holding the bust of Shakespeare that is being adorned with bayleaves by the three Graces; the sides are ornamented with the emblematic figures of Tragedy and Comedy; the back shows Garrick as Lear in the storm scene; its top and the edges are illustrated with motifs from the plays; and the whole box is sustained by four silver griffons.) On 11 May 1769 the box, containing the document, was ceremonially put in Garrick's hands, and he accepted the honour and responsibility of becoming the steward of the Jubilee. Preparations were made to transform a humble provincial town into a site worthy of celebrating the Bard. An octagonal amphitheatre was made of wood, the Rotunda, meant to resemble both a Roman circus and a church built for the worship of Shakespeare, and designed to be large enough to host a thousand spectators and a hundred musicians. By the riverside a summer residence was built in Chinese style; preparations were made for the fireworks, rooms were booked by future visitors, the press echoed even the smallest news of the approaching Jubilee and raised curious expectations of something unprecedented.

On 6 September 1769, at five in the morning bells and cannons proclaimed the first day of the celebrations. The actors and singers of Drury Lane theatre, with sooted faces and clothed in rags, gathered under the windows of the more distinguished guests and ladies to serenade them. In the old town hall the officials of the town elected their new mayor for the next year; then they marched to the new town hall where they inaugurated Garrick as Steward, presenting him with a steward's wand and a medal (with a small relief, set in gold, of Shakespeare's bust), both made of the (reputedly) authentic mulberry tree. The newly inaugurated steward expressed his gratitude for the honour and invited the guests to the ballroom for breakfast. Eight hundred people ate there, differing in rank and wealth, but all wore the same rainbow-coloured Shakespeare ribbon (that was meant to comprehend the colours of all the parties and symbolize Shakespeare's multicoloured genius) with or without a silver medal. After the meal, as between all the events of the Jubilee, Garrick's plan was to lead the participants to the site of the next programme, in a cheerful procession accompanied by an orchestra, reviving the custom of old English folk pageantries. By eleven o'clock they were at Holy Trinity Church where Thomas Arne conducted his oratorio *Judith*. Although some may have thought that an oratorio was too cold an introduction to such a joyous festival,[12] Garrick's scenario was meant to satisfy the emotional need for devotion that was thinly veiled by the apparent desire for profane entertainment. As soon became evident, he was right: Boswell not only called the performance 'admirable' (a curious comment since he arrived too late to judge its quality) but added that he would have wished prayers and a sermon as well. 'It would have consecrated our Jubilee, to begin it with Devotion, with gratefully adoring the Supreme Father of all Spirits from whom cometh every good and perfect Gift.'[13]

After the oratorio Garrick led the visitors to the birthplace, and contemporary newspapers and witnesses testify to the happy mingling of diverse ranks and social groups into a cheerful community of worshippers. The total cost of 49 pounds two shillings a participant complained to have paid for travel, tickets, food, lodging and the like may suggest that 'attendance was confined to the well-to-do';[14] yet by later (Victorian) standards the participants seem to have been a relatively mixed lot with no spatial or temporal segmentation during the programmes. The hierarchy of social order was temporarily suspended for the sake of what cultural anthropologists would call the experience of *communitas*: the communal sharing of a cultic ritual. Since people could read the detailed programmes of each day in advance, the participants knew what to expect and the unfolding ritual patterns fulfilled their expectations. Just as they could listen to the oratorio with Isaac Bickerstaffe's libretto in hand, now they could buy (in the very room where Shakespeare was said to have been born) copies of Garrick's *Ode* that was to be performed the next day, a collection of occasional poems entitled *Shakespeare's Garland*, and George Saville Carey's *Shakespeare's Jubilee, A Masque*. From there they went to the Rotunda where cannons greeted them, and at four in the afternoon a magnificent lunch was served for seven hundred people.

Here the meal, far from being a mere culinary event, more and more turned into a devout occasion of religious symbolism. After the toasts that cheered Shakespeare and Garrick, the mayor presented the actor with a goblet made of the Shakespearean mulberry tree and ornamented with silver. With well-rehearsed spontaneity Garrick returned the favour with a ballad he had written for the occasion; it was about Shakespeare's mulberry tree, and as sung by Joseph Vernon, the tenor soloist of Drury Lane, it suggested the proper behaviour of worship that was meant to be imitated by everybody present. Singing its first stanza Vernon actually demonstrated, with the goblet in his hand, how and why to pay tribute: 'Behold this fair goblet, 'twas carv'd from the tree, / Which, O my sweet Shakespeare, was planted by thee; / As a relick I kiss it, and bow at the shrine, / What comes from thy hand must be ever divine!' With a graceful simplicity that could not fail to impress, the subsequent refrain (that was to be repeated after each of the eight stanzas) completed the emotional and behavioural pattern Garrick sought to encourage: 'All shall yield to the Mulberry-tree, / Bend to thee, / Blest Mulberry, / Matchless was he / Who planted thee, / And thou like him immortal be!'[15] It is difficult to abstain from the usual aside that the scene greatly enhanced the popularity of Thomas Sharp's relic shop in Chapel Street, or that the mulberry relics, like the goblet itself, turned out to possess miraculous powers of self-multiplication. It is more important to note, however, that the behavioural suggestions of Garrick's ballad had far-reaching consequences as regards the norms of acceptable acts of reverence in the Shakespeare cult. A good example is James Boswell's ritual adoration of the Ireland forgeries a quarter of a century later: when he knelt down and kissed the manuscripts (saying that he would die contented because he had lived long enough to touch these papers), it was neither an unprecedented adaptation of religious symbolism nor just a pious improvisation on the spur of the moment but most probably an unconscious imitation of a ritual pattern he had seen at the Stratford Jubilee, authorized by Garrick's quasi-liturgical text ('As a relick I kiss it') and accepted by seven hundred enthusiasts on the spot and many more afterwards at the numerous Drury Lane performances of *The Jubilee*.

One of the episodes of the feast deserves special attention because it reveals the extent to which symbolic actions were inspired by a latent religious psychology and alluded to biblical scenes. As one of the participants relates, no sooner had the songs, catches and glees subsided than the merry company seized the goblet 'and nothing would satisfy them till it was filled with the best of Wines, that they might have the pleasure to drink to the Memory of the immortal Bard'. We can imagine the way the goblet 'went around very freely indeed, and the enthusiastic Joy upon the Occasion was very remarkable!' What is more, when the end of the lunch was signalled by everybody singing 'God Save the King' (one of the many early symptoms of the fact that the adoration of Shakespeare was intertwined with monarchical feelings), the custodian of the goblet was halted on his way home by a quickly growing number of friends who insisted on drinking some Shakespeare Ale from the goblet. As 'there was no refusing them', the common request was satisfied; the goblet was filled again and 'every one did Honour to it', until they felt contented enough to end the celebration 'with three Cheers for the divine Bard, and three more to his truest Representative Mr. Garrick'.[16] In one of the later book-length accounts of the Jubilee, this was reported as a mere 'amusing incident',[17] but in the light of its probable religious archetype it is much more than that facile expression would suggest. In addition to the atavistic revival of the belief in magic transfer by touch (Shakespeare planted the tree with his own hands, so he must be present in the holy wood of the goblet), the communal drinking of wine (or something less traditional but named after the Bard) to the memory of the immortal founder of the cult (and with his true representative being present) points to a familiar pattern that was well-known to the participants in Stratford. It is no exaggeration to think of the Eucharist itself, the ritual Christ bequeathed to his disciples on the eve of his death, with its liturgy of transubstantiation. The ritual performed at the Avon reveals an unconscious yearning for the bond of *communitas*, something immediate and without hierarchy. Those who drank from the goblet wanted to touch a relic and imitate a Christian liturgy within the quasi-religious context of a literary cult. They wanted to celebrate Shakespeare, to be sure, but what they also wanted, deep down, was no less than a *mystery* whereby their lives could gain a richer meaning and added significance.

The rest of that day promised a much less devout form of entertainment, but its symbolism was derived from the quickly developing mythology of Shakespeare and transcended the realm of the profane. The preparations for the evening ball were spectacular. The piles of wood burning everywhere around the Rotunda and the candles in the windows of Stratfordians transformed the night, as a contemporary theatre historian remarked, into a cheerful day.[18] The people flooded the streets, happily watching the enormous allegorical pictures, painted on transparent silk and illuminated from behind, like the copy of Sir Joshua Reynolds' composition that personified Time as it led Shakespeare, accompanied by Tragedy and Comedy, to Immortality.[19] In the windows of the town hall one could see Shakespeare on his soaring Pegasus, between two scenes from his comedies (with Falstaff and Pistol respectively) and two from his tragedies (with Lear and Caliban, the choice of the latter implying a classification of *The Tempest* as a tragedy or at least a play somber enough to be contrasted with the comedies). At the birthplace, in front of the room where Shakespeare was supposed to have been born, an emblematic painting showed the rising sun struggling through the clouds, representing 'the low Circumstances of Shakespeare, from which his Strength of Genius rais'd him, to become the *Glory of his Country'*.[20] Whether Domenico Angelo, the Italian master of fireworks added the splendour of his display to all these and imitated a rainbow to symbolize the multicoloured talent of the Bard, as several nineteenth-century accounts tell us, or it was postponed to the next day, is questionable,[21] but for the guests and the natives the orgy of light was dazzling enough. What is more, to enter the Rotunda one had to pass through a gate under a replica of the English royal crown made of coloured lamps – yet another sign of the early fusion of monarchic feelings and bardolatry. Once in the Rotunda, visitors could join a cavalcade of dancing, minuets till midnight, then cotillions and folk dances till three in the morning.[22]

The main spectacles promised for the next day, 7 September,

were heralded by bells, cannons and serenades, but the pouring rain seemed to jeopardize the costumed procession of Shakespeare's characters, the erection and crowning of the statue, a splendid display of fireworks and, last but not least, the masquerade. As Samuel Foote sarcastically remarked, the sudden torrent that washed away this magnificent plan was like God's punishment for vanity and idolatry. It is a remarkable proof of the irresistible strength of myth-making that in several accounts published in the next hundred years the events mentioned in this *cancelled* plan were vividly and elaborately described among the actual happenings of the Jubilee.[23] But the real event Garrick had to improvise in place of his thwarted plan worked wonders. The two thousand crammed into the Rotunda, many of them hungry and nearly all of them cold in their soaking wet clothes, forgot their miserable conditions at twelve o'clock when Garrick, with the steward's wand and gilded mulberry medallion, stepped up to the Shakespeare statue and recited his *Ode*, accompanied by orchestra and choir. The audience was carried away by the great actor and the unprecedented contrast of speech and music. The whole scene reminded James Boswell of the performances of ancient Athens or Rome because Garrick, 'inspired with an awful Elevation of Soul, while he looked, from Time to Time, at the venerable Statue of Shakespeare, appeared more than himself' and not only managed to fuse his passion into everybody present (and to create such an intense atmosphere that 'if any one had attempted to disturb the Performance, he would have been in Danger of his Life') but he seemed to personify no less than 'the Idea of a Mortal transformed into a Demi-god, as we read in the Pagan Mythology'.[24] Then Garrick modestly acknowledged the applause and, gazing at the statue, cited Milton's sonnet to warn that the true monument of Shakespeare is not 'in piled Stones' but 'in our wonder and astonishment'; finally he turned to the audience and appealed to what he called an even greater authority than Milton on the unequalled excellence of Shakespeare: *ask your own hearts*. This exhortation to accept the subjective inner voice as arbiter was later interpreted as 'typical of much that the Jubilee stood for: the new, romantic, uncritical worship of the creative genius'.[25] In the formation of a literary cult, however, Garrick's final rhetorical gesture represents further symbolic significance: as high priest of the ritual he implicitly declared (and thereby ordained) everybody present as full members of an intuitive, quasi-mystical community and suggested that every heart would testify to the same (affirmative) truth and confirm the same (positive) belief. Thus any possibility of dissent was henceforth precluded as heresy; this was promptly illustrated by the ensuing mock-debate between Thomas King and Garrick himself. The former, playing the role of *advocatus diaboli*, began to castigate Shakespeare and the Jubilee as vulgar entertainments far below a true gentleman's French taste; Garrick sarcastically rejected such over-refinement and hoped that 'we shall Entertain and content ourselves with that Heav'n has sent us in SHAKESPEARE'. Addressing finally the fair sex as the true protector of the fame of the poet (who was 'their Patron Saint') Garrick's eloquent prose culminated in a poetic *Epilogue to the Ladies*, including a myth-making celebration of his wand, proudly comparing it to a king's sceptre, and summarizing its precious genealogy with such shrewd psychology that it must have sounded like a gentle recapitulation of well-known truths: 'The Parent Tree from whence its life it drew, / Beneath his Care, its earliest Culture knew, / And with his Fame, the spreading Branches grew, / How once it flourish'd feeling crowds can tell; / Unfeeling Foes will mention how it fell.'[26] These allusions conveyed the reassuring message that there was a background knowledge all the participants shared and could resort to. Thus (with or without the much-debated 'oration in honour of Shakespeare, intended to be spoken by Mr Garrick at Stratford upon Avon during the Jubilee'[27] that was most probably left out of the actual programme[28]) the morning ceremonies struck the reassuring note of *communitas* again.

The same applies to the rest of the day that abounded in symbolic gestures pointing towards some kind of ultimate unity beneath any diversity. Even something as prosaic as the menu of the public luncheon in the Rotunda was exploited for such symbolic purposes: its main dish, an enormous turtle, was not only a culinary sensation but (as Garrick himself explained it in a speech) this animal was meant to unite all the other species of earth, air and water and thus to symbolize the multi-faceted talent of Shakespeare – just as the rainbow (on the Jubilee ribbon and in the fireworks) united the individual colours to illustrate Shakespeare's universal genius.[29] The *masquerade* of the evening ball also evoked a semi-conscious feeling of unity in diversity: the masks covered the features and thereby suspended the identities (and ranks) of the participants for a few hours. (This is significant even if some participants wore no mask; it is but one of Samuel Foote's mocking exaggerations in 'The Devil's Definition' that the Jubilee was, among other paradoxes, 'a masquerade, where half the people appeared bare-faced'.[30]) This temporary concealment of individual and social differences was symbolically authorized by allusions to Shakespeare and his work: William Kenrick personified the haunting spirit of Shakespeare himself, while three celebrated beauties of the period were masked as the witches of *Macbeth*. The sheer number of those present is revealing: dinner was served for no fewer than eight hundred people. After the meal the refined movements of minuets gave way to the vigorous exuberance of folk dances, signifying a harmony of cultures without condescension, and the common enjoyment did not subside before the light of dawn.[31]

The programmes scheduled for the last day, 8 September, were threatened by the unceasing downpour, but this could not prevent the main events and thereby the completion of a sequence that was soon to be regarded as an archetype for later Shakespeare festivals. The participants went to Shottery to see the horse-race for the Jubilee Cup. (The winner happily embraced the silver cup that was worth fifty pounds, admitting that he knew little about Master Shakespeare or his plays.[32]) By now the Rotunda stood in water, so the company had to form smaller groups and have lunch in different inns, to gather again for a display of fireworks, then for a last ball in the new town hall, where they could admire Mrs Garrick who 'danced a Minuet beyond description gracefully, and joined in the Country Dances'.[33] At four in the morning the steward resigned and the Jubilee officially ended. As the splendour vanished, Boswell bitterly remarked, the 'true nature of human life began now to appear'; it was difficult to find a post-chaise not yet spoken for and leave the place that now looked no more than a miserable little village.[34] The Rotunda, now dilapidated and dangerous, had to be removed; its material was sold by auction. Garrick returned to his country house, then went back to London and began to repay the deficit of the Jubilee, two thousand pounds, to Stratford. (No, thank you, the actor replied in 1770 when he was asked to assist in organizing a new Jubilee, but you should show your true love of the Bard by looking after this '*Holy-land*' because it is a disgrace that 'the town which gave birth to the first genius since the creation is the most dirty, unseemly, ill-paved wretched looking place in all Britain'.[35]) Sober reality prevailed again, though not entirely: in subsequent reports, recollections and theatrical adaptations the process of myth-making is unmistakable: no account, including our own, can be fully disentangled from the legend.

It is due to this elusive complexity that the queries about the *essential* meaning of the event have always been doomed to failure and leave ample room for less monolithic interpretations. In a letter to the *London Magazine* one of the eyewitnesses, James Boswell, answered his own question ('For what was the Stratford Jubilee?') by denying that it was 'a piece of farce', and pointing to its majestic archetype in classical antiquity: 'an elegant and truly classical celebration of the memory of Shakespeare [...] It was truly an antique idea, a Grecian thought, to institute a splendid festival in honour of the Bard.'[36] In modern scholarship this view was challenged by an argument that sought to establish the Romantic, as opposed to Boswell's idea of the Classical, characteristics of the event; the Jubilee thus 'acted as a catalyst to precipitate romantic attitudes toward Shakespeare'.[37] But one is no more convinced by this exclusive either/or than by Boswell's attempt to eradicate the farcical elements from the event. Moreover, the apparent paradox that the farcical had an integral part in the Jubilee and did not violate its classical grandeur indicates that the event followed not only Classical and Romantic modes of behaviour but also a partially secularized ritual of vaguely remembered or subconsciously desired religious cults. Cultural anthropologists remind us of how tribal rites or medieval Islamic and Christian pilgrimages ignored our modern distinctions between the serious and the playful, and how the gradual separation of work and leisure placed religion into the relatively unregulated and weightless leisure sphere, a transfer that would have endangered its social importance had it not been compensated for by purging religious activities of their ludic component and making them more and more exclusively solemn.[38] If interpreted as a half-conscious and partly secularized revival of an archaic (pre-division) religious festival, no part of the 1769 Jubilee has to be dismissed as incompatible with the rest. This underlying archaic pattern was able to reconcile otherwise antithetical elements of worship and pageantry, like a devout oratorio and a costumed procession, a laudatory ode and a mocking debate, a secularized enactment of the Eucharist and the fascinating suspension of identities during a masquerade. Moreover, it was by way of appropriating this undivided notion of religiosity and adapting it for a new cultural purpose that the Jubilee and other (less obvious) manifestations of the emerging literary cult tended to form a coherent system.

Performances of Shakespeare plays could have been fitted in this verbal and ritual system from the start, and it is a remarkable fact that Garrick, otherwise revelling in both adapting the plays and playing some of their main roles himself, did not include a single performance, indeed that amid 'all the odes and ovations at the Shakespeare jubilee not a word of Shakespeare was spoken'. However, this is not only (and perhaps not necessarily) yet another symptom of the 'misleading' or 'deliberately dishonest' strategy of his 'marketing claims',[39] but a sign of his fine sense of what that cultic event was about: the glorification, almost the deification, of a cultural hero, a rite of passage from the earthly to the quasi-transcendental, a mystifying ceremony where there is no place (yet) for the concrete historical figure simply as the author of certain works. True, Garrick was skilfully appealing to different and even conflicting expectations of his Stratford audience, and as a recent analysis of his *Ode* demonstrated he could magisterially accommodate the contradiction of deifying (that is, universalizing) and nationalizing Shakespeare, and could make it transparent that 'the timeless, the transcendent Bard must none the less be claimed as specifically and uniquely English', but neither his catering for anti-French sensibilities nor his probable allusions to the jubilees celebrating John Wilkes[40] were as decisive as his successful attempt to sanctify a pattern of quasi-religious behaviour in honour of a secular writer. The cult he thus initiated may justly be called (among other things) a 'national cult',[41] but its verbal and ritual manifestations alluded to a supranational religious heritage too clearly to be mistaken for a merely nationalistic affair. If Shakespeare had been deified at the Jubilee as the exclusive prerogative of the British, and if, to use Arthur Murphy's haunting phrase again, his cult had been established as the islanders' religion, then its language and ritual of celebrating Shakespeare could not have been so easily adopted by emergent European nations eager to define *their* national identity. Furthermore, the ultimate rise of bardolatry 'to orthodoxy as a *national* religion'[42] was a later phase, inseparable from the institutionalization of the cult in the nineteenth century, from the Shakespeare clubs and societies, from royal patronage, from the tercentenary *sermons* that

glorified Shakespeare as one of the main pillars of Victorian ideology. Garrick's Jubilee preceded all that, and preceded most other
symptoms of what Max Weber would have called the routinization
of charisma.

The immediate aftermath of the 1769 Jubilee reveals the irresistible drive of its underlying religious psychology. No matter
how satirical its first theatrical adaptations were meant to be, they
could not help fulfilling the inescapable patterns of myth-making.
In spite of all attempts at irony and detachment even the most
light-hearted stage enactments of the receding actual event
provided curiously indirect intimations of a former ritual. Evening
after evening audiences were encouraged to feel that they could
evoke a communal experience and take part in its ever more
haunting mystery. Fascinating through their evasive and unverifiable referentiality, such adaptations included Francis Gentleman's
The Stratford Jubilee, a two-act comedy that was staged in Stratford right after the Jubilee itself to entertain those guests who
could not travel home for some days. By 7 October Covent Garden
produced George Colman's *Man and Wife: or the Stratford Jubilee*.
The most popular of all, however, was Garrick's own stage version,
The Jubilee. First performed on 14 October in Drury Lane, a theatre
Garrick opened two decades earlier announcing that 'Sacred to
SHAKESPEARE was this spot designed',[43] this production had a
record series of 91 successful evenings in 1769–70 and 27 in the
next season, eventually reaching a total of 152 performances.

Celebrated as the greatest theatrical spectacle of its age, *The
Jubilee* most probably owed its great appeal to the unprecedented
extent to which it involved the audience and encouraged everybody to take an active part in the ceremony. The costumed procession, here an integral part of the play, entered the theatre from
the street, attracting and carrying away many pedestrians who
happened to pass by, wound through the auditorium and ended
up on the stage where, in the final scene, actors and spectators
sang Shakespeare's praise together in front of his statue, with
cannons thundering and bells tolling before the final outburst of
applause.[44] Just like the original Jubilee, Garrick's play seems to
have triggered an unstoppable proliferation of symbolic embellishment with many allusions to classical mythology. It was
performed in Dublin; from there the Dublin troupes took it to
Wales (where on 5 May 1772, under a mulberry tree erected on
the stage, the actor playing Shakespeare himself received

Prometheus' torch from the hands of an Apollo aided by Cupid). It was also staged in Edinburgh, and by the time it was published its text was much longer than Garrick's manuscript and hardly any part of the original was left intact. It managed to cross the Atlantic: *Boston Magazine* heralded it by giving an account of the Stratford event and its theatrical afterlife; then it appeared on American stages in New York (1788), in Charleston (1793) and in Philadelphia (1814). In the final scene of the New York performance a triumphal chariot carried the bust of Shakespeare, crowned by Time and Fame, accompanied by characters from his plays who were marching under a flag with symbolic trophies and transparent images; in Charleston the performance finally reproduced the Westminster Abbey memorial of the playwright.[45] Back in England Covent Garden renewed it to celebrate in four lavish performances the bicentenary of Shakespeare's birth; almost four decades later than the actual Stratford event, the audience responded to the stage version with undiminished enthusiasm.

The extraordinary appeal of the Drury Lane performance (and to some extent that of its various offspring) is best exemplified by the case of Johann Wilhelm von Archenholz (1741–1812), a former officer of the Prussian army, later the historian of the Seven Years' War, who went to London in 1769 and saw the play no less than 28 times. In his *England und Italien* he gives a detailed account of this performance as a telling example of the stage afterpiece, that is the theatrical adaptation of some important contemporary event, a genre he treated as the epitome of English culture and a clue to national character. The book was published in three volumes in 1785, an enlarged edition (five volumes) came out two years later, and it was translated into several European languages (including English, first via the French translation then from the original German), soon to become a representative and frequently quoted source of information about the English way of life, disseminating its author's admiration for *The Jubilee* even to countries (like Hungary) where the book as a whole was not published. It is from the German traveller that we learn about the painted scenery on the stage, representing the Stratford marketplace, where ('to the sound of instruments of music') a dignified procession started. Dancers appeared, they were followed first by nymphs strewing flowers, then the main characters of Shakespeare's comedies marched under a flag bearing the title of the play, then came 'a triumphal car' of Thalia, with

the statue of the playwright carried by a whole array of mythological figures ('the Muses, Venus, and the Graces; Cupids,
Nymphs, Fawns and Dryads'), then the principal characters of
the tragedies playing 'in *dumb-show*' representative scenes of *King
Lear, Richard III, Macbeth, Romeo and Juliet, Julius Caesar* and
Coriolanus, then the procession ended with Melpomene herself,
on a chariot, presumably a sublime and portentous figure, with
'an uplifted dagger in her hand'. The culmination of the show,
however, was the last scene, set in a majestic temple, its altar
ornamented with paintings about notable Shakespearean subjects.
The German visitor was fully conscious of the elevated symbolic
meanings suggested by the closing scene; he approved of all he
saw, being convinced that such a ritual deification was appropriate. 'This was a real apotheosis, for it was not literary fanaticism,
but a just admiration of everything that is truly great and sublime, which placed the statue of this immortal genius in the temple
of immortality.'[46] As Archenholz's approving description was read
throughout Europe, it exerted a converting influence, making his
readers accept and adopt ritual patterns of cultic behaviour in
relation to Shakespeare. This influence is difficult to limit in either time or place: in an article titled 'Shakespeare emléke' ('Shakespeare's memorial') Gábor Döbrentei enthusiastically reproduced
Archenholz's account as late as 1817 in the periodical *Erdélyi
Muzéum* (Transylvanian Museum) with the added didactic implication that such reverence for Shakespeare showed how every
civilized country should cultivate its great artists irrespective of
birth or rank. At the 1864 tercentenary two leading Hungarian
theatres (the National Theatre and the Buda Folk Theatre) supplemented their performances of a Shakespeare play with stage
enactments of the playwright's apotheosis.

FROM CRITICISM TO THEODICY: THEOLOGICAL
ANALOGIES IN THE RHETORIC OF APOLOGY

The apologetic arguments of early Shakespeare criticism tended
to follow latent theological patterns. To understand the genesis
of this curious similarity one has to ask a preliminary question
about the progressively more religious vocabulary of eighteenth-
century Shakespeare criticism in England: to what extent and in
what sense were all those sacred and transcendent qualities taken

seriously when attributed to a mere playwright? It would be hardly more than begging the question to point to the well-known humanist tradition of laudatory rhetoric that was ready to call a man of letters *divine* if his fame survived his mortal part. The psychology of that practice is nonetheless far from self-evident. When Petrarch, for example, gave the epithet 'divus' or 'divinus' to Roman emperors as well as to Homer, Cicero or Augustine,[47] all we can safely assume is that he did not mean it in the strictly theological sense. Besides, there is a striking difference between simply calling a poet divine and actually treating him as a perfect and unfathomable transcendental authority who is beyond criticism and deserves an elaborate system of quasi-religious metaphors and similes to glorify him.

Some elements of this sacralizing vocabulary, still mixed with a secular and heterogeneous language of praise, can be discerned as early as the 1660s and they are not rare in the writings of the major critics of the Restoration. But what exactly is the status of such rhetorical devices as John Dryden's admission in the 'Prologue' to his *Aureng-Zebe* (1676) that 'a secret shame / Invades his breast at Shakespeare's sacred name'? Or what is the status of the poetic statement in his prologue to *The Tempest, or The Enchanted Island* (1670) that 'Shakespeare's power is sacred as a king's'? And what degree of seriousness should be attributed to the adjective 'divine' in the 'Preface' to Dryden's *All for Love* (1678) where he 'professed to imitate the divine Shakespeare'? In his *Of Dramatic Poesy: an Essay* (1668) Dryden mentions 'the incomparable Shakespeare', but apparently he does not take his enthusiastic adjective literally; otherwise it would paralyse comparison and preclude relativity. For him Shakespeare is 'the man who of all modern, and perhaps ancient poets, had the largest and most comprehensible soul', which not only compares the incomparable and calls Shakespeare a *man*, but cautiously qualifies the praise with a disenchanting 'perhaps'. Characterizing Ben Jonson, Dryden relativizes his comparison even more unmistakably, despite his emotional preference for the latter. In his *Preface to Troilus and Cressida* (1679) he elaborates several contrasts between Shakespeare and Fletcher, and though finally the distribution of values is much more favourable to Shakespeare, their difference is certainly not that of God and man. In some respects Dryden condemns both playwrights, and Shakespeare receives the heavier sentence: 'In the mechanic beauties of the plot, which are the observation of the three unities, time, place, and action, they are both deficient; but Shakespeare most.' In his *Defence of the Epilogue, or An Essay on the Dramatic Poetry of the Last Age* (1672), having admitted that 'all writers have their imperfections and failings' (an admission that may sound harmless but is a powerful weapon against idolatry), he maintains that Shakespeare's and Fletcher's absurdities, their frequent and gross verbal improprieties, their 'lame' plotting and breaches of decorum can only be explained, though not explained away, by remembering the ignorance of their epoch and its relatively undeveloped state of language and literature. All in all, Dryden finds Shakespeare 'the very Janus of poets', with one face to admire, one to despise: he could write better than any other poet anywhere in the world, but 'he writes in many places below the dullest writer of ours, or of any precedent age'. The sporadic and casual occurrences of sacralizing epithets hardly invade and cannot control Dryden's critical procedures; he knew the difference between the occasions (panegyric, prologue, etc.) when excessive eulogy (of the poetry of Shakespeare or even the Earl of Dorset) could remain unsubstantiated and the realm of criticism proper where every literary phenomenon should be subjected to comparative analysis and relative evaluation.[48] He may have resented Rymer's '*blaspheming* Shakespeare', yet to say that the history of Shakespeare's deification began with the vocabulary of his 'immensely authoritative' criticism[49] is somewhat misleading: despite the sporadic sacralization of its vocabulary, the egalitarian procedures and uncompromising judgements of his Shakespeare criticism are still basically secular.

In the course of the eighteenth century the more and more frequent use of transcendental epithets, whether still coupled with analytical criticism or not, signalled a transformation of the intellectual climate. For Pope, Shakespeare is 'divine' (1737); for Johnson, despite some 'faults' in the plays, he is 'immortal' (1747); and for various authors in the last quarter of the century his genius is 'divine emanation', therefore 'inexplicable' and 'incomprehensible'.[50] When Elizabeth Montagu maintained (1789) that Shakespeare 'was approved by his own age, admired by the next, and is revered, and almost adored by the present', she did not exaggerate the sentiments of her contemporaries.[51] The propriety of quasi-religious adoration was reaffirmed by the communal presentation of eulogies. William Havard's *Ode to the Memory of Shakespeare*, set to music by William Boyce, was sung at the Drury

Lane Theatre in 1757, calling Shakespeare's inspiration 'yet more divine' than the Muse of Homer or the Delphic Oracle, declaring his merits so vast and various that they reveal, partly at least, their higher origin ('How can we sep'rate what's Divine?'), and in its final chorus appealing both to national pride and religious piety ('Then, Britain, boast that to thy Sons was giv'n / The greatest Genius ever sent from Heaven!'). Recommending this ode to the readers of the *London Chronicle*, Arthur Murphy emphasized that unlike most contemporary odes this is not a thoughtless patchwork of borrowed praises but something more balanced and substantial ('at the same time that it is poetical, it is a Critique on Shakespeare'); Havard's ode, however, is definitely *not* critical; in fact it applauds Shakespeare for soaring boldly high 'Above the Rules / Of Critic Schools, / And cool Correctness of the Stagyrite'.[52] David Garrick's *Ode* to Shakespeare (*An Ode upon Dedicating a Building, and Erecting a Statue, to Shakespeare, at Stratford Upon Avon*), partly recited, partly sung (with Thomas Arne's music) at the 1769 Stratford Jubilee, first calls Shakespeare a 'demigod', and 'the god of our idolatry', then wishes Fame to proclaim Shakespeare's 'lov'd, rever'd, immortal name', and in the final chorus exhorts everybody present to 'Sing immortal *Shakespeare*'s praise!'[53]

In Garrick's *Ode* the phrase 'the god of our idolatry', paraphrasing Juliet's adoring invocation to Romeo,[54] was meant to suggest no pejorative implications whatsoever; indeed, some years earlier it had already been used by Garrick in a resolutely apologetic sense, defending Shakespeare against Voltaire's objections.[55] Neither had its variant ('the god of their idolatry') disapproving overtones in the Advertisement in *Bell's Edition of Shakespeare's Plays* (1774), and in 1783 Joseph Ritson called Shakespeare '*the God of the writer's idolatry*' in a sentence that spelled out his own admiration for the infinitely varied art of 'this inimitable author'.[56] But the phrase (and the phenomenon) evoked much less enthusiastic responses as well. The 1769 Jubilee was meant to be pilloried by Francis Gentleman (oddly enough the editor of Bell's edition) when in 1770 he remarked dryly that it 'deserves no better title than theatrical idolatry'.[57] When in 1774 an anonymous treatise (written by Edward Taylor) blamed Shakespeare for ignoring the requirements of poetic justice, the three unities and other norms of dramatic composition, the reviewer of *Gentleman's Magazine* predicted tongue-in-cheek that 'the enthusiastic adorers of

Shakespeare will scarce forgive this sacrilegious attack on that *god of their idolatry*'.[58] The irony of such remarks revives Ben Jonson's sober preference for staying this side idolatry, and their polemic edge indicates the extent to which the psychology of adoration was felt to threaten the down-to-earth procedures of literary criticism. Whether or not the first transcendental epithets of Shakespeare were meant seriously, by now the criticism of his works was in danger of being castigated as sacrilege. Even some clergymen, though belonging to a profession otherwise ambivalent about the deification of a mere secular author, defended Shakespeare against adverse criticism like protecting the sacred against blasphemy: in 1779 the Reverend Martin Sherlock not only invoked Shakespeare as a superhuman being ('Homer was the first of men, but thou art more than man') but also insisted that his own adoring hyperboles were 'literally true' and should be weighed against the opinions of foreigners like Voltaire who 'profaned' Shakespeare's name.[59]

Among scholars we see a reluctance to accept the intimidating implications of the new quasi-religious worship. Attempting to restore Shakespeare's text by removing the errors of Pope's edition, Lewis Theobald confessed 'a Veneration, almost rising to Idolatry, for the Writings of the inimitable Poet', but (as if elucidating what he meant by the sober 'almost') he challenges the over-awed attitude of his predecessor. Quoting Pope's avowed principle of editorial self-effacement ('I have discharged the dull Duty of an Editor [. . .] with a *religious Abhorrence* of all *Innovation*, and without any Indulgence to my private Sense or Conjecture'), Theobald retorts that reverence should not paralyse editorial intervention, and recommends a similar strategy in religious matters as well, implicitly connecting Pope's attitude to his Catholicism:

> I cannot help thinking this Gentleman's *Modesty* in this Point too *nice* and *blameable*; and that what he is pleased to call a *religious Abhorrence* of *Innovation*, is downright *Superstition*: Neither can I be of Opinion that the Writings of SHAKESPEARE are so *venerable*, as that we should be excommunicated from good Sense, for daring to *innovate properly*; or that we ought to be as cautious of altering *their* Text, as we would That of the *sacred Writings*.

The policy of editorial non-intervention is all the more unjustifiable, argues Theobald, as the scholarly editorial work of Dr Bentley revealed 'some Thousands of *various Readings*' in the biblical texts themselves. The editor should not treat the text with tyrannical arbitrariness, but if he is overawed to the extent of shying away from all emendations, his behaviour will be 'almost as absurd as the Indolence of that good honest *Priest*, who had for thirty years together mistakingly, in his Breviary, read *Mumpsimus* for *Sumpsimus*; and being told of his Blunder, and sollicited to correct it, *The Alteration may be just,* said he; *but, however, I'll not change my old MUMPSIMUS for your new SUMPSIMUS.*' Having defended the rights of scholarly criticism in the editing of religious texts as well, Theobald makes no distinction between sacred and profane texts when he concludes that

> whenever a *Gentleman* and a *Scholar* turns *Editor* of any Book, he at the same Time commences *Critick* upon his *Author*; and whenever he finds the Reading suspected, manifestly corrupted, deficient in Sense, and unintelligible, he ought to exert every Power and Faculty of the Mind to [. . .] restore Sense to the Passage, and, by a reasonable Emendation, to make that satisfactory and consistent with the Context, which before was so absurd, unintelligible, and intricate.[60]

This last imperative, when employed indiscriminately, would overrule the principle known as *lectio difficilior* (the editorial assumption that out of any two variant readings it is the more unusual that is likely to be authentic), and it would often lead to a greater banality of the text. (It was this process textual critics had in mind when they forged the term *banalization.*) In his editorial practice, however, Theobald was alert to the possibility of obsolete words or strange usage, and after due consideration he acknowledged their authenticity even at places where his professedly devout and anti-innovationist predecessor chose a later variant for its smooth grammatical correctness. A good case in point is *Hamlet,* Act I, Scene 2, lines 36–7, where Pope (as well as Rowe) had accepted the 1676 quarto reading ('Giving to you no further personal pow'r / OF TREATY with the King, &c') and Theobald rejected it as an erroneous later correction: 'This is a Reading adopted, and of a modern stamp, as I take it; either from Want of Understanding the Poet's genuine Words, or on a Supposition of their being too stiff and obsolete.' He replaced 'of treaty' with 'to business', which he found in all his 'old Copies', explaining that 'to business' meant 'to *negotiate*, or *transact*' with the king, and quoting 'a few' (no fewer than 25!) examples to prove that it 'is a Licence in our Poet, of his own Authority, to coin new *Verbs* both out of *Substantives* and *Adjectives*; and it is, as we may call it, one of the *Quodlibet audendi's* very familiar with him'.[61] This is far from a Pope unhesitatingly eliminating the double comparative and superlative (mercilessly replacing 'This was the most unkindest cut of all' in *Julius Caesar*, Act III, Scene 2 with 'This, this was the unkindest cut of all'), and far from a Dryden confidently declaring that any reader ('who understands English') will find 'in every page' of Shakespeare (or Fletcher) 'some solecism of speech, or some notorious flaw in sense', listing cases of 'false grammar' or 'ill syntax' in *Catiline*, and finding enough in the first pages 'to conclude that Jonson writ not correctly'.[62] Theobald is far from such prescriptive dogmatism, though he is not always consistent in restoring the grammatically deviant phrase and defending the poet's right to differ from the accepted norms of later usage. Occasionally we see him wavering between the requirements of contemporary grammatical ideals (considered absolute by most editors) and the acknowledgement of Shakespearean (or generally Elizabethan) irregularities. Having collected examples of unorthodox pronominal usage (nominative instead of accusative), he ascertains 'a Liberty which *SHAKESPEARE* purposely gave himself', but this time, considering such cases unpardonable violations of grammar and idiom, he endorses Pope's emendations, and finds sufficient reason to make Shakespeare '*now*, at least, speak true *English*'.[63] At moments like this he seems to identify *true* and *contemporary* norms of usage, an identification haunting textual criticism ever since Dryden's evolutionist remark that Shakespeare and Fletcher, 'had they lived now, had doubtless written more correctly'.[64] But whether Theobald accepts or rejects Shakespeare's irregularities, his decision is always substantiated by wholly secular arguments, working on the assumption that it is both the right and the duty of the editor to exercise his reasoning faculty. Opinions may differ about Theobald's achievement as a whole, or whether (as a commentator of his controversy with Pope concluded in 1928) his rehabilitation went too far and his reputation increased 'far beyond his deserts',[65] but he was definitely fighting for the ideal of independent scholarship. Right or wrong, his voice is that of an undaunted professional protesting against the unconditional acceptance of dogmas, whether those of bardolaters or grammarians.

This reluctance to adopt an overawed editorial attitude *vis-à-vis* Shakespeare's texts was not the sole example of resistance. A recent analysis rightly criticized the 'tendency to present Theobald's work as an isolated instance of enlightened editing in a largely unenlightened discipline'.[66] There were other bulwarks of professional independence withstanding the rise of idolatry in eighteenth-century Shakespeare criticism. The culmination of what may be called the secularizing trend in Shakespeare scholarship was probably the achievement of Edmund Malone, whose editorial work has justly been portrayed recently as a construct of the Enlightenment and as the paradigmatic application of such scholarly notions as authenticity, periodization, biographical individuation and chronological arrangement.[67] One should accept the cogently argued thesis that for all his claims of verification Malone's Shakespeare was no less a construct, though different in kind, than those of his predecessors, yet it is worth noting that by having introduced 'chronological arrangement' he not only 'called into being a new mode of viewing the works: as development',[68] but also implied the possibility of less developed early plays (less subtle in characterization, more prone to punning, etc.), a relativizing implication omnipresent in Malone's work and clearly incompatible with the myth of Shakespeare's perfection and the imperative to explain away any deficiencies. It is deeply symbolic that it was Malone's ruthless investigation that annihilated the authenticity claims of the Ireland forgeries, the pseudo-autographs revered as relics, and put an end to their adoration.

Yet for all their sober efforts it was not the Theobalds nor the Malones who determined the overall character of the eighteenth-century critical and editorial discourse about Shakespeare. The dominantly apologetic arguments of contemporary Shakespeare criticism tended towards a barely secularized version of a pious genre which, although it originated in religious philosophy, pervaded the literature of the period: the *theodicy*, or the treatise that seeks to justify the ways of God to man. All the diverse and ingenious rescue operations that sought to explain away any flaws in Shakespeare's text relied on the assumption that the parts are manifestations of a design both perfect and unfathomable. There is an interesting similarity between the theological argument from design, the attempt to prove the existence of God by postulating that the coherent order of the universe must have required a supreme designer, and the amazement of late eighteenth-century critics who seriously wondered whether the inexplicable perfection of Shakespeare's design could have been invented and executed by a mortal author at all. Ironically it was the same age in which David Hume challenged the argument from design[69] that gave birth, to mention but one example, to Maurice Morgann's rapture of overawed self-humiliation in front of a dramatic *oeuvre* that seemed to have been planned and executed by a quasi-transcendental authority. In Shakespeare's works 'every thing seems superior', because in showing the motives and results of human behaviour he conveys an unmistakable sense of necessity, yet he 'submits himself so little to our judgement' that we are unable to account for it in any analytical way:

> We discern not his cause, we see no connection of cause and effect, we are rapt in ignorant admiration, and claim no kindred with his abilities. All the incidents, all the parts, look like chance, whilst we feel and are sensible that the whole is design. [. . .] I restrain the further expressions of my admiration lest they should not seem applicable to man; but it is really astonishing that a mere human being, a part of humanity only, should so perfectly comprehend the whole [. . .].[70]

Yet this admission of the critic's own (human) inadequacy to comprehend the full depth and intricate workings of Shakespeare's superior design was not followed by self-negation or surrender; in fact Morgann's essay analyses Falstaff's character to retrieve no less than Shakespeare's true intention and to refute the suggestion that the playwright 'ever meant to make Cowardice an essential part of his constitution'.[71] In spite of the critic's admiration, admittedly in danger of exceeding the degree 'applicable to man', he does not abstain from scrutinizing what the designer may have *meant* to make.

Neither does the Reverend Richard Stack in his reply, which refers to Morgann's essay as 'one of the most ingenious pieces of criticism' but objects to its misconception of Shakespeare's design that he feels confident enough to rectify by a close rereading of the entire play. He thinks 'it might be shown that Shakespeare has designed cowardice, rather than constitutional courage, to be a part of Falstaff's real character' and goes on to marshal evidence from details Morgann overlooked or ignored. The procedure is analytical, patient and painstaking; the argument is rational; and instead of Morgann's self-deprecating admiration in front of a superior intelligence the reply attempts to reconstruct the logic of an equal:

> Can we suppose then that Shakespeare, if he had designed to exhibit Falstaff as naturally brave, would in the first scene of our acquaintance with him have given strong intimation of his cowardice? which he has unquestionably done in the scheme laid for him by Poins, and in the observations made upon the probable conduct of Falstaff.

Demonstrating that by such self-serving omissions Morgann 'slurred over' details which could have revealed 'plainly the poet's design', and that to substantiate his erroneous view Morgann had to resort to 'systems of malice in the plot which certainly the poet never designed', the author of the reply seems to feel that he *proved* his own point with the certainty of any scientist concluding a decisive experiment. It is no mere coincidence that this thoroughly secular refutation was conceived by the Reverend Richard Stack, a priest, scholar and scientist, the vice-president of the Royal Irish Academy, whose energies were divided between writing studies of the Bible and an introduction to chemistry. In the role of literary critic a priest can be no advocate of evil, but Stack clearly refuses either to explain away or to exaggerate the moral problem implied in his own conception of Falstaff's character. He notices 'the strange arts by which Shakespeare has drawn our liking toward so offensive an object; or to speak with more precision, has contrived to veil the offensive parts of his character' but he does not condemn Shakespeare's art for demoralizing the audience.[72] The implication of his method suggests that for him Shakespeare criticism is not the proper occasion for over-awed worship, self-paralysing reverence or moral preaching.

It is only in view of these competing assumptions about Shakespeare's human or superhuman mind that one can understand the reasoning of Samuel Taylor Coleridge, deeply concerned with theological issues, but also endowed with diverse talents for psychology, philosophy and natural sciences that he sought to reconcile with his quest for a religious meaning of life.[73] A superficial glance at his Shakespeare criticism might show him as he is often taken to be: the paragon of bardolaters. On closer inspection, however, we discern a fascinating dilemma of secular and quasi-religious attitudes in his reasoning. In an intricate passage of his seventh lecture on Shakespeare and Milton, he mentions two distinct kinds of self-paralysis in the face of enigmatic details the critic finds too difficult to interpret. Although both are connected to 'a characteristic of Shakespeare, which belongs to a man of profound thought and high genius', Coleridge dismisses them as unnecessary and unacceptable. The first leads to giving up any hope of understanding a text because it seems (now or maybe forever) to transcend our abilities:

> It has been too much the custom, when anything that happened in his dramas could not easily be explained by the few words the poet has employed, to pass it idly over, and to say that it is beyond our reach, and beyond the power of philosophy – a sort of terra incognita for discoverers – a great ocean to be hereafter explored.

The other way of retreat is chosen by those who would accept and indeed revere disconnectedness as absolute, sublime, even sacred, treating 'such passages as hints and glimpses of something now non-existent, as the sacred fragments of an ancient and ruined temple, all the portions of which are beautiful, although their particular relation to each other is unknown'. (This simile may be more than a fictitious heuristic device; it may allude to actual sacralizing comparisons of this type, like the one whereby Elizabeth Montagu exhorted readers to admire the 'stupendous parts' of Shakespeare's works even when they remain ultimately inexplicable: 'Will not an intelligent spectator admire the prodigious structures of Stonehenge, because he does not know by what law of mechanics they were raised?'[74]) So far Coleridge's argument seems to imply the necessity of an alternative rationale, egalitarian and secular, to sustain the hope of intelligibility; but the subsequent refutation of critical surrender almost explicitly resorts to apologetic strategies Coleridge must have known from theological discussions. To maintain that it is not hopeless for us to understand Shakespeare ('study, and the possession of some small stock of the knowledge by which he worked, will enable us to detect and explain his meaning') Coleridge exhorts us to have confidence in the consistency of the superb order created by an intellect that knew even the 'most minute and intimate workings' of the human mind, a consistency reliable enough to be used as our aid in detecting scribal error and making sense:

Shakespeare [...] never introduces a word, or a thought, in vain or out of place: if we do not understand him, it is our own fault or the fault of the copyists and typographers [...] He never wrote at random, or hit upon points of character and conduct by chance; and the smallest fragment of his mind not unfrequently gives a clue to a most perfect, regular, and consistent whole.[75]

Surprisingly enough, Coleridge's argument resembles an eighteenth-century mode of thinking he treated with ever growing aversion: the operations of an excessively rationalist theological tradition that was still flourishing in his day. Reiterating that nothing is random in Shakespeare's works (excluding the possibility of anything accidental or unintended), considering even the smallest details of his text as necessary and justifiable parts in a perfect design from an omniscient mind, and attributing all the apparent obscurities to the frailties of transmission or those of the recipient, Coleridge (perhaps unwittingly) fuses the apologetic strategies we might call literary theodicy with the very technique of Christian apologetics he was otherwise more and more reluctant to accept: the argument from design. Just as William Paley (1743–1805) sought to prove the existence of a benevolent God by pointing to omnipresent 'evidences' of a transcendent design in nature, Coleridge exhorts critics to assume an all-pervading and perfect design in each Shakespearean play and to rely on this assumption whenever they are facing any problem in establishing the text, interpreting its meaning and ascertaining its value. One cannot but agree with the observation that Coleridge 'approaches Shakespeare with greater reverence than Paley approaches Holy Writ' and that 'this reverence involves a recognition of symbolic tension'.[76] Yet it is no exaggeration to add that Coleridge read Shakespeare precisely the way Paley read nature: with a firm belief in an underlying design of absolute authority and with the resolution to treat even the smallest detail as evidence of its manifestation.

Similar as these apologetic reading habits seem to be, they were applied to different phenomena; hence neither their philosophical value nor their moral impact could be the same. For the subtle analytical mind and ethically tuned religious sensibility of Coleridge it was but a question of time to discover the philosophical and moral problems lurking behind Paley's theology.

After a relatively brief period of youthful enthusiasm for Paley he began to suspect an untenable circular reasoning in the argument from design. In *Aids to Reflection* he mentioned the possibility that a crucial passage in Paley was impaired by 'dialectic flaws' like *petitio principii* and *argumentum in circulo*[77]; in *Table Talk* he suggests that even Kant failed when trying to prove the existence of God, and sums up the problem with admirable lucidity:

> Assume the existence of God, – and then the harmony and fitness of the physical creation may be shown to correspond with and support such an assumption; – but to set about *proving* the existence of a God by such means is a mere circle, a delusion. It can be no proof to a good reasoner, unless he violates all syllogistic logic, and presumes his conclusion.[78]

When applied to Shakespeare's texts, one might add, the self-serving circularity of such reasoning is no less evident, yet a wholesale condemnation of its impact would be unfair. Meant as an exhortation to unfold and discover, it encouraged analysis even if it triggered pre-structuralist analyses that precluded the possibility of any inner conflict or incoherence in the text as artistic flaws incompatible with the assumed unity of the author's supreme design. The results and conclusions of this apologetic method were difficult to falsify, at least within the orbit of its ruling assumption, but in literary interpretations a residue of circularity can be accepted as hermeneutical necessity. And one would think (innocently) that in Shakespeare criticism there is less at stake than in theodicy proper and that therefore the chances of philological self-correction are slightly better.

But are they? When reading late eighteenth- and early nineteenth-century Shakespeare criticism one has the uneasy feeling that the assumption of Shakespeare's impeccable design was largely responsible for fostering those soaring eulogies of pseudo-criticism an eminent scholar used to label *idolatry ad astra*.[79] Coleridge used and propagated the assumption so as to urge his contemporaries not to be overawed and to keep up their efforts to explore hidden meanings; nevertheless many of his fellow-critics followed an easier path. Reading these bardolaters one wonders about the actual moral impact of Paleyite apologetics both in theology and in Shakespeare criticism. Although Coleridge himself initially defended Paley's theology on moral grounds,[80] and in his Cambridge days once (1793) welcomed it as a means to pacify human discontent (including his own),[81] he soon realized that Paley's approach led to double-edged ethical consequences. In 1806 he severely criticized Paley's 'mode of defending Christianity' because it made people look outward instead of inward and thus it 'has increased the number of infidels',[82] and in *Aids to Reflection* (1825) he wages war on Paley's dangerously spreading doctrine: 'I believe myself bound in conscience to throw the whole force of my intellect in the way of this triumphal car, on which the tutelary genius of modern Idolatry is borne, even at the risk of being crushed under the wheels!'[83] In Shakespeare criticism the assumption of perfect design could have encouraged infidel behaviour in the good sense of the word (after all Coleridge used it to persuade critics not to treat enigmatic texts as sacrosanct ruins of some ancient temple) but in fact it served the tutelary genius of idolatry. Coleridge's own Shakespeare criticism is dominantly secular, and justifies the opinion that 'his *relative* freedom from idolatry [. . .] can be reasonably maintained if we admit the crucial distinction between extravagant praise and transmutation of the thing praised',[84] but the assumption he propagated could easily be assimilated by a quasi-religious transmutation of Shakespeare and his works. In addition to apologetic critical strategies, the manifestations of this transmutation included a whole range of devout (verbal and ritual) acts, from the worshipful use of transcendental epithets to the pious yet carnivalesque anniversary celebrations. The Shakespeare cult of his age, unlike that of Ben Jonson, was hardly this side of idolatry.

FROM JOURNEY TO PILGRIMAGE: THE RELIGIOUS PSYCHOLOGY OF THE STRATFORD VISITS

A journey through boundaries both spatial and spiritual, the pilgrimage often appears in the guise of tourism. If one analyses the behaviour of a rapidly growing number of people, from the eighteenth century onwards, as they travel to Stratford, as they collect and treasure souvenirs with a devotion fitting for relics, or as some of them explicitly testify to having experienced a kind of mystical illumination at Shakespeare's grave, one is reassured that everything falls into the latent pattern of the pilgrimage. The setting may be more and more institutionalized, technological, even commercial, yet the motivation at work preserves something ancient and fundamental. Indeed, some elements of their behaviour make sense only if we assume that as a whole it was patterned, whether they were aware of it or not, on the religious pilgrimage. Many of them, however, were fully aware of it; they applied the term 'pilgrimage' to their own journey. The metaphor itself is not our own retrospective imposition, even though it is our decision to take its implications seriously enough to analyse the Stratford visits as quasi-religious phenomena belonging to the same system of cultic appropriation as some forms of apologetic criticism or anniversary rituals.

To take the latent assumption of literary pilgrimages seriously enough to justify sustained attention and analysis, research is best conducted in a spirit of sympathetic agnosticism. Difficult as it is to suppress commonsensical doubts and commonplace questions, let us not enquire whether the great son of that little town had *really* been a transcendental being or not; if bits and pieces from the mulberry tree he once planted have been treated as objects of worship by the visitors, then these people behaved *as if* he had been more than human and *as if* religious forms of worship were appropriate. One need not share these assumptions to analyse their psychology, but it would probably be more detrimental to take an unsympathetic or hostile stance, and either to deplore all kinds of pilgrimage (including the religious) as anachronistic and superstitious, or to condemn literary pilgrimages as spilt religion, pathetic instances of misplaced devotion, nothing but ridiculous surrogates of the real thing. The quasi-religious is not necessarily secondary, let alone second-rate. Surrogate it often may be, and sometimes it admittedly is for the very people involved, but to label it ridiculous would be unwise (its motives resemble those of religious pilgrimages too much not to compromise them), unfair and unproductive. While we sneer at the devout feelings of visitors at Shakespeare's birthplace or his grave we could occasionally condescend to allow a more or less playful *metaphor* of pilgrimage, and could, at most, hint at its ironical adequacy, or try to explain it away by sweeping generalizations about, say, the English national character, its indifference to aesthetic pleasure, and its Puritanical sense of duty for which the excursion to Stratford feels vaguely pleasant as a rewarding moral accomplishment.[85] But giving the rein to such mildly patronizing impulses, or to stronger feelings either for or against the Stratford phenomenon, will foreclose any patient comparative study that could reveal their psychological connections with well-known types of religious pilgrimages. Even a mere juxtaposition with those types (the *prototypical* initiated by the founder or first apostles of a religion, the *archaic* fused with earlier faiths and symbols, the *medieval* originating between 500 and 1400 AD in Europe and saturated with the theological and philosophical notions of that period, and the *modern* developed after the Council of Trent and especially in the nineteenth and twentieth centuries as a form of Christian apologetics responding to the challenge of post-Darwinian secularization and using the new means of transport and communication[86]) would look grotesque unless one were prepared to give totally unorthodox manifestations of devout feelings at least the benefit of the doubt.

That juxtaposition, providing opportunities for instructive comparisons, is encouraged by anthropologists who discovered a continuity, embarrassing as it may sound to the dogmatic, between forms of behaviour that used to be thought of as antithetical. Often it is difficult or wellnigh impossible to tell how much in the feelings of a tourist is subconsciously governed by residual patterns of pilgrim psychology. As an appendix to the types of religious pilgrimage, anthropologists justly add examples of the secular type, arguing that religiously institutionalized or not, 'some form of deliberate travel to a far place intimately associated with the deepest, most cherished, axiomatic values of the traveler seems to be a cultural universal'.[87] On the surface the motivation of those making such journeys seems to differ greatly, but a latent yearning for the transcendental is not difficult to detect. When surveying the different varieties of covert pilgrimages anthropologists include the Soviet millions who used to visit Lenin's tomb as a token of political reverence (and as, let us add, a barely secularized enactment of an old pre-burial rite memorably incorporated in Dostoevsky's *The Brothers Karamazov*); they also include those millions of Americans who participated in 'a sort of secular jubilee' in 1976, the bicentenary of the birth of their country, by visiting memorable places of the liberation struggle and singing 'secular psalms' of patriotic feeling. More surprisingly, but with no less justification, they include the multitudes in certain unguarded moments of their vacation: 'When people bury themselves in anonymous crowds on beaches, they are seeking an almost sacred, often symbolic, mode of *communitas*, generally unavailable to them in the structured life of the office.'[88] The journey to Stratford generally preserves much more of the ritual and psychology of the religious pilgrimage than these diverse symbolic activities do. It is an intermediary version between religious and secular practices, much nearer to the former than half way between the two. As regards its forms of behaviour and their motivation it is closely related to the so-called *modern* type of religious pilgrimage, but the complexity of its sustaining traditions resembles features of the *archaic* type, although it appeals to (and gratifies) religious needs in a much more indirect way and it is often characterized by various forms of divided loyalty between the sacred and the secular.

The more and more widespread recognition and acceptance of the journey to Stratford as a meaningful social custom is clearly evidenced by some of its prominent early practitioners, who recorded their experiences and feelings on the way; no less revealing is the story of custom formation told by statistical figures. It is evident from both types of sources that the house revered as Shakespeare's birthplace, his last home (known as New Place), and his grave in Holy Trinity Church made the little town increasingly attractive to pilgrims. Although the town was no longer the same as it was in the poet's youth (in 1594 and 1595 approximately two hundred houses were burnt down, and an additional 52 fell victim to another fire in 1614) the sites of the beginning and end of his life retained an air of authenticity for those longing to see, hear and touch everything the Bard saw, heard and touched. In the seventeenth century this was not yet a custom, and the sporadic visitors were motivated by miscellaneous needs like Thomas Fuller (1608–61) who came to compile material for his *The Worthies of England* (published posthumously in 1662). The first known visitor to be considered a literary pilgrim is a certain Mr Dowdall who in 1693 was given something like a guided tour of the church by an old verger who supplied him with some local episodes from the poet's life. Shortly after this, in 1694, a young man called William Hall arrived from Oxford with the purpose of visiting the ashes of the great Shakespeare.[89] The first significant actor to make a pilgrimage to the birthplace was Thomas Betterton. Once the admired Hamlet of the Restoration period, he gratefully paid his tribute, probably in 1708, and searched through the town archives and church register to find out more about the creator of his great role. Garrick's Great Jubilee in 1769 contributed more than anything else to the social acceptance of Stratford as a pilgrim centre. Before the Jubilee he predicted, apparently with the wish to make a self-fulfilling prophecy, that long after the architectural beauties of the town had ceased to be admired the humble birthplace would still attract visitors who 'will rush thither to behold it, as a pilgrim would to the shrine of some loved saint; will deem it holy ground, and dwell with sweet though pensive rapture, on the natal habitation of the poet'.[90] He was fully conscious of the economic implications: shortly afterwards, in 1770, he urged the modernization of the town with the suggestion that a well paved and well lighted place would 'allure everybody to visit the *Holy-land*'.[91] It reveals the quasi-religious feelings the Jubilee seemed to sanction that its aftermath abounds in devout gestures: in 1770 Dr Paul Hiffernan made an elaborate 'PLAN of a permanent TEMPLE, to be erected to the Memory of SHAKESPEARE'.[92] But the birthplace itself was felt to be something like a temple; a royal princess fell on her knee at the threshold. The way visitors responded to this humble secular building was more and more akin to their feelings and behaviour at Shakespeare's grave in the church; by the turn of the century at both places many felt and behaved as if they were entering a shrine of some remote yet familiar and permissive denomination, and as regards psychological function by then a shrine it was.

By giving prominent symbolic roles to Shakespearean objects in the Jubilee ceremony it was also Garrick who effectively sanctified the transubstantiation of souvenirs into relics. It is not only that the steward's wand and medal he wore had been made of the famous mulberry tree that had been planted by Shakespeare himself, but he set an example for a transparently quasi-liturgical use of a goblet reputedly made from that tree. Acquiring a tangible memento of the Stratford trip was no longer a sheer tourist habit; there is more to it than the deceptively secular, often monetary, transaction would suggest. As Horace Walpole recorded in 1777, visitors cut off pieces from 'Shakespeare's chair' as souvenirs; in 1785 Sir John Byng tells us that the old flooring of the bedroom had fallen victim to similar enthusiasm, and he reports the testimony of an inhabitant of the house that it was only after the Jubilee that people began to think so highly of the chair. Sir John bought a tempting little piece (for the time being because later he purchased the whole lower crossbar) and was sufficiently enthusiastic to steal a tile from the grave.[93] The diary of John Adams, who visited the place with Thomas Jefferson in 1786, reveals that such behaviour was usual by that time, and one may conjecture, perhaps, that some less devout visitors simply felt the need to comply with expectations. 'They shew Us an old Wooden Chair in the Chimney Corner, where He sat. We cut off a Chip according to the Custom.'[94] It would be too much to assume that every visitor who followed that custom was prompted by strong quasi-religious feelings, but their behaviour would often be inexplicable without some such motives or at least by a half-hearted approval of its latent psychology. Even somebody as sober as Georg Lichtenberg (1742–99), natural scientist and literary critic, in principle opposed to any cult of genius, an enemy of both mysticism and sentimentality, must have felt at least some sympathy with the hidden irrational need of literary enthusiasts. In a letter to Johann Christian Dieterich on 18 October 1775 he gave a brief account of his own behaviour at the birthplace, and its motivation looks far from simple.

> Neulich reisste ich durch Stratford am Avon in Warwickshire, dem Ort wo Shakespeare gebohren ist. Ich sah sein Haus, und habe auf seinem Stuhl gesessen, von dem man anfängt Stücke abzuschneiden. Ich habe mir auch etwas davon für 1 Schilling abgeschnitten. Ich werde es in Ringe setzen lassen, und nach Art der Lorenzo-Dosen unter die Jacobiter und Göthiter vertheilen.[95]

At first sight this gesture is motivated by no more than the sense of propriety of an accomplished literary gentleman who refers to Sterne's *Sentimental Journey* where Yorick was presented by Lorenzo with a snuff-box (a motif taken over by Friedrich Heinrich Jacobi in his *Winterreise* in 1769), and it requires no personal involvement to buy a splinter from Shakespeare's chair with the intention of mounting it in rings to be distributed at home among devotees of Goethe and Jacobi. But even if Lichtenberg's brief account of the event reveals a touch of irony, it is not the testimony of a mere outsider. His more committed gestures must not be ignored and cannot be explained away: he sat in Shakespeare's chair himself; the letter about his Stratford visit is only one in a series of glowing, occasionally rhapsodizing reports about Shakespeare performances and Garrick's acting seen in England;[96] as late as in 1791 the first sight of the Boydell edition prompted him to exclaim ecstatically in his diary that he saw the *divine* Shakespeare ('Den göttlichen Shakespeare gesehen!!'[97]). Hence one cannot exclude the possibility that when sitting in the famous chair even he hoped, maybe subconsciously, to receive some sort of inspiration from its touch. The visitors' desire to sit in Shakespeare's chair was so irresistible that the chair exhibited at the birthplace had to be supplied with a new seat (made of hard oak) every three years.[98]

Surveying the Shakespearean objects revered as relics in the late eighteenth century one finds that their common denominator was the claim to have been touched by the poet. It is only by assuming a vague and atavistic belief (or a willing suspension of modern disbelief) in the sacralizing power and somehow life-enhancing magic of the original touch that we can explain why visitors seem to have been possessed by a common desire to touch and be touched by something that Shakespeare had touched. This need and its latent logic was so irresistible that it overruled the alternative criterion of relics, that is their belonging to a sacred and hence consecrating locality (such an object was not required to have originated in Stratford) and it eroded in everybody but the most austere-minded the determination to submit the object to a severe test of its authenticity. As we have seen, the reception of the Ireland forgeries[99] is a case in point: when (early in 1795) they were first exhibited in London, James Boswell knelt down in front of the allegedly Shakespearean manuscripts, ceremoniously kissed them, thanked God that he was allowed to see these invaluable relics, and said that after *this* he would die contented. Although the manuscripts could not deceive the textual expertise of Edmond Malone, all parties seem to have assumed that there was more at stake than sheer philological truth. No manuscript unless taken as a relic and treasured for that sacred touch could justify the tormented sigh of old Samuel Ireland when he told his son (after their frustrated hunt for manuscripts in Stratford) that he would give all his rare books for a single line written by Shakespeare's own hand.[100] And this yearning of the father would not have prompted the zealous forging activities of his son had the latter not been conditioned from his early childhood by many an after-dinner session of reading together and extolling the plays of this divine author to admire Shakespeare as an incomparable and immortal genius. It was probably rightly assumed that the historian of Stratford (Robert Bell Wheler), the forger of the Shakespeare manuscripts (William Henry Ireland), the painstaking scholar who proved that they were not genuine (Edmond Malone) and many others shared a tacit 'assumption that life would be infinitely richer from touching what Shakespeare's hand had touched, an assumption of the immanence and indwelling of the god of their idolatry'.[101] It is somewhat less convincing, however, to interpret this common element as 'a romantic belief that the spirit is immanent in matter, that genius can hallow the common earth it touched briefly long ago'.[102] The belief that justifies the reverential attitude towards relics (religious or literary) may have been revived and was definitely fostered by Romanticism but it is much older than the Romantic age and relies on ancient notions about magic transfer and spiritual survival. As my analysis of the Garrick Jubilee demonstrates, the ritual use of relics in 1769 followed underlying biblical patterns established many centuries before. The entire collection of curious Shakespeareana exhibited at the birthplace in the late eighteenth and all through the nineteenth centuries[103] (the Birthday Museum was opened in 1859) was too miscellaneous not to contain many objects that had no religious archetype, but even the most profane-looking of them belonged to the same quasi-religious system, whether their genuineness could be demonstrated or not. (And whether this demonstration was decisive or not, the gradual institutionalization of testing also followed latent ecclesiastical archetypes: in the mid-nineteenth century the Birthday Trustees defined the criteria of authenticity and commissioned a curator to inspect objects closely, though such measures could not safeguard against dubious items.)

In the early nineteenth century many observers recorded the popular feelings behind the Stratford movement that grew to an unprecedented magnitude and left its quasi-religious imprint on the nascent secular and commercial genre: the guidebook. In his *History and Antiquities of Stratford-upon-Avon* (1806) Robert Bell Wheler made his best not to sound condescending about local enthusiasm and to confirm the pilgrim spirit as something not unworthy of an educated visitor. When he comes to describe the church Wheler makes a characteristic remark, guarded, controlled, studiously detached, that both describes and justifies contemporary religious sentiments evoked there by Shakespeare's grave. 'A recollection that it covers the ashes of our admired Bard, contributes, to some degree, to the reverence this sacred mausoleum inspires; and by the enthusiastic native in particular, some extraordinary adoration, even with a religious zeal, may justly be offered to the manes of his immortal townsman.' *Justly* offered: the adverb confirms and reassures all the more as it surfaces in cool, balanced and meditative prose. This tone is sustained all through the book, and the admiring epithets ('Our immortal Bard', 'the pride of nature and paradigm of poets') will be all the more emphatic as they appear amid prosaic biographical data.[104] In a similar book with the epoch-making title of *A Guide to Stratford-upon-Avon* (1814) Wheler's persuasive rhetoric both suggests and endorses pilgrim mentality from the very beginning of his narration. '*Stratford-upon-Avon* is possessed of peculiar attractions', he writes in his first sentence, 'and by every admirer of the matchless Bard to whom it gave birth [. . .] is approached with sentiments that few places inspire.' Wheler pronounces not only that Shakespeare's name 'confers immortality upon his native town', and that his genius illuminates the surrounding countryside, but implicitly suggests that the unequalled excellence of his dramatic poetry justifies his own sacralizing vocabulary as well as the behaviour he observed. The whole opening paragraph is reassuring; it is meant to inform readers about a custom and convince them of its propriety. 'So natural, and so laudable, is the curiosity which induces every inquisitive and enlightened traveller to visit this classical and consecrated ground, that very few leave unexplored any part of the town that bears the slightest memorial of the divine bard, who was and ever will be its greatest pride and ornament.'[105] A dignified opening for a guidebook, a novelty at the time, and familiar to us only because in its wake that is how Stratford guidebooks have sounded over the centuries.

Around 1806, the year when Wheler's proto-guidebook was published, the warden of the birthplace (between 1793 and 1820 a certain Mrs Mary Hornby, whose rather dubious character is preserved in several vivid, though not exactly flattering descriptions) was receiving about 1,000 visitors annually, a considerable figure when compared to the 2,500 inhabitants of the town.[106] The reverence of these visitors varied in intensity from the playful and willing suspension of disbelief to the most serious devotion. For those with the former disposition the inevitable intrusion of the profane and commercial in Stratford was but a nuisance, tolerable because amusing; for those with the latter it was downright blasphemy. As for the former type, Washington Irving was a good and influential example: the essay (in his *Sketch Book*) on his Stratford trip was widely read, disseminating the charms of an elegant non-commitment that was both warm and cool, sympathetic and aloof, nostalgic and disillusioned. He went to Stratford 'on a poetical pilgrimage' in 1815 and saw that the authenticity of the relics exhibited by Mrs Hornby, 'a garrulous old lady', was questionable and in some cases clearly false, not to speak of her claims 'to a lineal descent from the poet' that she wanted to demonstrate by a drama of her own. Yet he thought it wise to accept the rules of the game. 'I am always of easy faith in such matters, and am ever willing to be deceived, where the deceit is pleasant and costs nothing,' he tells us, arguing that whether the relics and legends offered are true or false, we should try to 'persuade ourselves into the belief of them' with the enlightened attitude of 'resolute good-humoured credulity'. He managed to do so, and tactfully concealed his doubts when listening to Mrs Hornby and inspecting 'the relics with which this, like all other celebrated shrines, abounds'. In addition to the famous chair he mentions the stock of Shakespeare's matchlock, his tobacco box, the sword he played Hamlet with and an array of objects made from the mulberry tree 'which seems to have as extraordinary powers of self-multiplication as the wood of the true cross; of which there is enough extant to build a ship of the line'. At Shakespeare's grave, however, where his emotions were 'no longer checked and thwarted by doubt', the unquestionable authenticity of the place evoked the devotion of the true pilgrim: here he admitted to having been overwhelmed by 'the idea, that, in very truth, the remains of Shakespeare were mouldering beneath my feet. It was a long time before I could prevail upon myself to leave the place.'[107]

In spite of this final exaltation of feelings, Irving's account is rich in overtones of subtle and affectionate irony and suggests a certain distance from the cult. The documents of the other visitors of the period, like the Hungarian Baron Miklós Wesselényi, display an entirely different attitude: they found anything profane abhorrent and considered the commercial contamination of tourism there a sacrilege. 'It was with sacred reverence that I looked at the birthplace of that great man,' Wesselényi wrote in his diary in 1822; 'I saw the church, Shakespeare's grave, his house, and several relics of his [. . .] and reverently made my tribute by writing *in Hungarian* in the book that contains the names of everybody who makes a pilgrimage, with or without sacred feelings, to this sacred place.' Nothing could be more characteristic of his own sacred feelings (mingled with the pride of the patriot representing his nation) than his fierce reaction when confronted with the intrusion of even the smallest profane phenomena, be it the real goosefeather pen in the statue-Shakespeare's hand or the obtrusive and shop-minded talkativeness of the warden.[108] As can be expected, he declared himself to have been disgusted and infuriated by Mrs Hornby's behaviour; his indignation was so intense that one suspects a latent biblical analogy governing his interpretation of the situation: money-changers in the temple.

Shrine, relics, pilgrimage: the same religious notions are used in the accounts of both visitors, but whereas Irving is ironically playing with the possibility of quasi-transcendence and comes very near to suggesting a similar stance towards its religious archetype as well, Wesselényi displays an almost equal reverence to both. It is safe to assume that the majority of early nineteenth-century visitors felt more like him than the American writer, but their behaviour shows traces of a more popular sort of quasi-religious worship. The blank walls of the house, and especially the room where Shakespeare was supposed to have been born, were not left intact for long. To cover the whitewash with names proved to be an irresistible temptation for visitors yearning to record their arrival, and the proliferation of signatures revealed 'the idolatry manifested for the chamber wherein Shakespeare first inhaled the breath of life'. This latter opinion comes from John Wilson whose catalogue of Shakespeareana (1827) could not have been compiled without a residue of a not entirely different attachment; he tells us that in the previous twenty years visitors had written their names over 'the ceiling, sides, projecting chimney, in short, every portion of the surface'.[109] The inscriptions on the walls testified to the social diversity of early nineteenth-century visitors. As Irving recorded a decade earlier, the 'walls of its squalid chambers are covered with names and inscriptions in every language, by pilgrims of all nations, ranks, and conditions, from the prince to the peasant'.[110] Wilson deciphered names from the realm of art, like those of Moore, Scott, Kemble and Kean, many autographs of politicians from both Houses of Parliament, and some persons of even higher standing, such as the regent who was to become George IV, Austrian and Russian princes and Lucien Bonaparte. Thomas Carlyle cut his name in the window-pane during a visit in 1824. Seized with sudden enthusiasm, Tennyson added his name to the many on the walls in 1840, though he was somewhat ashamed of it afterwards. All in all, an impressive list, even if some of the autographs, like that of the Duke of Wellington, may not have been genuine.

To illustrate how pilgrim psychology coheres with the rhetoric of apologetic arguments and the ritual of occasional celebrations in this period the most telling example is *The First Annual Jubilee Oration Upon the Life, Character, and Genius of Shakespeare*, delivered by an American actor, George Jones, at Stratford-upon-Avon on 23 April 1836. Dedicated to King William IV and addressed to the Royal Shakespearean Club, the oration was subsequently published (in the same year) with the telling motto 'palmam qui meruit ferat' (he who deserves the palm should take it), aptly epitomizing the gesture whereby a visitor from a far-away land testifies to the well-deserved worship of Shakespeare. In his dedication to the king Jones described himself as 'a Pilgrim from the New-World' who came 'to the Shrine of the "time-honoured" Bard'; later in his speech he considered the humble birthplace 'to the poetic pilgrim far more dear than the sceptred palace', remembered 'that all ranks worshipped there', and felt (with no trace of irony) that to shed a tear was 'but the pilgrim's tribute to "the God of his idolatry"'. At the grave he could not suppress the pious wish that long 'may future Pilgrims esteem the *Man*, when they venerate the *Poet*'. After several other references to the underlying pattern of pilgrimage Jones reaffirms his status as 'the Pilgrim from the New-World', and closes his oration with a hymnic parallel, indeed equation, between the worship of Shakespeare and that of God, based (with full seriousness) on an article of apocryphal theology: 'the praise that is offered to thee, O! Shakspeare! is but gratitude to a mightier power; [. . .] it ascends on the voice of thanksgiving, to the throne of that GOD, who ordained thee to receive THE VENERATION OF THE UNIVERSE.' The life of Shakespeare is narrated by Jones to illustrate that adversity is good for the development of character, and his death is imagined and extolled as the exemplary Christian death ('his once fiery eyes were dimmed [. . .] by the joyful tear of a dying Christian', 'dying in moral and religious quietude, his Soul must have mounted on the smile of tranquility, to the eternal presence of his Creator and his God!'); moreover, the entire story is offered as something like a parable with a transcendent lesson since it 'should teach us that that Power which governs even "the fall of a sparrow," is not unmindful of the image of Himself'. These ideas dovetail with several apologetic arguments in the oration; though Jones professes to be an advocate of Shakespeare and not his apologist, he argues that the plays' alleged anachronisms are but translators' errors, he maintains that anything obscene, vulgar or careless in them must have been interpolated by the actors, and he accepts the allegation about Shakespeare's lack of classical education only to demonstrate the great creative power of the poet's 'unassisted' mind.[111] The pilgrim may have come from the New World but the quasi-religious system of his ideas must have sounded familiar to his English audience.

By the mid-nineteenth century the steps of many a visitor (by 1856 their annual number reached 3,000[112]) were directed by a thoroughly romanticized sense of pilgrimage. The title page of Charles Vaughan Grinfield's book (1850) indicates the ease with which the two traditions dovetailed: the title is *A Pilgrimage to Stratford-upon-Avon, the Birthplace of Shakespeare*, and the motto extols the incomparable genius: 'Thou Genius, who hast never met thy peer, / Who shall with thee contend – with thee – SHAKE-SPEAR!' The book itself was meant to foster this attitude; the author admitted at the beginning that the 'design of this little "PILGRIMAGE" is to supply the numerous visitors [. . .] with a pleasant companion and guide', and the first pages were filled with quotations from laudatory verses including Warton's invocation at the Avon ('O Goddess, guide my pilgrim feet!') and at the church ('I muse, that here the BARD DIVINE, / whose sacred dust you high-arch'd aisles enclose'), reinforcing the quasi-religious interpretation of the situation. To write a *guidebook* for literary *pilgrims* who come here to see the birthplace of 'the greatest genius that the world has seen' is a paradoxical task Grinfield justifies by referring to Shakespeare pilgrimage as an already widespread practice that can be supported by the value judgement of a great Romantic authority: 'thither, attracted by the charm of the wonderous productions of this "myriad-minded man," – as Coleridge has emphatically called him – hundreds of admiring, and almost worshipping pilgrims are constantly resorting [. . .] to the shrine of the nativity of the sweet Bard of Avon.' But however well-established the custom was, every now and then the author found it necessary to spell out the code of proper behaviour. We are reminded that 'a pedestrian ramble' from

Leamington to Stratford not only reveals hidden beauties but it
'is the true way of making a "Pilgrimage"'; we learn that coming
from Alveston to Stratford we glimpse an elegant spire which
'points out to the pilgrim's eager eye the sacred spot where
reposes the mortal part of the immortal Bard'; at the shops we
are reassured that to buy and carry away 'Shakesperien memen-
tos' is a laudable custom; at the birthplace, this 'shrine of genius'
on Henley Street, we are subtly reminded of the association
between St George, Shakespeare and true patriotism (here, 'nearly
three centuries ago, on the day dedicated to the patron saint of
old England, this greatest of Englishmen first saw the light'); in
the room where 'our inimitable bard drew his first breath' we
are told that visitors may write their names into a book and that
the autographs of many famous people (Scott, Schiller, Edmund
Kean, Emerson, Duke of Clarence) can be read on the walls and
windows; before arriving at the church, the 'last scene of all', we
are prepared by Warton's lines again for seeing the aisles that
enclose the sacred dust of the divine Bard; at the end of the
journey we are reassured that Shakespeare's town 'will ever fill
the mind of the enthusiastic literary pilgrim with the most delight-
ful associations', and the all-pervading presence of the poet will
be with him in the later years of his life.[113] All these reminders
indirectly prescribe the behaviour of the newcomer, they help to
condition his or her mental and emotional state; the book is not
only a manual for accomplished literary pilgrims but, more importantly, an aid for the initiation of candidates, the scenario for a
solemn rite of passage. All through the book the contemporary
reader must have felt an unmistakably elegiac voice musing over
the great contrast of time, decay and eternal glory, a motive familiar
since Wheler's 1806 *History and Antiquities of Stratford-upon-Avon*,
and a tone that was to become the dominant mode of Stratford
guidebooks for a long time to come. Even the quotations, whether
in prose or verse, are brooding over transitoriness to accentuate
the Bard's abiding value. 'Many houses of far more imposing
respect, have crumbled into dust; new houses built upon their
sites have all vanished, and even their successors are in decay;
yet still *that* house remains, the goal of a thousand pilgrimages.'
Sentences like this (quoted from an 1849 article in the *Edinburgh
Review*) convey a sense of having arrived at the boundary of earth
and heaven, and this is meant to be the reader's final impression, as the carefully chosen last quotation harks back to it with

a memento of the pilgrim's own mortality: 'Revolving years have flitted on, / Corroding time has done its worst; / Pilgrim and worshipper have gone / From Avon's shrine, to shrines of dust; / But *Shakespeare* lives unrivall'd still, / And unapproach'd by mortal mind.'[114]

Yet this attitude to the cult of Shakespeare is far from uncritical, and certain clues in the book can be interpreted as symptoms of a bad conscience haunted by almost theological worries about propriety. Occupying the narrow, indeed (in both spatial and anthropological sense) liminal no man's land between the sacred and the secular, the literary pilgrimage was suspect from both directions: its quasi-religious character was too obvious not to evoke fears about the possibility that it would conquer, usurp and profane the realm of religion proper; on the other hand some of the naive and popular manifestations of this quasi-religiousness prompted down-to-earth ironical responses that refused to take its aspirations seriously. Grinfield seems to be more than dimly aware of both kinds of unsympathetic views and tries to preclude them by different strategies. Quoting approvingly the religious strictures from a poem ('Lines written after seeing the house at Stratford-upon-Avon, in which Shakespeare is said to have been born April 23, 1564') by a certain T. G., he implicitly but unambiguously assents to the priority of the worship of God over the cult of a man. 'Yet steals a sigh, as reason weighs / The fame to *Shakespeare* given, / That thousands, worshippers of him, / Forget to worship heaven!' Weighed by reason, found disproportionate and scolded for the impious behaviour it may foster: if this sounds like the evaluation of the Shakespeare cult by a clergyman, we are not mistaken because the author of the poem, T. G., was most probably Reverend Thomas Grinfield, MA, whose book titled *Remarks on the moral influence of Shakespeare's Plays: with illustrations from Hamlet* was advertised together with that of Charles Vaughan Grinfield, MD. But his testimony about the ultimate object of worship can be quoted in this book precisely because it defines the upper limit of quasi-religious devotion but it does not amount to an unqualified dismissal of the Shakespeare cult. The lower limit is likewise defined throughout the book by carefully distancing the devout mentality of Stratford pilgrims from the credulity that feeds on apocryphal stories and fake relics. Commenting on 'curious biographical memoranda', like the claim that Shakespeare's father was a butcher or that he himself was a schoolmaster in his youth, the author quotes Halliwell's advice of how to deal with them and their confabulators: the only effective strategy is 'to read, be amused, then examine his inconsistencies, and believe nothing'. It is worth noting that the high serious- ness of quasi-religion is defended here with the help of a *scholar* who is safeguarding the dignity of his profession against the same enemy. Halliwell's advice is similar to that of Washington Irving, whose Stratford essay is often quoted by Grinfield, except for the characteristic scholarly admonition to examine. The differ- ence between authentic and dubious is carefully noted when- ever the exhibited objects are mentioned in the book, and the phrasing seems to be deliberately sceptical: a square of glass with the initials 'W. A. S. 1615.' is a 'probably genuine relic'; the 'Shakspeare's desk' of the grammar school, from which 'the relic hunters' carved off many bits, was perhaps 'only so named from its being the oldest-looking, and in the worst condition'; the oak chair of the birthplace bought by Princess Czartoryska 'was considered to be the only undoubted relic of Shakspeare's time'; the other pieces of furniture sold (with five volumes of manu- scripts) for £180 in 1847 'had no absolute connection with the poet', although they included a small bust of Shakespeare, made 'from the veritable mulberry tree'. The word 'veritable' is also undermined by Grinfield's account of the mulberry story. Quot- ing as sceptical authors as Malone and Johnson, and adding (with- out referring to Irving) that the small objects carved from the tree by Thomas Sharp 'have since somewhat miraculously multiplied', Grinfield subtly and perhaps unwittingly qualifies the traditional and solemn elements of his narration, such remnants of former narratives as the condemnation of Gastrell's deed as a 'sacreligious act', or the quoted assertion that the tree had 'supplied such relics as devotion holds still sacred, and preserves with pious care'. This insistence on ascertaining the degree of genuineness and certainty, and on qualifying the claim of an object for the status of a relic, is supplemented by a condemnation of all kinds of interference that would violate the original integrity of anything Shakespearean: Malone is no less condemned for having the bust painted white and thus destroying its original colours and features, than for having 'marr'd' the plays. At a time when some other visitors felt the pristine whiteness of the bust more in harmony with the shrine of Shakespeare than the rather harsh former colouring would have been, Grinfield's main concern is that 'Malone's meddling and unscrupulous impertinence' injured the noble features of the only true and even phrenologically correct likeness of the poet.[115]

No wonder that the problem of relics in the context of the quasi-religiosity of the literary pilgrimage prompts diverse and passionate responses: their place in religion proper is no less contested, and the clashing theological tenets of different denominations are often discernible as they lurk behind differing appraisals of the thriving mulberry industry. To illustrate the crucial role of theological convictions in the pre-formation of attitudes in the Shakespeare cult it is worth comparing the respective sentiments of a Protestant minister and a Catholic priest who went to see Stratford roughly at the same time, and recorded their experiences in sufficient detail. One of them, the Reverend John M. Jephson (1819–65), the youngest son of Reverend John Jephson, was at the time of his visit Chaplain of Hutton near Brentwood, soon to become Vicar of Childerditch. He arrived at Stratford on 3 September 1863, and wrote a book about it afterwards, *Shakespeare: His Birthplace, Home, and Grave. A Pilgrimage to Stratford-on-Avon in the Autumn of 1863*, to be published in 1864, and intended (according to its title page) as 'A Contribution to the Tercentenary Commemoration of the Poet's Birth'. Although individual and idiosyncratic motives cannot be excluded, the distance Reverend Jephson tries to keep from some manifestations of the cult is inseparable from his Protestant outlook. Not that he would feel less reverence for Shakespeare and his works than any other visitor; nor would his sensibility be antagonistic to a more comprehensive, not clearly protestant religious pattern as an underlying archetype for the literary cult. Referring to his grand-uncle, Robert Jephson, who had tried to revive Elizabethan drama, he admits in his preface that from his childhood he has 'heard Shakespeare discussed, extolled, acted, and quoted', because 'an especial veneration' for the playwright has been 'hereditary' in his family. Accordingly, he defines the purpose of his visit with the humility of a religious pilgrim: 'I was glad of an opportunity of visiting the place which is especially consecrated to his memory, and of adding my tiny grain to the volume of incense which will rise in his honour on his three hundredth birthday.' Knowing that in some places from the seventeenth century onwards the Anglican eucharistic ceremonial restored the use of incense, and that in the wake of the early nineteenth-century Tractarian Movement incense and other non-verbal symbols, albeit still considered

a controversial issue, were reluctantly accepted,[116] historically there
is nothing necessarily unprotestant in this metaphorical reference
to the honorific use of incense, though ahistorically it may also
reveal a wider, more comprehensive and denominationally inde-
terminate archetype of worship. Perhaps significantly, there is
no trace of iconophobia in the generous compliment he makes
to Ernest Edwards, the 'coadjutor' who provided the illustrations
for the book: if his own speech faltered, like that of Moses, his
shortcomings would be made up for by the photographer 'whose
camera is almost as great a worker of wonders as was Aaron's
rod'. All in all his disposition is not hostile to the very idea of
the religious pilgrimage either, be it Christian or otherwise, but
he makes no secret of his preference for its literary variant. After
lingering over the objects in the room where Shakespeare was
born he compared his own feelings to those for which pilgrims
presumably go to Jerusalem or Mecca. Early in his opening chapter
he makes a comparison between fourteenth-century pilgrims who
'rode from every shire's end of England to kneel at the shrine of
Becket, "the holy, blissful martyr," and to kiss his blood-stained
vestments' and their nineteenth-century literary counterparts who
take the train to Warwick and then the omnibus to Stratford so
that they may 'gaze' on Shakespeare's cottage and grave. He concludes that on the whole the latter type has the advantage of
having been inspired by poems representing the exquisite taste
of a consummate artist, whereas the minds of their medieval predecessors 'were prepared to adore in the gorgeous temple where
the relics of the saint were enshrined in gold and precious stones,
by the perusal of legends written in defiance of Nature and Taste.'
Characteristically, the only thing that he thought to have made
his own journey (on horseback) inferior to the one which started
from the Tabard around 1383 and headed for Canterbury was
the lack of such jolly company as depicted by Chaucer. And yet,
reading his text more closely, a Protestant interpretation and
evaluation of the Shakespeare cult becomes evident.

On arrival his gloom is aggravated not only by a town he found
rather dull, shabby and disagreeable, but by his apprehension
that the approaching anniversary festival might revive the horrifyingly vulgar and undignified pageantry of 1769. He sneered at
a painting showing 'the mummery which was acted in the streets
of Stratford under Garrick's auspices at the Jubilee' and sincerely
hoped that Shakespeare's memory would 'not be desecrated by

a repetition of such folly next Spring'. It would be difficult to explain, unless by assuming a dose of puritanical religious essential-ism, why Jephson (who still felt it necessary to defend the plays against the strictures of neoclassicism) condemned Garrick for having 'presumed to alter and adapt Shakespeare' and treated with less than usual trepidation the famous topoi of the mulberry story, be it the Reverend Francis Gastrell's 'selfish act' or the 'cup from which Garrick drank when he sang the foolish song composed for the Shakespeare jubilee'. Although to transport Shakespeare's house to Boston would have been an 'act of sacrilege', and he also admits that 'it is well to keep up our veneration for genius by respect for the place consecrated by being the scene of some of its happiest creations', Jephson's ambivalent, slightly self-contradictory attitude to literary relics surfaces whenever he is confronted with concrete objects related to the poet's life. He remarks that such palpable 'trifling remains' have no 'intrinsic connection' to the man and his work, and it is but 'by some wayward and irrational, but still natural process' that the human mind connects Shakespeare's wonderful plays with a mulberry snuffbox. Whether due to a reflex of anti-ritualism, iconophobia and a preference for the purely spiritual over the tangible, or simply to a streak of utilitarian rationalism not uncommon at the time (another Stratford visitor remarked in the same year that 'the men of the Iron age demand that the Beautiful shall be combined with the Useful'[117]), Jephson disagreed with those eager to erect a memorial statue of presumably little aesthetic value and no apparent use. As opposed to such plans he emphasized the *aere perennius* monument of the plays themselves and argued that the only thing worthy of the great occasion would be to 'found a theatre in which the Shakesperian drama could be acted and a school of acting maintained', and it would be 'the most rational and noblest homage' they could pay to excellence 'to provide for the adequate representation of Shakespeare's plays'. His interpretation of *adequacy* unwittingly but unmistakably testifies to his latent and ultimately religious aversion to mediatory altera-tions of an a priori substance and excessive material aids to its representation: 'There can be no doubt that a public which can be drawn together to hear stupid lectures and orations about things in general by popular preachers, would flock to hear Shakespeare's plays declaimed exactly as they were written, and without any of the factitious attractions of elaborate scenery and dresses.' (In the church, this 'most interesting relic of all', which the Reverend kept for 'the last station' of his pilgrimage, he carries this extolling of Shakespeare over the preachers even further: this poet was, and will be 'till the crack of doom', the 'benefactor' of the world, because 'divines may preach and philosophers may theorise' but they will never speak so intimately to our conscience or convey such practical wisdom as the author of *Hamlet*, *Lear* and *Othello*.) The latent anti-Catholic thrust of the argument is already manifest in the first chapter, where the author, having compared the way Stratford lived on the memory of its great son to Rome living on the relics of the apostles, goes on toying with a more elaborate version of the parallel. 'What a capital plan it would be, by the way, to set up a Shakesperian high-priest at Stratford, whose function it should be to regulate the devotions of the pilgrims and employ himself in the *culte des ruines*, and who should be inspired to pronounce an infallible judgment upon Shakesperian criticism.' This high-priest should decide once and for all whether the contested plays like *Titus Andronicus* or *Pericles* 'were canonical or apocryphal', which folio should be considered 'the received text', which readings and commentaries could be accepted as valid. The latent anti-Roman tendency is reaffirmed by the conclusion that such a high-priest would abolish all divisions and uncertainties, and at last 'the republic of letters might repose upon infallible authority'. Realizing that the town hall badly needed restoration he suggests in a similar, playfully ironical tone that they should resort to the well-tried medieval method of finding, 'providentially', some relics of their saint in the neighbourhood, enshrining them, and then renovate the building with the help of the 'pious offerings' of the people who would flock there 'to pay their devotions'.[118] For all his devotedness to Shakespeare, the Reverend Jephson's Anglican sensibility finds something embarrassing, with more than a merely subliminal awareness of a threat to ecclesiastical, even theological, propriety in the alarmingly familiar emotional transactions that he suspected of taking place in Stratford.

The latent Protestant pre-formation of this attitude becomes even more evident in juxtaposition with that of Jácint Rónay (1814–89), a Hungarian Catholic priest who fled to London in 1850, after having taken part in the 1848–9 fight for independence, and who visited Stratford a decade and a half later. In spite of his 16-year exile his life exemplifies a rising career in the Catholic

church, from entering the Benedictine order in 1831, studying
theology in Pannonhalma, and being ordained in 1839 to becoming a provost in 1877 and finally a bishop. When he visited Stratford
on 3 September 1865, as a member of the British Association for
the Advancement of Science, his diary (later published in ten (!)
copies) reflected a pattern of behaviour governed by an untroubled and dominantly Catholic attitude to relics and pilgrimage.
Of the four excursions offered by the Association he chose the
one to Warwick and Stratford admittedly because of his desire
to see Shakespeare's town and house, and with the intention not
to return with the group that evening but to stay longer 'to visit
everything connected with the immortal poet'. In Warwick castle
he kept asking himself at each step whether Shakespeare had
really been there, and he was more and more annoyed by what
he felt to be insensitively commercial elements in the quickly shifting official programme; distancing his own pilgrim mentality from
that of the tourists he felt relieved only when they arrived (by a
train called *William Shakespeare*) at 'Stratford, the Mecca of Britain,
where every thinking and poetically feeling person is longing to
go in England'.

Once in Stratford, his comments or behavioural responses reveal
an unquenchable thirst for authenticity and an uncompromising
demand for religious propriety. In the Henley Street house he
felt offended by the news that only the oak floor, the ceiling and
the walls were kept intact, but the windows and the fireplace
had been changed: he deplored this symptom of a 'lack of piety'.
His isolation among the others became even more conspicuous
when, deeply immersed in his contemplations, he was suddenly
alarmed by the noisy crowd rushing to the windows to see the
name of Walter Scott, 'engraved with a diamond but in bad taste'.
Rónay was pleased to see that the thousands of names on the
wall had been whitewashed; obviously he found the unbroken
whiteness more appropriate in the shrine. In the east wing of
the house he was similarly disappointed by the small number of
Shakespeare relics and especially by their 'lack of authenticity'.
Inspecting the relics one by one he refers to their supposed genuineness in a painfully hypothetical way, be it the dilapidated stone
basin from Holy Trinity Church which was used, reputedly, for
christening the infant Shakespeare, or the famous jar whose claim
to have been used by Shakespeare he finds dubious, though he
seeks consolation in the thought that 'Garrick certainly drank from

it at the 1769 centenary celebrations, for the memory of Shakespeare and the glory of himself!' Seeing a copy of the 1623 folio exhibited in the centre he laments over 'the saddening poorness' of the manuscript and document collection, and wonders whether it is due to indolence or impiety. Leaving the museum he worries over the future of the house, 'this dear relic of the past', haunted by the burning of York Minster (a significant association) some years ago, and finds consolation in the idea that whatever happens, it cannot perish altogether because there are reliable reminders like its small replica in the Sydenham crystal palace, complemented by a fully detailed drawing and an accurate description. On the marketplace he enthusiastically recalls the decision the Shakespeare Committee made in 1864 to erect a 60-foot memorial statue for the poet; at the town hall he admires the Shakespeare statue donated by Garrick and the paintings by Wilson and Gainsborough (showing the poet and Garrick respectively); at New Place he narrates the mulberry story with great empathy and inevitable commitment, admittedly 'deeply moved' by the ruins, and indignantly pillories the Reverend Gastrell, the shameless vicar, for his disgraceful act. In Holy Trinity Church, the last station for this group of tourists too, Rónay's devotion soars even higher, and it is at Shakespeare's grave that he refuses to leave with the others: he stays there, spellbound, as a true pilgrim should, while everybody else rushes on. Characteristically, he is disappointed by the coloured bust: unlike Jephson, he would have preferred pure white stone. (Scholarly impulses, however, seem to be compatible with the piety of the pilgrim: Rónay copies out data from the exhibited parish book for the biography he is planning to write about the poet.)

Next day his devout attachment to intact and genuine relics becomes manifest over and over again. In Shottery he is happy to find Anne Hathaway's cottage 'still the same as it must have been in Shakespeare's time', and there is no shade of irony in his voice when he describes his encounters with the legendary items to be seen there: in the garden he welcomes 'Shakespeare's well from which the poet reputedly used to drink many times and from which visitors are usually offered a glass of water'; in the living room he is pleased to see the old armchair known as 'Courting-seat because it was on this chair that the 19-year-old Shakespeare reputedly courted Anne'; upstairs in the small attic room he has nothing irreverent to say about the bed that used to be (reputedly) the poet's. The same high seriousness characterizes his attitude at all other stations of this complementary phase of his pilgrimage: in Wilmecote he is deeply moved by the humble little house where Shakespeare's mother lived as a young girl, in Charlecote the castle of Sir Thomas Lucy evokes in him only respectful sentiments about the poaching story but he keeps tactfully silent, not to offend Lady Lucy who guides the visitors herself; in the Castle of Kenilworth he wonders whether, at the third visit of Queen Elizabeth, Shakespeare as a child had been here; in Bosworth he is eager to see the battlefield, quotes the appropriate line from *Richard III*, adding (almost ecstatically) that an ancestor of Shakespeare, probably named so because of the enormous spear he used to shake, may have been one of the brave soldiers awarded here by Richmond (Henry VII) after the victory, though his great descendant was too modest to include this glorious family event in his play. Although these secondary places of pilgrimage may have represented an anticlimax for others after the culminating point in Holy Trinity Church, and we learn from the diary that to reach some of them was a tiresome job at the time, Rónay's true pilgrim spirit makes even this second tour a deeply satisfactory experience, and his closing sentence reveals his sense of having breathed the air of another world. 'Having seen the places whose memory will not vanish but with Shakespeare's plays, I returned to Birmingham contented, and on 14 September I was in London already, where the startling news of Mrs Kossuth's death bitterly dispelled my poetic musings, and reminded me of the transitoriness of all earthly fights.'[119] Thus from the *Mecca* of Britain our pilgrim returns to the earth of mortality. From his first words to his last the entire self-interpretation of his journey testifies to the untroubled compatibility of his religious ideas and sentiments with his experiences as a literary pilgrim. Moreover, he can interpret his experiences all the more approvingly because his expectations had been pre-formed by his Catholic upbringing; on the other hand whenever he condemns something, be it Gastrell's iconoclastic deed, the profaning of the diamond-cut name of Walter Scott on the window-pane, or the lack of piety responsible for the poorness and careless storing of the relic collection, his judgement is in no less perfect congruence with his Catholic stance. The transfer of his religious attitudes to the realm of the Shakespeare cult is performed with natural ease, just as that of Jephson's was; hence the clear contrast between the Protestant minister who finds the relic worship and other cultic phenomena there *too much* and therefore a threat to the primacy of spiritual essence, and his counterpart the Catholic priest finding it either satisfactory or (if faulty at all) *not enough* compared to a fully-fledged religious cult.

Despite their telling contrast, the heightened theological awareness of the two visitors makes their respective attitudes equally different from those of most laymen in the mid-nineteenth century and later. The Romantic heritage of the notion of genius as a quasi-transcendental authority to worship was to become both supra-denominational and supranational, something over and beyond the usual divisions and demarcations of social life, providing (in the anthropological sense) a complementary anti-structure[120] and the gratification of otherwise frustrated desires. Due to their unusually keen sense of denominational propriety, Jephson and Rónay hardly realized that they had made a pilgrimage to a denominational no man's land, but for the less ecclesiastically minded it is precisely this common spiritual realm that makes the journey worth the effort. A significant late example of a literary pilgrimage transcending denominational limitations, assimilating Romantic motives and culminating in a mystical experience is the journey of the Hungarian writer Magda Szabó. Though a Calvinist, she longed all through her adult life to realize her childhood wish to travel to England and *kneel down* at Shakespeare's grave, 'so that I could kneel down once in my life as people of other faiths do'. When she was given the opportunity, in 1962, the psychological unfolding of her whole trip followed the successive phases of religious pilgrimage: starting from London where she visited Hampstead to pay tribute to Keats's greatness, then going to Yarmouth (for Dickens), then to Oxford (Keats again and Galsworthy) and finally to Stratford, her own account reveals a gradual, if temporary, liberation from worldliness, a step-by-step preparation for the final act of kneeling that suddenly gave the moment, 'one of the most significant moments of my life', a dazzling sense of eternity.[121] The same common ground is provided for different nationalities: Carlyle's prediction of a Saxondom united by King Shakespeare, 'the noblest, gentlest, yet strongest of rallying signs', is quoted in 1892 in a review of a photographic album by the American typographer James Lyon Williams, titled *The Home and Haunts of Shakespeare*,[122] but Stratford became a place of pilgrimage not only for English-speaking nations: after the tercentenary celebrations of 1864 the annual number of visitors grew to more than 5,000, and by 1887 it reached no less than 16,500, coming from 40 countries, 5,000 of them from the United States.

These figures still represent a cosy and human scale when compared to the multitudes that the more and more gigantic traffic of the twentieth century brought to Stratford, and their behaviour indicates that literary pilgrimage is not merely a thing of the past. In 1908 nearly 45,000 visitors paid for their admission at the birthplace. (The eighteenth-century custom of voluntary donation was replaced by a compulsory six pence in 1896, this was subsequently raised to two shillings and six pence by the middle of the twentieth century,[123] and in 1995 the ticket for adults cost £2.75.) By the First World War the birthplace was seen by about 100,000 visitors per year, and although the press occasionally challenged the authenticity of the birthplace and its relics, the statistical figures show no trace of disillusionment, and by the early 1960s the annual number reached almost a quarter of a million. They were from about a hundred and fifty different countries; more than one tenth of the visitors came from the United States. By then nearly £60,000 worth of books and postcards were sold here in a year, and this commercial figure is not devoid of spiritual significance either. The books and other kinds of printed matter that people can buy at the birthplace, the church and even in the shops are often designed to foster the special attitude favourable to pilgrimage. Guidebooks declare Stratford a pilgrim centre and draw parallels, seriously, with Jesus' birthplace. An attractive little volume called *The Shakespeare Birthday Book* offers an enigmatic Shakespeare quotation for each day of the calendar and thereby encourages people to interpret the lines allotted to their birthdays so as to find some hidden and ultimate meaning capable of illuminating their lives; there is evidence that even a sceptical minded visitor may be inclined to meditate upon possible correspondences.[124] No less rewarding is the little certificate, inserted in the book by some shrewd psychologist of the Shakespeare trade, with an etching of the birthplace and the inscription: 'This book was purchased at Shakespeare's Birthplace, Stratford-upon-Avon.'[125] This cunning sentence can wake up the pilgrim dormant in many tourists: it reminds them of the merit of actually taking the trouble to make the journey to the only authentic place where a genuine admirer of the Bard can acquire (and thus deserve) this little book, which is, in its turn, more a quasi-relic than a mere souvenir.

In addition to the birthplace, New Place and the church, the Shakespeare pilgrims of today have several places to visit in and around Stratford. The New Place Garden, planted in 1919, was visited by 33,000 visitors in 1959; they came to see and smell all the flowers mentioned in Shakespeare's plays. Our pilgrims can take a walk of a mile to Shottery and visit the birthplace and home of Anne Hathaway, who was to become Shakespeare's wife. The system of places resembles the structure of religious pilgrim centres described by anthropologists as sacred complexes with a successive arrangement of stations preconditioning (both spatially and psychologically) the pilgrim's progress up to the momentous final climax at the most significant shrine.[126] This climactic inmost shrine is not easy to locate in Stratford: several pilgrims testify to having experienced something exceptional at Shakespeare's birthplace or at his grave; it was an experience they had hoped for and desired, and yet the sudden gratification always came as a surprise, differing only in degree, from the moving to the shattering. The grave is usually mentioned in a tone suggesting a more cathartic experience than the birthplace; here the pilgrims often feel the mystical presence of something sacred or transcendental.

The similarities with the pattern of religious pilgrimage are still unmistakable, though they should not be stressed beyond a certain point. No sick person makes the journey in the hope of a miraculous recovery. But healing need not be physical: many expect, consciously or otherwise, a sort of spiritual recovery or a renewed faith in the meaningfulness of life. In many cases the psychology of the spatial journey that leads through all sorts of outer and inner boundaries to Stratford resembles those 'interior salvific journeys' that mystics make in their contemplations or that religious pilgrims exteriorize in their pilgrimage, the 'extroverted mysticism' which is often 'the great liminal experience of the religious life'.[127] If the resemblance is usually difficult to recognize, it is because the profane scenery of commercialized tourism diverts our attention from those subtle traces that give away the latent pattern. To recognize it the journey to Stratford needs to be seen in the context of the cult as a whole system: together with relics worship, myth-making, ritual, hymn and other such manifestations of unconditional reverence and quasi-religious devotion.

FROM TRANSCENDENT UNITY TO VICTORIAN HIERARCHY: THE SOCIAL INTEGRATION OF RITUAL

Garrick's Jubilee became the archetype of many a memorial celebration for a long time to come; its ritual was always modified
to some extent but its spirit haunted several generations. Of course
the initial frequency was difficult to keep up for long: on 6 September 1770, Stratford celebrated the first anniversary of the Jubilee,
and this was duly repeated each September for six years. In 1776
when the founder of the tradition retired from acting, several
London theatres renewed the stage versions of the original event,
and Stratford paid its tribute by organizing a three-day jubilee
with a programme of procession, singing, public breakfasts, evening
balls and cockfights. In these years the procession had become
an opportunity not only for parading the costumed characters of
the plays together with dancers and singers but also for allowing the artisans of diverse crafts to march in their respective groups,
each in allegorical costumes identifying their trades. Jersey combers,
for example, followed Jason and were accompanied by the Golden
Fleece. One could see Bishop Blaize on horseback, the saint healing
sore throats, personified here as a playful allusion to the painful
result of the flooded 1769 Jubilee. These were also the years when
the organizers of the jubilees were wise enough to accommodate
any local event in the programme: in 1793 it was even shifted to
June to merge with the inauguration of the Shakespeare Masonic
Lodge; in the next century it was grasped as an opportunity for
pious fundraising to repair Holy Trinity Church. In April 1816
bells and cannons heralded the new jubilee that was to commemorate the bicentenary of Shakespeare's death with the familiar
programmes of a public breakfast and dinner, fireworks and ball,
with replicas of Garrick's medal and ribbons, with toasts celebrating
both Shakespeare and Garrick, and with pouring rain, nature's
nostalgic contribution to full authenticity. In 1819 the fiftieth
anniversary of the great Jubilee was celebrated, a self-reflecting
moment in the life of a literary cult, somewhere between taking
stock of its own heritage and turning it into an institution, a
half-way house between the receding act of the founder's inspired
innovation and the inevitable routinization of charisma. This was
also the moment when the organizers felt the need to provide
something like a scholarly justification for the event (and for the
respect of Shakespeare): John Britton gave what he called a *Lecture*

on the Peculiar and Characteristic Merits of Shakespeare.[128] It is an interesting paradox of the times that whereas English Shakespeare criticism could rarely stay this side of verbal idolatry, the jubilee's ritual idolatry had to be rationalized by a learned antiquarian as part of the programme.

Justification worked both ways, and not only between the transcendental analogies of critical language and the ritual apotheosis of Shakespeare at the festivals. There was a similarly mutual vindication of Shakespeare and that sacred patriotic symbol, the Patron Saint of England, St George. Since April 1808 John F. M. Dovaston in Westfelton, Shropshire, organized annual celebrations of Shakespeare's birthday, and the Stratfordians more and more realized a coincidence that enhanced the attraction of the April date as opposed to their Garrickian September: 23 April was not only the day of Shakespeare's birth and death (it is well known that the merging of these two dates owes more to myth-making needs than to archival evidence because it is only the day of his death that we can prove) but it is also St George's Day. In 1824 the jubilee procession was led by St George on a white horse. It seems that the symbolic unification of literary, sacred and patriotic values was well received: from then on Saint George led the procession whether the festival was held in April or not. By 1835 the cult-forming collective imagination completed its act of retrospective implantation: Saint George was made to appear on pictures representing the Garrick Jubilee. When the newly established Shakespearean Club (conceived in 1816 but born only in 1824) successfully revived the the three-day Garrick Jubilee in 1827, at least 20,000 people saw how St George ('ably represented by Mr. Wm. Tasker, jun. of Stratford') rode his grey horse with martial dignity in the company of the mayor, the representatives of the club, the Muses of tragedy and comedy, and the protagonists of Shakespeare's plays. This 'gallant Champion' was 'clad in a splendid suit of Grecian armour', wearing 'a golden helmet, over which majestically waved a plume of 16 ostrich feathers', and holding an 'ancient sword [. . .] which, according to tradition, has been used for similar purposes, since the period of Edward III'. They marched to the birthplace, this 'hallowed spot', to adorn a bust of the 'Immortal Bard' with a wreath of bayleaves, then to the churchyard around the Collegiate Church to sing. (Some regretted this but some felt to have been saved from profanation when hearing that the vicar had refused to let the procession into the church itself for performing an adaptation, at the very grave, of the gravedigger scene from *Hamlet*.) Finally they went to the garden of New Place, to lay down the foundation stone of a future New Theatre, with 'enthusiastic cheers', an orchestra playing 'God Save the King', followed by a chorus and solo composed for the occasion and including the couplet 'To Shakespeare's name we build a shrine, / To celebrate his works divine'.[129] Although in 1828 and 1829 the enthusiasts had to be content with more modest celebrations, the choice of toasts at the birthday dinner indicates the firm establishment of symbolic unity: glasses were raised not only to 'The Immortal Memory of William Shakespeare' and to that of David Garrick, but just as importantly to the King, to England and St George, even to the Duke of York and the Army.

It was in 1830 that St George was fully integrated into the ritual of the Shakespeare cult. The celebration was called 'The Second Royal Gala Festival', but it was the first with the proud claim to be a *royal* event. George IV, who adopted 23 April as his own birthday, granted his eager Stratfordian subjects the precious privilege of referring to him as Royal Patron and listing him with less distinguished though indispensable 'Vice Patrons' from the local community. When the Committee of the Shakespearean Club received the good news in a letter from the Right Honourable Robert Peel, then Secretary of State for the Home Department, a meeting was called (on 29 March 1830) and a resolution unanimously agreed upon to acknowledge this majestic favour:

That the KING'S most gracious ASSENT to the request of the Committee, that his Majesty would be pleased to PATRONIZE the SHAKSPEAREAN CLUB, and sanction them in their endeavours to pay a Tribute of Respect of the Memory of the Bard who has conferred Immortal Honour on his Native Land, demands our heartfelt gratitude.

George IV must have been no less grateful for the occasion: identifying himself with Shakespeare and St George was probably an attempt to boost his popularity. Much to the annoyance of the rival True Blue Shakespeare Club it was likewise resolved 'That in consideration of his Majesty's munificent Boon, the Club assume in future the name of "The ROYAL SHAKSPEAREAN CLUB".'[130] (The two organizations had their respective programmes side by side, a parallel that signalled processes of institutionalization and schismatization at the same time.) There was a sufficient number of allusions, solemn or playful, to justify the motto of the festival 'The King, the Poet, and the Patron Saint'. When listening to the new jubilee song, written by J. Bisset, to the familiar tune of 'God Save the King', those present may have felt a similar emotional fusion of loyalty to the monarchy and respect for the Bard as had been experienced six decades earlier by the guests of the jubilee ball who had to enter the Rotunda under a large replica of the royal crown composed of coloured lamps. The difference was, however, that with the appearance of such an analytical motto everything was spelled out, suggesting an order of established priorities, something like a new trinity. The social integration of cultic behaviour was conscious and conceptual, highly rationalized and neatly programmatic, leaving hardly anything to the subliminal awareness of intuition and spontaneity. A contemporary account of the festival, published in book form 'By a Member of the Royal Shakespearean Club' later in the same year, displays this elaborately defined and carefully coordinated system in no uncertain terms. Already the title page manages to epitomize the message, offering what at first sight may look like mere data of relevant information but what turns out to be for us a distilled essence of studied simultaneity in ritual appropriation: 'A Descriptive Account of the Second Royal Gala Festival, at Stratford-upon-Avon, In Commemoration of the Natal Day of Shakespeare, the King's Adopted Birth-day, And the Festival of St. George, On the 23d, 24th, 26th, & 27th of April, 1830.'

The details of those four days testify to the double purpose of reviving the Garrick Jubilee and confirming faith in the trinity of the king, the poet and the saint. On that Friday morning, 23 April, cannons and bells signalled the beginning of the festival; the participants hurried to the pavilion, built for the occasion, to have their traditional public breakfast, while the rain outside contributed to an authentic evocation of the true Garrickian spirit. But it was sunny enough by two o'clock for the procession to start, a lively spectacle with the members of the Royal Shakespearean Club wearing new replicas of Garrick's medal and the rainbow-coloured ribbons he had initiated as a symbol representing both the entire political spectrum and the all-inclusive diversity of Shakespeare's genius. The march was duly led by Saint George, personified by the young and controversial Charles Kean whose

horse followed Garrick's hallowed footsteps before turning towards
a new destination where the cornerstone of the Shakespeare
Theatre was to be laid down. It was more than a mere customary
gesture and reveals an awareness of the fruitful connection
between cult and culture that the cornerstone contained mementoes
of the 1769 Jubilee. The crucial question must have been obvious
enough not to escape the attention of the corporation responsible for the festival: how could a small place like Stratford afford
to build and maintain a theatre if it had not been for the nationwide tradition of cultivating the birthplace and thereby attracting a potential audience far beyond local possibilities? The
organizers had to realize that even the *Descriptive account* of the
event could not have been published without an appeal to this
larger readership; on a separate page the book is 'most respectfully dedicated by the publisher' to three communities with overlapping but distinct memberships widely different in size: 'To
the admirers of Shakspeare generally; to the inhabitants of his
birth-place particularly; and to The Committee and Members of
the Royal Shakespearean Club individually.'

It is no mere coincidence that the Second Jubilee revived the
long forgotten idea of performing plays to supplement the ritual
designed to celebrate the playwright. Curiously and perhaps significantly, the last time plays were performed at a Shakespeare
festival was 1746, and even Garrick himself, despite his insatia-
ble desires both to act and to adapt Shakespeare, conducted his
Jubilee without a single play being performed. Now, however,
as if to demonstrate the compatibility, indeed the interdependence, of diverse functions, worshippers were allowed to turn
into audience. After the procession that was coloured with about
75 characters of Shakespeare's plays (an integral part of the procession in its own right but also anticipating the evening performances), there was a late lunch prepared for about 300 people,
and the participants reassembled in the evening to see plays by
Shakespeare and Garrick. The programme included *As You Like
It*, *Catherine and Petrucchio* (Garrick's adaptation of *The Taming of
the Shrew*) and as a self-reflexive addition *Paddy Whack's Dilemma
at the Jubilee*, based on Garrick's own *The Jubilee*. The day, however, was not allowed to end there; it was not felt complete until
the masquerade, inherited from the first jubilee, could provide a
welcome opportunity for a playful suspension of identities. During
the following days, though there was no longer any procession,

the programme showed the same combination of ritual and theatre, the performances were likewise set between a ceremonious lunch and a glamorous ball, with Kean reputedly excelling in *Richard III* and in Philip Massinger's *A New Way to Pay Old Debts*. All this was supplemented by the entertainments provided by the rival True Blue Shakespeare Club, either in the elegant Royal Saloon (lavishly illuminated by 4,000 coloured lamps) or outside where a 30-foot-high 'Choragic Monument' was erected to Shakespeare (with a transparent portrait of the Bard), and a grandiose spectacle of fireworks was coupled with the show of an American acrobat on a tightrope at the breathtaking height of 80 feet. (All this was expensive, of course, and the Royal Patron promised no financial support whatsoever, but by now Stratford had proudly adopted the jubilee tradition, and its corporation was willing to repay a deficit of £3,000 after the festival.[131]) It was in this colourful context of pageantry that the reappearance of the theatre sealed the newly forged alliance of Shakespeare, St George and the King, confirming the unity of literary, religious and monarchist loyalties that was to provide much of the vitality of the English cult of Shakespeare and was to offer a reservoir of encouraging cultural unity in later periods whenever the life of the nation was threatened by the dragons of history.[132]

All these changes reveal the latent tendency of post-Garrickian festivals; their social implications, however, could not be sufficiently ascertained before the fully-fledged new pattern had had an opportunity to surface. The price to be paid for the growth of the literary cult into a large-scale movement seems to have been the quasi-secularization of the quasi-religious. Nevertheless the latter could not be (as it hardly ever is[133]) completely demolished; over and over again it was restored and maintained by a tenacious psychological need for its revival. It was in 1864, at the festival organized to commemorate the third centenary of Shakespeare's birth, that the Stratford tradition turned into a gigantic movement, and the literary cult reached its full institutionalization. It was then that the legacy of an inspired and charismatic founder was taken over by official and routinized committees, and in the process of social integration the membership acquired an internal hierarchy of its own. Even the ritual practice itself was redefined so as to divide a hitherto loose, unstructured and more or less unified body of adherents into separate units along the worldly demarcations of rank and wealth. The background to these processes of differentiation looks familiar – it is because this was already an age of railways, nationwide committees and international communications. To travel from London to Stratford in the early 1860s visitors could take a train stylishly called *Will Shakespeare*, yet to keep the tercentenary in Stratford the organizing committee of the little town had to fight off the rival claim of mighty London. The London committee, with no less than 400 vice-presidents, argued that the capital of the nation would be the proper place for such an important *national* celebration even if Shakespeare, merely born in Stratford, had not made his fame in London. Unable to mobilize their forces, they had to surrender when *The Times* sided with the Stratfordians, though the support of the decisive article (on 20 January 1864) was not unqualified. Speaking 'with perfect impartiality', the Editor was not enthusiastic about the plan for erecting yet another memorial monument: 'There are monuments enough.'

The Stratford committee was contented with their victory and were neither surprised nor disheartened by the objection. Had they not been familiar with such misgivings already, they would learn about them later that year (still before the festival) when reading the Reverend J. M. Jephson's *Shakespeare: His Birthplace, Home, and Grave, a Pilgrimage to Stratford-on-Avon* whose author had similar mixed feelings about the approaching anniversary in a grey little town neither antique nor elegant enough for his taste, about a festival that might revive the horrifyingly undignified pageantry of Garrick's Jubilee, and about one more useless and presumably ugly statue.[134] As regards the taste of its own members, the organizing committee was no less purist, and would have been in favour of solemnity and high seriousness, a jubilee largely confined to events like a presidential opening address, an oratorio, a concert and theatre performances. (Even the traditional banquet and ball, if they could not be eliminated altogether, were to be reserved for a restricted number of carefully selected people.) But the committee also knew that the masses wanted pageantry, something colourful and carnivalesque, with the tangible result of a memorial statue. The compromise of these two conflicting priorities was reached in typically Victorian fashion: it was decided that the tercentenary commencing on 23 April 1864 would offer two distinct, separate and subsequent festivals: first, minutely planned, a serious and stylized event for the well-to-do, then the 'people's week' with its more spontaneous and exuberant entertainments.

Despite this declared bifurcation, for a while the preparations seemed to promise a revival of the unifying Garrickian tradition all over the town. The committee (with an impressive list of 200 vice-presidents including the Poet Laureate Alfred Tennyson as well as distinguished foreigners like the American ambassador, Victor Hugo and Theodor Mommsen) proposed that the participants should wear the same badge, ribbon and medal, all three made specially for the occasion. The duodecagonal Grand Pavilion built in a meadow between New Place and the church was both an allusion to Garrick's legendary octagonal Rotunda and a clear indication of the ambition to outdo it in scale and splendour. The impressive wooden construction, held together by more than four tons of nails, was 74 feet high and 152 feet in diameter, thus large enough to accommodate an audience of 3,000 people and an orchestra of 530 members. We may remember that Garrick's amphitheatre was designed to host 1,000 spectators (though eventually it hosted twice as many) and 100 musicians. The new building also contained a stage, unlike the Rotunda, and the drop curtain in front of it portrayed Shakespeare in a vestibule, providing a central symbolic presence similar to that of the bust used by Garrick a century earlier. (As if to supplement this pictorial representation with textual authorization, the pseudo-Elizabethan interior was interspersed with quotations from Shakespeare.) The town outside looked eager to participate: nearly every house was repainted, available buildings were turned into temporary hotels, flags appeared everywhere, the place that the Reverend Jephson had found almost hopelessly miserable was now all of a sudden revitalized, festive and flourishing. The town hall exhibited a collection of 300 paintings, works by Reynolds, Maclise, Frith and other celebrities, 25 different portraits of Shakespeare, and Sir Thomas Lawrence's portrait of John Kemble as Hamlet, a painting lent for the occasion by Her Majesty the Queen. In the town hall one could also see the relics, similar to the ones used by Garrick as psychological props of quasi-sacralization and myth-making: this time the main items were the poet's walking stick and jug, and it was in their hallowed and hallowing vicinity that visitors could buy little statues and, yes, photos. (These souvenirs must have been felt to be removed further from the authenticating sacred origin than the little objects made of the mulberry tree had been in 1769, because that tree, planted by the Bard himself, was probably felt to be magically imbued with his spirit; but by now the souvenir industry could safely rely on the psychological impact of a long tradition, the one founded by Garrick's ritual and quasi-liturgical efforts to transubstantiate profane knick-knacks into relics and thus to foster and confirm pilgrim attitudes.) On the bright morning of 23 April, a Saturday in 1864, everything seemed perfectly prepared for the great revival, and by two o'clock, when the festival was to begin, distinguished guests gathered (including Lord Leigh, Lord Carlisle and the Archbishop of Dublin) and even a German delegation arrived, with greetings from the Goethe Society paying tribute to the playwright whom they considered theirs as well, implying the notion of *unser* Shakespeare in both senses of the word, a great mutual poet of the brotherly Angles and Saxons, and the one most intimately appropriated and best loved (after Goethe and Schiller) by Germans. But no crowd appeared on the street, nothing comparable to that of Garrick's Jubilee, no vivacious simple folk mingling with their superiors, no overflow of carnivalesque spontaneity and, therefore, no cultic suspension of social hierarchy either.[135]

The psychological reasons for this anticlimax are not far to seek, and reveal the problems created by the official integration of a literary cult into Victorian society. All through the whole first week subtle but strict regulations were used to ensure that participation be restricted to the well-to-do. The opening banquet, with its unmistakably graded and guarded access to luxury, is a case in point. Probably it was the grandeur of the tercentenary and (by implication) the precious cultural value of the Bard that the organizers meant to accentuate with their veritable orgy of exquisite dishes: the four kinds of fowl, a gorgeous selection of pork, beef, lamb and fish served with vegetables and rolls, followed by a choice of fresh fruit, and washed down generously with ale, beer and champagne. But this feast was available only to those who could afford the price of one guinea (i.e. 21 shillings), a sum way beyond the possibilities of the wider public. Those who could and would pay 5 shillings, however, were allowed to *watch* the eating and drinking from the gallery and to *listen* to the numerous toasts. In those days 5 shillings was far from being a nominal sum, and most probably it proved to be an insurmountable obstacle for many, a device in effect demarcating a third class of people who were excluded altogether. But even among the ones who could afford it, the dilemma of participation was not easy, and not only because, to borrow an apt phrase from a later commentator, five shillings 'must have been a heavy price for gorging the eyes alone'.[136] The psychological problem must have been much deeper than that, touching, indeed stirring, the very depths of cultic gratification. Whereas in other contexts gorging the eyes can be felt a treat in itself, and the middle classes have often been prone to a snobbish curiosity that induces them to tiptoe and peep through the window of aristocratic elegance, it is hardly compatible with a *cult*, literary or religious, to cater to this latent need at the expense of the much more relevant desire for a sense of (now transitory but ultimately essential) belonging together. Although the banquet is reported to have been attended by 750 guests and was considered successful, for the people compelled to stay outside it must have reinforced a sense of being excluded, and even those relegated to the gallery may have felt a dubious pleasure when listening to the sequence of toasts, first to the Queen, then to the Prince and Princess of Wales, to the memory of Shakespeare, to the Archbishops and Bishops and clergy, to the Army, the Navy and related forces, after a while descending to the poets of England, Ireland, Scotland, and America and concluded by toasts to the Mayor and Corporation of the Borough.[137] After this the 63 items of the fireworks that could be seen from Warwick Road must have provided a rather different experience for those who went to see it contentedly from the festive table and for those who had not eaten. Little wonder that the number of spectators was much less here than expected at such a popular form of entertainment.

Next day (Sunday) both the morning and afternoon sermons in Holy Trinity Church tended to accentuate this latent message of hierarchical separation, equating it with the righteous acceptance of a sacred order and making it sound like a hallowed article of faith. In the morning Dr Trench, the Archbishop of Dublin, suggested that Shakespeare was worthy of admiration in this respect, and elaborated the point that 'those who mould a nation's life should be men acquainted with God's scheme of the universe, cheerfully working in their own appointed sphere the work which has been assigned to them, accepting God's world because it is His.'[138] At the afternoon service Charles Wordsworth, Bishop of St Andrews, was pleased to follow his old schoolfellow from Harrow, and devoted his sermon to the transcendental and earthly implications of obedience, but raised this theological issue so as to meditate on questions about the religious and moral propriety of revering Shakespeare, dilemmas he seems to have felt timely at the beginning of such a large-scale institutional celebration of the Bard. As his text he chose Psalm CXIV: 10. ('All Thy works praise Thee, O Lord; and Thy saints give thanks unto Thee') and made his ultimate message predictable already in his opening sentence: 'When the Psalmist tells us [. . .] that all the works of God praise their Creator, he means that by their beauty and excellency they testify to His skill and power; but he also means that [. . .] they severally obey the laws which He has imposed upon them; and such obedience, it may be said, is the higher praise.' Applying this universal idea to the tercentenary festival, 'an event which is felt to be of national, nay, of worldwide importance,' and to the admirable works of Shakespeare, the Bishop's sermon began with a warning that revealed his worry about the blasphemous possibility of idolatry.[139]

He was not the only priest, we may remember, to be alarmed by this danger; a similar fear of misplaced (and, well, papist) religiosity had already provoked Reverend Jephson's playful but deeply ironical suggestion to set up a Shakespearean high-priest in Stratford to regulate worship and act as the infallible final arbiter in criticism.[140] The latent anxiety underneath Bishop Wordsworth's pious warning ('never, never let us forget that the author of those works was himself a work of God') was due to his feeling that the festival could far too easily and sinfully lose sight of the proper object of ultimate admiration.

And if as men we naturally feel, and desire to express, a greater interest in the excellency of a fellow-man than in that of any other of God's works, [. . .] yet, in order to render such interest not only innocent and rational, but in the highest degree pleasurable and beneficial to ourselves, [. . .] in honouring our great poet, we shall be led to magnify God in him, as a truly divine and matchless work; and [. . .] to bless God for him, as an inestimably precious and most glorious gift.

The vocabulary reflects something of the speaker's religious (Protestant) essentialism activated by his presentiment of possible heretical behaviour in a quasi-religious context. The anxiety to keep our interest in (and reverence for) Shakespeare not only innocent but *rational* is similar to the concern informing Reverend

Jephson's final remark that to found a theatre and a school of acting for the authentic representation of Shakespeare's plays 'would be the most rational and noblest homage we could pay to his greatness'.[141] The emphatic *we shall be* is meant here in the biblical sense of we *should* and *must* be: this imperative to worship nothing but the divine or at least the divine in man (as opposed to the merely human) was next applied to the 'scruple' Bishop Wordsworth anticipated as a preacher in a church, on the holy day of St George, at a festival organized to celebrate the greatness of a *man*.

It was a delicate, contradictory and potentially controversial situation for a clergyman who knew only too well (and hastened to declare) 'that the Church is no proper place for panegyric, save in honour of Him Who is above all praise'. To overcome this scruple of impropriety he argued that there was enough of the divine in Shakespeare to justify reverence because he was not just an example of intellectual superiority (which, 'merely as such', would not be recommended by the Bible for glorification) but also an example of things pleasing to God: he conquered the temptation of wealth, coveted no worldly goods, his life was one of virtuous sacrifice. Moreover, the obedience to Christian norms is implicitly attributed to Christ-like qualities: due to his 'characteristic meekness' the reputedly 'gentle' Shakespeare is worthy of the Church of Christ because 'in him, *as a man*, the Gospel has exemplified that truest element of the Christian character, of which it is written – and fulfilled as on this day – "Blessed are the meek, for they shall inherit the earth."' *As on this day*: the tercentenary celebration itself is taken to be an implicit proof of Christian meekness ultimately rewarded, the proof of inheriting the earth rendered all the more convincing by the preacher's immediate approval, on quasi-theological grounds, of having the festival in the tercentenary year of the poet's birth but on the day of his death: 'as the church has ever been wont to celebrate not the birthday, but the deathday – as being the truer and more glorious nativity – of her saints and confessors.' Similarly, the preacher felt entitled to confirm the widespread assumption (without which, he added, this grandiose celebration surely would not have taken place at all) that 'the works of Shakespeare are plainly on the right side; [. . .] on the side of virtue and of true religion'.[142]

This vindication of Shakespeare's impeccably Christian morality, both in his works and in his life, seems to have been a prerequisite of what was (logically) the next step: referring to the general consensus about 'our poet's nationality' and declaring him England's representative poet of patriotic significance: 'Like Homer to the Greeks, he is *the poet* of us Englishmen.' He is 'to us Englishmen the national, the domestic Poet, whom we love as we love our own homes'. What is more, the works of this eminently English poet provide an antidote to the far too mechanical and material pursuits this practical nation is prone to indulge in; his plays will refine, enlarge and elevate the English. It is for his inspired *oeuvre*, domestic and yet divine, reflecting 'no uncertain image of the Word of God', that both English and foreign visitors were exhorted to contribute some (well, financial) 'thank-offering' for the maintenance of the 'consecrated edifice', all of them having come here as 'pilgrims to this shrine of Christian genius'.[143] The last phrase, coming from a bishop at such a decisive moment in the institutional confirmation of a literary cult, amounts to an almost unqualified ecclesiastical approval of quasi-religious attitudes, language and ritual, an acceptance of the special treatment of Shakespeare (Christian genius and national poet) that was overtly analogous to a religious cult.

The implied endorsement, suggested indirectly by a coherent set of religious metaphors, makes a virtue out of necessity. The initial problem of the clergyman, that is how to refute possible charges of idolatry and how to negotiate the theological objections to (and his own sense of impropriety about) glorifying a man in the house of God, was solved in a way that demonstrated (just as the triadic motto of Shakespeare, the King and the Patron Saint did) the ultimate integration of all the principal literary, transcendent and patriotic values into an all-pervading ideology of the Victorian establishment. And precisely because the ecclesiastical approval was not offered easily and was *earned* only after a long and painstaking meditation (something like the subtle reasoning of bad conscience) on the dilemma, it exercised and accentuated the right of ecclesiastical control, just as the right of royal supervision was foregrounded when King George agreed to be listed as Royal Patron of the festival. Moreover, it seems that the symbolic legitimizing processes worked both ways: transcendent and monarchic symbols joined forces to legitimize Shakespeare's elevation to the status of cultic object, but in turn he helped to reinforce, with the authorizing prestige of a widely acknowledged and acclaimed genius, the political and religious elements, indeed the entire moral structure of Victorian ideology. Last but not least, by working out an ecclesiastical vindication for the cultic admiration of a poet the bishop reinforced the sacred origin of poetry itself ('in him, *as a poet*, Poetry has filled every purpose for which in the mercy of God she was given to our fallen race as, next to Revelation, His most precious boon') and thereby gave literature a very dignified status of utmost moral importance and high seriousness, second *only* to God's own words.

This high seriousness prevailed over the carefully planned programme from Monday to Friday, and even the few items of lighter entertainment were controlled in a way that left no room for reckless joy and suited a limited number of participants. True, on Monday at noon nearly two thousand people went to hear Handel's oratorio, *The Messiah*, performed, as the official programme heralded it, by a 'band and chorus of five hundred performers',[144] and the audience seems to have filled the two classes of reserved seats (21 shillings for the 'Area' and ten shillings and sixpence for the Gallery) as well as the unreserved seats (five shillings), in spite of the prices that were twice as high in all the three categories as those of the evening concert, 'A Grand Miscellaneous Concert of Music Associated with the Words of Shakespeare', which was meant to be more on the popular side. At a concert, of course, those sitting in the humblest places are not excluded from full participation, and the division between Area and Gallery was not as absolute here as the one at a banquet between those who eat and those who watch them eating. The rest of the week, however, showed a decline of interest. On Tuesday afternoon there was an excursion to Charlecote (where young Shakespeare reputedly poached) and other places of alleged biographical connections. To get on one of the carriages necessitated buying an excursion ticket for five shillings, not a high price in itself but together with all the other costs of the week the sum was already considerable. In the evening a performance of *Twelfth Night; or, What You Will* by the Theatre Royal (from Haymarket, London) was applauded (the role of Sir Andrew Aguecheek was played by the famous comic actor Charles Buckstone), but the afterpiece, a French 'Comediette' titled *My Aunt's Advice*, was less well received. (The tickets had the same range of prices as those at the Handel oratorio.) On Wednesday evening *Romeo and Juliet* and *The Comedy of Errors* attracted a larger audience, though there were complaints later about the barely intelligible foreign accent of Mademoiselle Stella Colas as Juliet, and about the short and stout J. Nelson as a not exactly irresistible Romeo. Thursday began with a concert of 'instrumental music and glees from Shakespeare's plays'; this was also the occasion to read a poem (as Tennyson failed to write the memorial ode requested, it was John Brougham's rather poor sonnet that had to continue the tradition of panegyric inherited from the 1769 ritual). In the evening it was *As You Like It*, again for the same prices of admission. The most exclusive event, however, was yet to come.

The prominent first part of the festival ended on Friday night with 'A Grand Fancy Dress Ball' designed to be more grandiose and more restrictive than anything Stratford had witnessed over the first seven days or ever before. The official programme of the festival, printed and distributed before the event, declared the conditions of admittance in no uncertain terms: first of all 'no one will be admitted except in Fancy Dress, Court Dress, or Uniform', costumes were requested to be ('so far as possible') 'Shakespearian', and 'No Mask, Dominoes, or Pantomime characters will be admitted'. Although tickets were very expensive (21 shillings including 'Refreshments and Supper', otherwise either ten shillings and sixpence or five shillings for the spectators in the galleries who were also required to wear 'Evening Dress') precautions were taken to ensure that only the right kind of people would obtain them. To have money was a necessary but not a sufficient condition; the prices of the tickets were listed only after a preliminary demarcation to safeguard the privilege. 'Tickets (not transferable) will be issued only on production of a Voucher, or Letter, signed either by the President, one of the Vice-presidents, or Local Committee, or by a Lady Patroness or Steward [. . .]'. (The President was The Right Hon. The Earl of Carlisle, KG, Lord Lieutenant of Ireland; among the many Vice-presidents one finds a considerable proportion of aristocratic names and titles; and the list of the patrons, patronesses and stewards abound with Lords, Earls, Sirs, Countesses and Ladies.) It indicates the scale of the event that the lucky few meant three or four hundred people who were able to dance till five in the morning and enjoy a sequence of dance music ('Arranged expressly for this occasion') that began with an English country dance followed by 20 items of quadrille, valse, lancers and galop.

It is little wonder, though not easy to explain, that the number of participants over the first week was a fraction of what had been expected by the Stratford organizing committee. The land-lords who turned their houses into hotels were disappointed; artisans and vendors lamented their deficit. Having deemed the situation hopeless, a travelling circus called Wombwell's Menag-erie left almost as soon as they arrived. Yet it sounds too facile an explanation to say, as two later commentators would have us believe, that the problem was the lack of a sufficient number of snobs in Warwickshire or in England as a whole to make this snobbish first week worth the investment.[145] Most probably it was due to a violation of cult psychology that the first week, meant to be exquisite, turned out to be too exclusive and was marred by a lack of wider participation. In contexts other than that of a cult there are occasions when the poor may watch contentedly the happy few acquiring and consuming goods that poverty could only dream about; within a cultic context, however, participa-tion is expected to be direct, immediate and preferably nonhierarchical (or at least structured by the alternative hierarchy of the cult itself). Hence in the ritual process nobody is seeking to be represented by somebody else, let alone an institutional-ized body of the privileged. Here, more than anywhere else, indi-rect representation would be resented as a thinly veiled form of exclusion, an alienating experience at odds with the yearning for a sense of ultimate belonging, a moment of quasi-transcendent *communitas*, that flickering ray of heaven on earth Garrick's legendary Jubilee captured for a few rainy days a century earlier.

As if to compensate, the subsequent 'people's week' offered 'popular entertainments', and although it was but half a week (in fact only three days), it was teeming with life. Accepting the separate occasion reserved for them after their more privileged brethren left, the simple folk participated more fully on any one day from Monday to Wednesday than during the whole preced-ing week; thousands came by railway (special arrangements were made for 'excursion trains') or any other conceivable vehicle to the pageantry. Mr Ginnett, the famous equestrian, was the moving spirit of most events: he put up his enormous tent by the river-side, no match for the Grand Pavilion but it provided the people's week with suitable headquarters of its own. His orchestra led the procession on Monday; he lent the costumes (mostly Shake-spearean) to make it more colourful; his troupe, clothed as Shake-spearean characters, mingled with the visitors marching under the usual banners of St George and escorted the customary triumphal chariot of the poet himself surrounded by his most notable creations. The procession was immensely successful (so much so that it was proposed to be repeated the following day); without the participation of the upper classes it could not match the carnivalesque suspension of hierarchy achieved a century earlier, but what was lost in comprehensiveness was compensated for by the ease, abandon and sense of kinship enjoyed by people of similar status. The concert (in Mr Ginnett's inelegant but spacious circus tent) attracted 500 people, not much less than the performance of Handel's oratorio could boast on the previous Monday. Although on Tuesday the much awaited spectacle, 'Coxwell's monstre Balloon', failed to ascend (it would have needed more gas than the town could supply), in the evening a large audience was allowed to fill the Grand Pavilion and see *Othello*, produced 'under the superintendence of Mr Creswick', for conveniently cheap tickets that nevertheless reproduced the spatial separation and financial hierarchy, on a lower level, of the previous week. (This time reserved seats were four shillings, First Tier three shillings, Area two shillings, Lower Tier one shilling, so in each category the tickets cost only a fraction of what the well-to-do paid for the same seats a week before, and much less than what the banquet's *voyeurs* had to pay for their admittance to the gallery.) On Wednesday a similarly large and happy audience enjoyed *As You Like It* and the trial scene from *The Merchant of Venice*.[146]

Although these three days with their moderate prices could not make the whole festival profitable (the final deficit was £2,000), they proved that people of lower social standing would be attracted to a play or a concert no less than to pageantry. The success of the plays also indicated that Shakespeare had not been appropriated by the emerging elite culture exclusively and irreversibly, although this period was already marked by a growing cultural differentiation both in Europe and America with far-reaching consequences for the status of Shakespeare's works as well.[147] The behaviour of the audience may have been somewhat different from that of the spectators during the preceding week (it is a pity we don't know much more about that), but the difference was most probably less striking in the Grand Pavilion than outside. It reveals both the exuberant vivacity of these days (in sharp contrast with the 'ominous quietude' of the beginning of the festival) and the secret fears of the organizers, that the secretary of the Stratford Committee, Robert Hunter, felt relief at the end of the people's mirth seeing that 'no widow or orphan associates his or her bereavement with this joyful occasion'.[148] This anxiety about the possible damage caused by recklessness is perhaps symptomatic of the prime Victorian concern about the imperturbable dignity and decorum of social life, and it testifies to an awareness of where the inner drives of certain cultic events may sometimes lead, as carnivals of all ages have often been dangerous and (almost as if demanding some human sacrifice) left behind casualties. All those ingenious measures, designed to control, restrict and structure the festival, were means whereby to make an exceptional occasion predictable and manageable, one that fits safely into the smooth daily routine of a powerful establishment.

Yet all these various measures of restrictive differentiation also indicate the routinization of charisma. Just as that haunting Weberian phrase reminds us of the adjustments required before official acceptance, these regulations reveal what may happen to a spiritual tradition before it is institutionalized as a legitimate social practice. In sharp contrast with its mid-eighteenth-century antecedents, the social integration of the Shakespeare cult as a sanctified code of behaviour in Victorian culture reached its point of no return at the post-romantic moment when the cultic (and subconscious) unity of the quasi-sacred and the secular was finally disrupted and conscious efforts were made to control their ideological reintegration. In 1769 even the seemingly profane amusements gave an opportunity to transcend the hierarchy and reveal the ultimate oneness of separate identities. (The masquerade, though obviously not open to *all* classes of society, was a symbolic, carnivalesque and mildly subversive game in which differences of rank or status were temporarily obliterated and any disclosure of identities gained special significance.) The tercentenary regulations sought to underscore hierarchical differences (not only between the two large divisions but within each of them as well) and tended to preclude even their imaginary subversion. As we may remember, the organizers announced well before the festival that at the fancy dress ball no masks would be admitted and no tickets were allowed to be transferred. In 1864 even the sermons echoed, with theological confirmation and sonorous religiosity, the omnipresent and overruling idea that the social order is to be maintained just as every creature has to accept its allotted place in the great scheme of beings. The same applies to the family, of course: the Bishop of St Andrews was pleased to point out that *King Lear* castigated filial ingratitude just as Shakespeare himself had been a paragon of obedience to parents. A century earlier the Jubilee did not include sermons at all, and Boswell who would have liked an opportunity for common prayer as an expression of gratitude[149] had to content himself with the oratorio as a devout experience (not only because he wanted to please his pious fiancée[150]), but then the programme was full of quasi-liturgical and ritual reminiscences, studiously or spontaneously revived and adapted, so the whole event was permeated with religiosity. Now, on the other hand, religious elements were given a separate and institutional form, adjusted, like Shakespeare and practically everything else, to ideological requirements within a social and ultimately secular framework. The tercentenary festival, no longer a jubilee in the Garrickian sense, broke away from the *jubile* tradition and its symbolic restoration (through ritual enactment) of primordial oneness, eliminated its possible theological associations with the (etymologically unrelated) medieval *jubilaeum* and even with the (etymologically related) Old Testament *yobel*, and lost touch with its residual sense of an all-inclusive *communitas*. Institutional but no longer inspired, the Shakespeare cult was now supported by the very pillars of Victorian society. In return it had to serve that establishment. Recruited at a time of ideological warfare, it had to give up some of its former aspirations. To make a potent and down-to-earth ally for class-consciousness and national pride, it traded its birthright to other-worldly mystery and transcendent compensations for those more tangible benefits a prosperous nation could provide.

3

A Middle European Case Study: The Development of the Shakespeare Cult in Hungary

The historical phases discernible in the Hungarian reception of Shakespeare follow a sequence largely governed by an almost Aristotelian entelechy with a quasi-religious inner logic of its own. Though inseparable from the history of literary taste and theatrical opinion, and by no means unrelated to the changing concerns of cultural and political history, the five historical epochs in the Hungarian reception of Shakespeare can be interpreted as subsequent phases of literary cult formation: it proceeds from an age of *initiation* and then goes through the stages of *mythicizing*, *institutionalization* and *iconoclasm*, culminating in a twofold period of *secularization* and *revival*.

The first of these, from the 1770s to the end of the 1830s, can be called the age of initiation. Numerous articles in the press made people aware of the verbal and ritual manifestations of the reverence the English felt for their beloved Shakespeare; an ever-widening circle of writers and readers were introduced to this special code of social behaviour. The message communicated to them (more or less explicitly but always with the unmistakable approval of the mediator) was that all those sacralizing forms of reverence, seemingly unprecedented and excessive when lavished on a secular figure, are not out of place or undeserved in the case of an English playwright called William Shakespeare. It is important to add, however, that the adoption of quasi-religious praise and ritual could scarcely rely on firsthand experience, whether in performance or print, of Shakespeare's originals. Initiation meant learning to revere before getting to know.

Second, there followed the age of mythicizing, from the early

1840s to the tercentenary celebrations in 1864, when a retrospective justification was sought for the sacralizing ritual by ascribing mythical qualities and transcendental powers to Shakespeare. In Hungary this was the time when the language of Shakespearean criticism turned into a close-knit network of religious metaphors, similes and allusions. Thus raised to the heights of divine sovereignty, the playwright was considered to be beyond comparison, unfathomable and infallible, and not amenable to any set of critical norms.

Then comes the age of institutionalization, from the 1860s to the early 1920s, which witnessed the formation of the first Hungarian Shakespeare Committee in 1860 and of its successor in 1907, institutions whereby something like a priesthood was founded with an official character and a professional hierarchy of its own. More and more integrated into the legitimized social establishment and enjoying the approval and financial support of the state, these committees both organized and controlled the translation of Shakespeare into Hungarian. This included the moral and ideological supervision of the first complete edition, in 19 volumes, between 1864 and 1878. Such cultural activities as the production and dissemination of Hungarian editions of Shakespeare were nevertheless inseparable from cultic events like the centenary ceremonies of 1864 and 1916. A good example of their interdependence is the success-ful attempt of the Committee to publish the first volume of the complete Hungarian Shakespeare by April 1864 to add to the splendour of the celebrations.

The fourth stage, which ran from the early 1920s to the late 1950s, can be labelled an age of iconoclasm. It is characterized by renewed attempts either to desacralize or to overthrow the whole established system of bardolatry – or at least to denounce and demythologize the current conception of the revered Bard and replace it by another. The latter, invariably called 'the real Shakespeare', was usually resurrected by virtue of its being conveniently nearer to the aesthetic ideal of the new literary trend that sought to legitimize itself by finding a divine ancestor. The first of these attempts, hopeless from the start, had been triggered off by the Hungarian translation, published in 1922, of Tolstoy's mutinous treatise on *Shakespeare and the Drama* (1906); its polemical arguments became a constant subtext even of those idoloclasts who were motivated much less by Tolstoy's Christian conservatism than by the zeal of the social reformer. The obvious failure of any attempt to overthrow Shakespeare and his cult led to the second kind of venture, in the 1930s and 1940s, that sought to appropriate the apparently unshakeable prestige of this sacralized author for gaining power in the all too secular world of warring literary coteries. From the late 1940s to the late 1950s, the darkest years of postwar Hungarian history, Shakespeare's plays became a site for a tug-of-war between the oppressors and the oppressed: the attempts to appropriate Shakespeare were either demagogical manoeuvres trying to legitimize a totalitarian regime or subtly (yet bravely) subversive moves to resist it.

This heralds the coming of the fifth stage, i.e. the age of secularization and cultic revival, from the early 1960s to our own day. The main trend in this period has been towards secularization: the cultural processing of Shakespeare's work, whether scholarly, theatrically or educationally, is mostly done with a professional expertise and ethos no longer determined by quasi-religious attitudes. Underneath the secular workings of this Shakespeare industry, however, one can spot traces of a repressed transcendental symbolism. In unguarded moments the rational analysis of the critic still gives way to the devoutly apologetic gesture of theodicy, not to speak of the unmistakably religious psychology of those now undertaking pilgrimages under the profane cloak of literary tourism. By the 1980s such atavistic recurrences of quasi-religious attitudes and behaviour together with a renewed upsurge of passionate interest in the dramas both as texts and performances amounted to a renaissance of the Shakespeare cult in Hungary.

THE AGE OF INITIATION: LEARNING TO REVERE BEFORE GETTING TO KNOW

The late eighteenth century was the first time in Hungary when readers of periodicals and newspapers became aware of those diverse forms of reverence whereby the British paid tribute to their Bard. A number of laudatory articles described and disseminated the symbolic expressions of respect, whether verbal, ritual or institutional, the contemporary visitor was witnessing in England. These articles made no difference between social behaviour we would now conceive of as the quasi-religious manifestations of a literary cult and those we would consider as secular procedures of our culture. They exhorted Hungarians to emulate

the British in all those hitherto unknown practices: in performing quasi-religious rites at the Stratford Shakespeare Jubilee in
1769, in erecting memorials to their deceased writers and scientists
(and not only to kings or statesmen), in providing a decent living
for the intellectual even though he did not come from a noble
family, in founding charitable institutions to relieve the burdens
of the poor, in subscribing to nicely made books, and so on. The
self-confessed aim of these articles was to 'polish' the nation and
to exert a civilizing impact by transplanting new cultural values.
However, due to their explicit approval of the worship of
Shakespeare, the readers of these articles got accustomed to the
idea of raising a mere writer to heights verging on the transcendental, and the dissemination of this idea enhanced the prestige
of letters in general. Learning the Shakespeare cult and its latent
religious patterns was part of an undifferentiated cultural experience that fostered the growth of Hungarian culture.

The indirect acquisition of reverential behaviour

The Hungarian periodical *Mindenes Gyűjtemény* (*Miscellanea*, published in Komárom between 1789 and 1792) pointed to England
as an example, as indeed the very pinnacle of civilization, and
exhorted Hungarians to follow suit. In 1789 an anonymous article
entitled 'Az Ánglusokról némelly Jegyzések' ('Some notes about
the English') maintains that there are three things that indicate
how far the English have progressed: their institutions of charity, their level of public education and the way they respect their
intellectuals. As regards the first, the societies meant to help the
poor, the article mentions four laudable examples: the *Humane
Society* that was trying to save lives otherwise unprotected, the
Kent Dispensary which was an organization providing free medi-
cal treatment for the poor, the *Lying in Charity* catering for penni-
less women in childbirth, and a fourth society organized to set
free those who were imprisoned for minor debts. As regards the
level of public education, England is praised as the paragon of
high literacy and widespread reading habits. 'In England mere
common people see things more clearly than the nobility elsewhere, and this is caused by the reading of many good books
and newspapers.' In London alone 83 different newspapers were
being printed daily, and some journalists reached 10,000 to 15,000
readers. How enviable! Even the fishwives of the open market

began their day by discussing the latest events in Parliament. It was this love of reading, the article maintained, that had led to a general enlightenment of the British. As regards the status and prestige of the man of letters in England, well, 'if a writer publishes a beautiful work in England, he will be not only respected, but his revenue will suffice for the rest of his life'. One of the examples given is the sermons of Hugh Blair, which first earned the author a handsome sum of money, and then after a year the publisher gave him a share of the profit. Another example was the translation of the *Iliad* by Alexander Pope, which earned the translator 150,000 forints and in addition 'he was honoured so much that many lords and the Prince of Wales himself visited him frequently'.[1]

This last fact was mentioned not only to boost the morale and self-esteem of the Hungarian intelligentsia, but also to convert the Hungarian aristocracy to the cause of Hungarian letters and culture. As potential sponsors they were to be reminded of *noblesse oblige*, i.e. that their wealth conferred on them the responsibility for the well-being of writers. As if to make the addressee of this appeal even more explicit, another article of the same issue mentioned that Hungary had a bigger and wealthier nobility than any other country (several princes, 97 families of counts, 87 barons and several thousand smaller noblemen) and yet 'all these people are reluctant to spend a few forints on Hungarian books that could polish our language, although they spend many gold pieces on dogs; they ignore the possible glory of our nation that could be achieved by cultivating the language and by publishing good books'. What is worse, some of them are expressly against books and consider literature pernicious. 'What would the English or the French think of our nation if they knew this?'[2] As a contrast, another small article in 1790 makes the point that as soon as a beautiful volume of Shakespeare's works was offered for subscription in England there were more than ten thousand subscribers even though each had to pay more than eleven hundred forints. Again, the exhortatory lesson to be learned from this is made clear in the last sentence: 'How much the English love their language and the glory of their nation!'[3]

Nearer to propagating traditionally cultic forms of reverence, another major article, entitled 'A' Nagy embereknek temető helyek Westmünster' templomában Londonban' ('The burial place of great people in Westminster Abbey in London'), reveals a different kind of example for Hungarians to follow. Although the architecture of the church is praised as one of the most beautiful in the world, its main claim to fame is said to be that there are many great personages buried here and the monuments commemorate not only kings and ministers but men of letters, scientists and other people of spiritual excellence. The article was probably taken over from a foreign periodical, nevertheless its lavish superlatives are endorsed by the Hungarian translator. Its main theme, that the merit of one's own achievement is no less than the distinction of noble birth, was very dear to the heart of those that edited and wrote the periodical *Miscellanea*. 'There has never been a place that instilled more respect and devotion in the visitor than this Abbey; especially the student or the man of learning can feel at home here because wherever they look they can see the names of their famous predecessors immortalized in marble monuments.' In an almost hymnic praise of self-made greatness there is even a hint, a very courageous one in those days, that such men of letters and men of science deserved their place in the pantheon *more* than many crowned kings. Among the tombs of ministers, admirals and military commanders are to be found those of philosophers, poets, scientists and famous artists because 'the English, this wise nation, pays tribute not only to generals and triumphant kings, who would not, by this alone, deserve to be called great people, but the English acknowledge the greatness of those who made the whole of mankind happy not by blind chance or good luck but by the indefatigable work of their exquisite minds'. The article reminds us that whereas many kings are buried here without a monument, Newton's memorial was given the most beautiful place of all, and you can see even distinguished foreigners like Handel decently commemorated. 'And that immortal Shakespeare has a memorial with no inscription on it; thereby the English wanted to indicate that this great person is beyond any praise.' There are only a few lines engraved from one of his own works, *The Tempest*, about the transitoriness of all earthly things. The article adds that at the time of Queen Anne the Parliament donated £4,000 sterling per year for the maintenance of this church. The latent message of all this is made explicit at the end: ever since the ancient Greeks no nation has had so many great personages as the English, but this is no wonder because no other nation has ever revered its intellectuals as much as the English.[4] The implied lesson is unmistakable again: Hungarians should revere their outstanding men of letters in the same way. Having read this article the contemporary reader had to contemplate the idea suggested and endorsed, that it is all right to commemorate a great writer of humble origin by a monument that was previously reserved for distinguished statesmen of noble birth. Erecting memorials in a church and then paying tribute to them is nearer to the ritual of a literary cult than the theme of the previous article was, the exhortation to subscribe books, to spread literacy and to disseminate civilized reading habits.

Erecting memorials, however, is not yet, in itself, a literary cult, and it does not require a transplantation of religious ideas into the realm of secular literature. It is in the next article to be considered that the contemporary reader was exposed to the sight of a fully-fledged cultic ritual being transferred into the realm of letters. This article, published in two parts in 1790 under the title 'Shakespeárnak Jubileuma' ('Shakespeare's Jubilee'), is not original – it probably draws on more than one foreign source – but it is adopted so as to persuade the Hungarian public, especially those wealthy enough to support the cause of Hungarian letters. 'Shakespeare was respected in his lifetime by Queen Elizabeth, King James I and many English lords who wanted to make English literature prosper. Among others there was a lord who sent him 1,000 pounds sterling as a present. This would sound a fairy tale in any other country but in England it did happen because here merit is both respected and rewarded.' This motive must have been familiar to the readers of the other articles, but here it is only an introductory paragraph that was meant to prepare the reader for the splendid description to come, the description of the Jubilee that would show how the English paid tribute to their great playwright. The reader was to be prepared to accept all the surprising procedures that followed as something approvable, indeed as something laudable and worth imitating. 'That famous comedian Garrick who is respected all over England so much that even lords and princes talk to him, devoted a public Jubilee or celebration to the memory of Shakespeare in 1769 in summer at Stratford where this immortal poet had been born.' We learn that David Garrick invited the noble and refined circles of England for this national day of celebration, and so many guests flooded into Stratford that many could not find a lodging in the town, and they put up tents on the meadow or slept in their coaches.

We would expect a description of the Jubilee itself, but the article goes on to give an account of the one and a half hour theatrical version that Garrick wrote after the event. 'On the stage many people sang verses on the memory of Shakespeare and then drank wine out of a wooden goblet that the Magistrate of Stratford had made out of the mulberry tree that Shakespeare had planted by his own hands, and this the peasants told each other and showed great respect towards the goblet.'[5] This little episode must have evoked religious associations in the contemporary reader. To learn that the Magistrate of Stratford found it necessary and normal to make a goblet out of the mulberry tree that had been planted by Shakespeare himself, or to read that at this jubilee the devotees of Shakespeare drank wine out of this goblet and that the peasants were overawed by this, must have evoked either the Eucharist itself or some kind of quasi-religious rite resembling the Eucharist. The underlying religious pattern behind this rite is too obvious to be missed. And to learn that a mere playwright, who is, after all, a secular person, was considered worthy of such worship was a very important step towards accepting the idea of a literary cult. But for the contemporary reader this allusion to liturgy was presented in a secular context of English cultural values such as the high standard of literacy, the system of subscription to books and the institutions of charity. It was within a matrix of secular values that readers had to come to terms with this strange quasi-religious cultic way of worshipping a writer. The system of values that had been transplanted into Hungary must have seemed very heterogeneous, yet the approving tone of the narrative suggested the wholesale and unconditional endorsement of the Hungarians passing on the message.

The religious psychology or the deep magic structure of the whole scene is not difficult to work out. By touching and planting the mulberry seed Shakespeare not only gave life to the tree but he himself must have continued to live in it, long after his death, in some magic way. Once the tree was cut, its wood, sacralized by its Shakespearean origin, gave life to the goblet. Shakespeare was not only represented by the goblet but he was somehow *present* in it. Drinking wine from the very goblet that contained Shakespeare's sacralized essence, and drinking wine from it as a celebration of his memory (and thus repeating a sacred rite well-known from the Bible) must have meant, for the Hungarian reader, something with unmistakable religious overtones. The subtle hint that the peasants respected this goblet very much is a further step towards myth-making. In addition, Hungarian readers could learn the implied message that the Magistrate of Stratford, the famous actor (who had talked to lords and princes), the humble folk of England, indeed a wide cross-section of English society, endorsed this jubilee ritual, so there was nothing wrong in this kind of practice.

The second part of the article both completes and confirms the emerging pattern of quasi-religiosity: there follows a description of the great pageantry staged by Garrick, 'a splendid procession that no theatre has ever seen in the world'. It is very important from the point of view of initiation into a cult that the article calls this a *procession*, since in Hungarian this word has primarily religious meanings and the contemporary reader must have understood it that way. Its detailed description must have reassured this quasi-religious interpretation. First the characters of Shakespeare's comedies marched onto the stage, groups of actors carrying a banner with the title of the comedy they represented, then Thalia herself drove in on a spectacular chariot of triumph, then the Muses, Venus, the Graces, Nymphs, Dryads, Fauns and others followed Shakespeare's portrait, singing, one after the other. And then the characters of Shakespeare's tragedies marched in, followed by mythological figures like Melpomene. So the procession, a refined blend of mythological figures and Shakespeare's own creations, was half-way between an ancient classic march of triumph and a religious procession. But it was crowned by something vaguely but unambiguously religious although perhaps not entirely Christian. The scene shifted to the temple of immortality. Painted on the altar you could see the masterpieces of the playwright, and then in the middle there was a monument of Shakespeare, a replica both in size and shape of that in Westminster Abbey. And then the Graces and Nymphs surrounded the memorial and put a wreath on it.[6] This symbolic act of deification in the temple of immortality (aptly called by a later article Shakespeare's *apotheosis*[7]) was the final symbolic transfer from mortal to immortal, profane to sacred.

Put all these three things together, first a quasi-religious rite resembling the Eucharist, then a pageantry that the article itself calls a procession, and last but not least Shakespeare's apotheosis, and you can approximate the impression made on the contemporary reader: Shakespeare was (and should be) worshipped in a way that resembles the religious forms of devotion preserved for a transcendental being. This sacralization of the profane was approved of by the mediator, it was presented as something normal, appropriate and acceptable by the English, so Hungarians should accept it as well. It may look unusual, the implied argument suggested, but there is nothing extravagant, exalted or disproportionate in this kind of quasi-religious reverence. The article mentions at the end that Garrick's Jubilee was performed 97 times a year, and a 'wise traveller' (who remains unnamed but he must have been Johann Wilhelm von Archenholz[8]) saw it 28 times and in his opinion (quoted) each performance was a new and unique and unforgettable experience. The final paragraph is like the ultimate seal of approbation: the English ever since the Jubilee have shown an unlimited respect for their Bard: streets and inns and cafés are named Shakespeare, in many homes you can see his portrait and even the peasants sing his praises in the pubs. The closing sentences are worth quoting: 'And now the English again show their respect to the immortal ashes of this poet by publishing his works with the most splendid printing, with exquisite etchings in twenty volumes, and although each volume costs 6 pound sterling, there are more than 10 thousand subscribers.' And then the last exhortation, with added significance: 'My dear country, when will *you* do this much?'[9]

So from the colourful pageantry and the solemn ritual of the theatre to the praise of the beautifully printed books and the system of subscription this article has to make one little, barely perceptible step. Since all these forms are considered by the Hungarian author different manifestations of the same attitude, the tacit logic of the article is that if you want to cultivate the memory of a writer then cultic and cultural forms of reverence are equally good for the purpose. It is almost as if the common etymology of 'cult' and 'culture' in *colere* (to cultivate) would be re-enacted by this cultural transfer; it is in the spirit of their original inseparability and interdependence that no difference is made here between the publication of beautifully printed books and the ritual worship of Shakespeare. The aristocracy making friends with an author or presenting him with donations, streets named after an author or his portrait hanging in homes, quasi-religious rites in the realm of literature: these are all laudable manifestations of the same respect, and the ascent and endorsement of the mediating Hungarian is unconditional in each case. The writer of the article is something like a missionary, eager to initiate his readership into the ritual of the Shakespeare cult; he does it with a zeal that does not make a difference between values we would today call cultural and values we would call cultic. From this moment we can witness a very fruitful coexistence, indeed cooperation between secular and quasi-religious patterns of behaviour, much as the purists of both sides have been protesting against what they suspected to be a dangerous contamination of their respective sphere of interest.

The conclusions to be drawn here pertain to both the peculiarities of cultural transfer and the general characteristics of socialization. The first step towards transferring cultural values is to disseminate the social practices whereby those values have to be cultivated. We sooner acquire the ways of responding to certain values than the values themselves. Late eighteenth-century Hungarian readers were taught to admire the English who lavishly printed Shakespeare's works and who subscribed to purchase these books, thereby financially supporting their publication, and eventually bought them at a high price. The readers were also taught what kind of memorial Shakespeare had at Westminster Abbey, hence (by implication) what kind of grandeur he *deserved*. Last but not least they were taught the quasi-religious ritual whereby Shakespeare was worshipped at the Jubilee. To sum up: Hungarian readers in the late eighteenth century were taught how to publish and buy, how to bury and how to worship an author they still had had little opportunity to read. Learning the proper ways of reverence preceded any considerable firsthand acquaintance with the works of Shakespeare. The texts of the plays that could have justified the excessive claim to cultural values were to be studied later. And they came to be studied in a frame of mind already prepared for values verging on the transcendental. The first steps of cultural transfer were the acquisition of a proper psychic attitude towards the cultural values that were to be imported. The proper attitude was to be inferred from learning the ways of reverence people cultivated in the home country of those values. Just as some cultural anthropologists maintain that myths grow out of reflections on ritual practices and not vice versa, at an early stage in cultural transfer the awareness of exquisite values is born out of reflections on ritual forms of reverence rather than vice versa. First we learn how to behave by imitating a model, and then we try to find sufficient justification for our behaviour. We begin to read Shakespeare so as to justify the exceptional greatness attributed to him by those diverse social practices of reverence we have acquired. And it is only much later, if at all, that we begin to discern the heterogeneous elements of that acquired set of social practices and values, only to realize that in this curious mixture the sacred and the profane are no longer separable.

Authorial prestige and the role of translations

Nowadays it is hardly more than a commonplace that both the principles and the practice of translation differ from age to age because their function changes with the shifting emphases and modified requirements of their cultural contexts. To understand the peculiar rationale and procedures of early Hungarian translations of Shakespeare in the age of initiation it is indispensable to bear in mind the paradox that in Hungary Shakespeare was revered before he was known. As the emphasis was on learning an imported ritual and verbal system of reverence rather than on acquiring reliable knowledge of Shakespeare's original texts, translations were neither expected nor meant to provide a faithful rendering of the original, whatever faithfulness meant or may mean today. (I am aware of the odious ring of words like 'faithful' for some historians of translation,[10] yet if one can point to late eighteenth-century translators who explicitly stated their preference for radical alterations as opposed to following a text as closely – by their own standards – as possible, then to say that they gave up the ideal of faithfulness is merely to sum up their own position and not to castigate them anachronistically. In such circumstances the elimination of the word – and problem of – 'faithfulness' would be no more than over-zealous and futile clinging to the untenable positivist dogma, fossilized in some quarters of current translation studies, that descriptions can and should be purely descriptive and non-evaluative.) No textual fidelity was required at this stage to warrant the sacredness that was attributed to the playwright by this newly learned code of behaviour. Moreover, sometimes in the first period certain kinds of textual transformations were positively recommended, though the guiding principles behind those transformations were still rather uncertain and by no means universally applied.

It is not easy to find the religious archetype of this attitude to translation. The wholehearted acceptance with which diverse textual deviations were met is certainly at odds with the tradition of literalism in Bible translation, which is based on the postulate that the message of God is contained even in the ordering of the words and consequently requires the holy text to be copied as scrupulously as possible. But encouraged by Frank Kermode's suggested parallel between the diverse types of ecclesiastical constraints on Bible interpretation and the types of institutional control on Shakespeare criticism,[11] one can search for a more positive parallel here as well. Maybe the readiness of the custodians of Shakespeare's sacred original to accept and disseminate translations of obvious verbal inaccuracy is similar to the ecclesiastical decision to italicize those words of the translated biblical text that the translator had interpolated with a view to bridging the gap between the source and target languages. These italics worked as subliminal reminders of the ultimate futility of any attempt at an adequate rendering of the sacred original. Their special typographical quality may suffice to evoke a sense of transcendence and mystery in the reverent reader. Similarly, an unconditional reverence for Shakespeare can convert the apparent (intended or unintended) deviations and even the very shortcomings of the translations into suggestive indications of the supreme excellence of originals they seem unable to reproduce. The inevitable imperfections of those early Hungarian translations of Shakespeare, if and when noticed at all, could be taken as indirect evidence of the unfathomable depths of their divine original. Normally translators cannot win; in the initiation phase of a literary cult they can hardly lose.

The curious paradox of revering the inaccessible is confirmed when one considers the theatrical background of all the sonorous praise lavished on the playwright. As we have seen, the press initiated Hungarian readers into the ritual whereby the English worshipped their Bard: in the late eighteenth and early nineteenth centuries Hungarians could read detailed accounts of the Stratford Jubilee of 1769 with its ceremonies often revealing a latent religious pattern.[12] University students were taught to accept the apologetic strategies of Shakespeare criticism; famous English, German and French authors were quoted to praise Shakespeare.[13] The first Hungarians who visited Stratford in the early nineteenth century called it 'a sacred place', considered themselves literary pilgrims and behaved accordingly.[14] And yet in the contemporary Hungarian cultural context most of this reverence simply *could not be* inspired by theatrical or reading experiences of Shakespeare in the original, nor of translations based on and trying to follow those original texts. Prior to 1837 there was no permanent Hungarian theatre; the German theatres in Hungary, whether in Pozsony, Buda or Pest, rendered invaluable services to late eighteenth-century Hungarian culture by spreading the social custom of theatre-going, but they performed Shakespeare in versions drastically shortened and adapted, so that even the German-speaking spectator could scarcely get access to something more authentic than a thoroughly transformed version of the plays. The German theatre in Pozsony performed *Hamlet* as early as 1773 and 1774, but they used Franz Heufeld's adaptation, with nearly half the play omitted and the rest geared to a peaceful ending. The *Macbeth* they performed in the same years was the adapted version by Gottlieb Stephanie Jr, which can more justifiably claim to be considered a new play in its own right than a text representing Shakespeare's famous tragedy. Strangely enough, when (in 1775) director Karl Wahr decided to perform an unabridged *Macbeth*, probably in Wieland's translation, it was received less favourably than expected, apparently because audiences were not used to the striking features of the original.[15] Those free adaptations may have suited the occasion, yet the art they offered was hardly that of Shakespeare.

A different kind of theatrical experience was provided by the Hungarian wandering troupes who worked heroically amid all sorts of difficulties, usually on makeshift stages, often in barns. What they could offer from Shakespeare's dramas was but a scene or two of one of his plays together with popular pieces by other playwrights to make an attractive and profitable bill. One of these troupes, led by director István Balog (1790–1873), kept an account book they called *Cassa Protocollum* (Cashier's Record); from this document we can reconstruct the programmes of their performances between 1820 and 1837. Whereas from 1820 to 1835 they used to couple an act or even less of *Hamlet* (for example the gravediggers' scene) with an act from some popular comedy or musical play, from 1835 to 1837 it was replaced by a fragment from *Romeo and Juliet* similarly coupled with other pieces of miscellaneous entertainment.[16] What this shows is not only that Shakespeare was integrated into popular culture as well and had not yet become the exclusive property of high or elite culture, as was to happen by the second half of the century in Hungary no less than in America,[17] but also that the growing fame of the author, and the news about the excessive tribute he was being paid in England, had to be accepted without the opportunity to test it against a representative performance, in Hungarian, of any of his dramas.

The Hungarian translator knew only too well that his work was bound to be curtailed and marred owing to the miserable theatrical conditions at that time. In 1812 Gábor Döbrentei, the translator of an unpublished and no longer extant *Macbeth*, had to reduce the number of *dramatis personae* and consequently sacrifice entire scenes so as not to exceed the number of actors available at Kolozsvár, even though the theatre was owned and sponsored by Baron Wesselényi's family. One can sympathize with the same translator when he prefaced his second and more ambitious translation of *Macbeth* (1830) with the pious desire that he would like to see it performed on a Hungarian stage 'but preferably not in a plank theatre resembling a barn'![18] (Partly it was due to such down-to-earth problems, and not only to those of decorum, that the subtitle of this volume promised a *Macbeth* 'adapted to make it performable nowadays'.) Before the opening of the first permanent theatre the quality of acting also left much to be desired and may have often increased the distance from Shakespeare's art. Before translating *Hamlet*, one of the most outstanding Hungarian writers, Ferenc Kazinczy, expressly abstained from going to see the play in Kassa, 'fearing that the bad or – which amounts to the same thing – the mediocre acting would kill in me what I was longing for'.[19] Although such performances didn't necessarily disappoint their audiences and may well have paved the way for a more appropriate staging and reception of Shakespeare in later periods, what they conveyed to the audience would not have been enough to do justice to Shakespeare's art or to vindicate his soaring reputation – unless by dint of a preconditioned reverence strong enough to prevail over any deficiencies. Shakespeare had to be revered before he was known because up to that point there was no way to acquire any sufficient knowledge of the plays, or if and when there was, one can detect a certain reluctance to expose preconceived aesthetic expectations to whatever might clash with them.

As they were meant to be published as literary texts, and very rarely performed, the first Hungarian translations could provide but fragmentary knowledge of an author otherwise wellnigh inaccessible. György Aranka translated a few scenes of *Richard II* in 1785, in prose, working from Wieland's German prose translation, while the *Romeo and Juliet* translated by Sándor Kun Szabó in 1786 was actually the sentimental adaptation by Christian Felix Weisse; both translations were twice removed from an original unknown to the translators. Even the *Hamlet* (1790) of the great Kazinczy was based on the German adaptation, mainly in prose, of Friedrich Ludwig Schröder; the translation itself also retained the prose, evoking an atmosphere completely alien to Shakespeare's blank verse, and rendered the occasional verses in rhyming alexandrines. Schröder's *Hamlet*, with its distinct *Sturm und Drang* flavour, was already far from its original, and Kazinczy's Hungarian version went even further not only by abandoning any attempt to be faithful to Schröder's text but also because it is a 'Wieland-Heufeld-Schröder 1776-Kazinczy adaptation', prolonging and incorporating a whole chain of mediations: it is 'based on Schröder's first, 6-act rendering, which in turn was based on Heufeld's adaptation and on Wieland's translation of the Pope-Warburton text of Shakespeare's *Hamlet*'.[20] Kazinczy's subsequent revisions of this translation display his concern with artistic excellence in his own way but no urge to improve it by bringing it closer to its German model. Kazinczy's translation of *Macbeth* (1791), based on Gottfried August Bürger's translation, is a similar case in point. Not until Gábor Döbrentei's 1812 version of *Macbeth*, still in prose, do we find a Hungarian translation based on Shakespeare's original, and it is only his second translation of the same play in 1830 that reproduces its metrical pattern as well. But this remains the exception, not the rule, in what I called the age of initiation.

It would be misleading, of course, to call these translations inadequate, and it would be unfair to ascribe their deviations from the original to the incompetence of the translators. True, most of them knew no English, had little experience and were rather poor poets. But their *ideal* was different from that of the translators of most later periods. Instead of aiming at representative adequacy, they wanted to create a new work of art that was to be beautiful in its own right, fitting *their* (basically neoclassical) standard of beauty and thus surpassing the original. This principle was already implied in the prevailing method for teaching Latin at school: to develop skills of writing, children were trained to compete with ancient authors by free *imitatio* or *aemulatio*. A similar ideal of translation was advocated by d'Alembert and accepted by some

Hungarian writers. This inspired József Péczeli, the editor of the excellent periodical *Mindenes Gyűjtemény* (*Miscellanea*) as well as a translator of French and English poetry, to persuade his fellow translators to 'fight with the writers' of foreign masterpieces like champions and recreate their thoughts as vernacular works 'just as beautiful' or 'even more beautiful' than the original.[21] Péczeli expounded this tenet in the preface to his own translation of Voltaire's *Henriade*; no wonder that the translation itself is often wellnigh independent of its original, especially in its idyllic parts and battle scenes. On occasion Péczeli would go as far as to defend the idea of conscious mistranslation: when translating Young's *Night Thoughts* and other poems in 1787 he promises his reader that his version 'will surpass not only the German and French translations but the original itself inasmuch as the compelling beauty of the Hungarian language mostly purged this work of that sombre melancholia that might otherwise alienate some readers'.[22] Thus, even though he had learnt English as a student of the Debrecen Reformed College and mastered it to the point of reading its great literary works in the original and planning to translate Shakespeare's revered dramas, he translated Young's poems from French adaptations and clearly endorsed a reader-oriented ideal of translation allowing the removal of unwelcome features. The same ideal is implied in an anonymous article published in his periodical in 1789, urging Hungarian writers to purify Samuel Richardson's *Pamela* and *Sir Charles Grandison* by translating it from a mediating language: 'If somebody does not understand English, he can surely work from the French translation because in most cases the French translation is like a fine sieve, so that if there is some bran in the original work, it cannot pass through it.'[23] Translation is here seen as a means to alter and transform in order to adjust, submit, domesticate. This is exactly the opposite of our prevalent and rarely challenged notion of the ideal translation as an equivalent replica or true likeness that can adequately substitute for the original.

Much as the translator was authorized to alter the original, his translation was not considered a completely new work of art. In fact, writers in this period were largely unaware of the theoretical consequences of the freedom given to the translator and naively identified the translation with the original. Whether Juliet died at the end of the play or not, and whether Hamlet survived the last act or not, did not seem to matter when the plays were identified as Shakespeare's *Romeo and Juliet* or Shakespeare's *Hamlet*, so much so that the translator's name was often omitted from the theatre bill. (This belief in the undestructible identity of Shakespeare's art in spite of excessive interference with his text is not unlike the mentality of those English playwrights and critics of the Restoration who acknowledged Shakespeare's genius but not as something that 'resided in the words he used to express his ideas', and who felt free 'to treat his works as a plastic material which could be reshaped at will'.[24]) This naive identification is implied in the terms of a dramatic competition advertised by a Vienna-based Hungarian newspaper in 1790: a prize of twenty gold pieces was to be awarded to the author of the best Hungarian historical drama *if* it turned out to be successful in German translation when performed in a noted German theatre. This condition was meant as a guarantee of artistic excellence, and it may have served that purpose well; nevertheless it ignored the fact that the appeal of the German version of any play for a German audience would not necessarily indicate the quality of the original play in Hungarian. Yet this competition was expressly designed to foster the work of new Hungarian Shakespeares![25] Thus the essence or identity of a work of art was thought of as something universal and indestructible, something that could not be impaired by mediation even if it meant transplantation into a different language and a different cultural context altogether.

Most Hungarian writers of the period knew little or no English and if they read Shakespeare's dramas at all, they did so sporadically and in translation (mostly German, sometimes French). On closer inspection the soaring praise with which they promulgated the British author turns out to be derivative: far from being inspired by their own reading, it was simply taken over from a prestigious foreign authority, sometimes almost verbatim, and their subsequent (and scanty) personal experience of the plays could not but support Shakespeare's established reputation, which involved much goodwill, persuasive ingenuity and something like a missionary zeal. An inherited value judgement preceded and predetermined the knowledge they sought to disseminate. This applies even to György Bessenyei (1746–1811), the moving spirit behind the Hungarian Enlightenment, who served in the Hungarian Guards of Maria Theresa and thus lived in the thriving cultural milieu of Vienna from 1765 to 1782. In a fictitious letter to a friend, written in French and published in 1777, he articulated his views on the English writers as follows: 'Vous demandez mon avis sur les auteurs anglais. J'en ai lu quelques-uns en français; et je puis vous dire que ce sont des gens très sensés et sublimes dans leur raisonnement, où ils vont quelques fois si loin, qu'ils semblent passer les bornes de l'imagination humaine. Ils ont de tems an tems [*sic*] des pensées effrayantes, mais toujours sublimes.' ('You want to know my opinion on the English authors. I read some of them in French, and I can tell you that they are very sensible and sublime in their reasoning, sometimes they go so far that they seem to transcend the boundaries of human imagination. Their thoughts are occasionally frightening but always sublime.') The advice given to his imaginary addressee is also meant to convince a wider readership: 'Lisez *Milton, Shakespear, Young,* et vous verrez comment la raison humaine peut devenir à la fois majestueuse et terrible.'[26] ('Read Milton, Shakespeare, Young, and you will see how the human mind can be both majestic and terrible.') If we survey the varying views Voltaire expressed on Shakespeare in 1734, 1748, 1768 and 1776, ranging from reluctant admiration to bitter disappointment, their common denominator all through the changes in his opinion seems to be a very similar sense of something both grandiose and shocking. On the whole there is more endorsement and less reservation in Bessenyei's attitude than in Voltaire's, but their characterization of Shakespeare is similar to the point of both using the same adjectives. In Voltaire's texts 'belle' and 'grand' are coupled with 'terrible', and so is 'bizarre' with 'gigantesque' or 'sublime'; in Bessenyei's text 'effrayant' is coupled with 'sublime', and so is 'majestueuse' with 'terrible'; both writers clearly noted the contrast between 'terrible' and 'sublime'. That Voltaire had an immediate impact on the views of the Hungarian writer is plausible enough, if only by Bessenyei's own (slightly boastful) admission in 1779 that he perused all the 36 volumes by the 'famous French writer', reading them 'carefully, two or three times, through and through'.[27] In fact, scholars who have examined Bessenyei's *oeuvre* are unanimous in emphasizing how much his intellectual development owed to Voltaire's inspiration. Without greatly overstating the case one could claim that 'he devoted his entire life, with apostolic fervour, to spreading the ideas of this great French writer and philosopher'.[28] There may be some exaggeration in the opinion that Voltaire's early judgements on Shakespeare 'simply echoed those he had heard expressed by the Bolingbrokes and the Chesterfields whom he frequented',[29] yet even its partial truth is enough to indicate that Bessenyei's pronouncement had a genealogy far beyond his own personal experience.

Voltaire's impact and the decisive role of second-hand critical judgement in this case become more than probable in view of the possible translations of Shakespeare the Hungarian writer may have used. He admitted having read Shakespeare, Milton, Pope and Young in French, but we know that most of the contemporary French translations of Shakespeare were hardly representative of their originals. In an introductory epistle addressed to King Louis XVI, Pierre Le Tourneur contended that prior to his own translation Shakespeare's dramas were available to the French public only in debasing versions no better than travesties.[30] It may be argued that the translations by Pierre Antoine de La Place (who thought that the translator was entitled to correct whatever he perceived as errors in the original, and who omitted parts of *Hamlet*, interpolated embellishments of his own and gave but a prose summary of some scenes), or the work of Jean-François Ducis (who knew no English, produced adaptations from the translations of others, and reworked La Place's *Hamlet* into a tearful neoclassicist play 'having no discernible resemblance to Shakespeare's beyond the names of the principal characters'[31]) deserved no better than Le Tourneur's harsh comment. Yet such were the translations Bessenyei may have read to justify the admiration he preached. Le Tourneur's own excellent prose rendering of the plays was published in 20 volumes between 1776 and 1783, so at the time when Bessenyei published his letter in 1777, the first two volumes could have been at his disposal in Vienna. We have, however, no evidence to substantiate this. There is of course a more probable origin of his knowledge of Shakespeare: he must have seen the translations of Shakespearean fragments contained in Voltaire's essays or his free adaptations of Shakespearean material. But this way could lead to no reliable knowledge either; Voltaire was notorious for his strongly biased representations of Shakespeare. In the preface to the second edition of *The Castle of Otranto* (1765) Horace Walpole challenged Voltaire's 'severe criticism [. . .] on our immortal countryman' by doubting his sufficient command of English.[32] Voltaire's incompetence was also criticized severely by Elizabeth Montagu's book, *An Essay on the Writings and Genius of Shakespear*, with a subtitle promising 'Some Remarks Upon the Misrepresentations of Mons. de Voltaire'. Published first in London in 1769, then in Dublin in the same year, the book went through four English editions just in the next decade (1770, 1772, 1777, 1778), as well as a German (1771) and a French (1777) translation, so it reached a readership wide enough to undermine the credibility of Voltaire's views on Shakespeare,[33] though there is no evidence that such anti-Voltaire diatribes ever reached Bessenyei. His Voltaire-like worded admiration for Shakespeare remained unchallenged, yet no translation or any other form of written mediation available to him could have inspired, let alone justified, the admiration he professed.

As Bessenyei lived in Vienna, and in a triumphant period of that imperial city, one might surmise there must at least have been *theatrical* experiences that would have conveyed to him Shakespeare's dramas in a form nearer to their originals. However, as far as one can reconstruct the situation, again, this was hardly possible. We may assume, though not prove, that he saw *Hamlet* in the Burgtheater in 1773, but this *Hamlet* was in fact Franz Heufeld's adaptation of the play – a sentimental melodrama, very much abridged with the so-called vulgarities such as the gravediggers' scene removed altogether and Hamlet kept alive at the end. (It indicates the early simultaneity and contrast of high-brow versus low-brow cultural appropriations of the plays that the gravedigger scene here omitted was one of the popular parts that Hungarian wandering troupes singled out for their performances.) There were several other layers of mediation between the Hungarian spectator and the Viennese performance. Heufeld's adaptation was based not on the original but on Wieland's translation. The German text had to be grasped, moreover, by a Hungarian who had been learning German only since 1765 and could not possibly have mastered it to the point of appreciating all its poetical subtleties, especially as he had no access to the original and had no idea what to expect or look for. True, there was a French theatre in Vienna too, but up to its closing in 1772 it had never performed a single play by Shakespeare, in sharp contrast with their frequent performances of Voltaire's dramas, including *Brutus*.

Considering the excessive praise Hungarian writers lavished on Shakespeare around the turn of the century one may be surprised to realize how little the available translations, if they were known at all, could justify such enthusiasm and reverence. One is tempted to assume that, having acquired that reverent attitude, they looked for a justification for it hard enough to find it

at all costs. The translations did not have to be either representative or terribly good: the incipient literary cult needed texts for
veneration, but primarily it was the veneration that required texts
rather than vice versa. The strange case of György Alajos
Szerdahely (1740–1808) has made several twentienth-century scholars suspect that sometimes a reverent attitude to Shakespeare
was not supported by any knowledge of any Shakespearean drama
whether in translation or in the original.[34] Szerdahely, a Jesuit,
had been teaching aesthetics at the university of Nagyszombat
from 1774, and as the university was moved first to Buda in 1777,
then to Pest in 1784, he continued his lecturing and made his
students more and more aware of both the exceptional greatness
of Shakespeare and the unique way he was treated by the critics.
Szerdahely's printed works, written in Latin, reveal his growing
effort to initiate both his student audience and his readers into
the ritual of Shakespeare worship. As early as 1776 a transcript
of his lectures mentions the eminence of Shakespeare; in his
Aesthetica (1778) Shakespeare is ranked with Homer, Aeschylus
and Sophocles; in his *Poesis Dramatica* (1784) he goes as far as
studying the anatomy of bardolatry. He maintains that Shakespeare
was considered a miracle of nature ('prodigium naturae'), and
an idol of the world of tragedy ('Idolum Tragicorum'), and that
whenever critics found some flaw in one of his plays they were
intimidated by his great name and emphasized the excellence of
its successful parts and hence of the drama as a whole. Although
Szerdahely goes into considerable detail to characterize Shakespeare's art, in 1914 a thorough and scholarly examination of his
book concluded that he actually borrowed his ideas from the works
of Johann Georg Sulzer, Henry Home and Christian Heinrich
Schmid, and probably had no firsthand knowledge of Shakespeare's
works at all.[35] Szerdahely's borrowings were far too pretentious
not to cast suspicion on his flashy erudition:

> If it is true what Farmer and others maintain, i.e. that
> Shakespeare was not equipped with either a command of ancient
> languages or a knowledge of various sciences, then it has to
> be considered nothing less than a miracle that by nature alone
> he could reach a degree of dramatic excellence unsurpassed
> by the most learned of men and the greatest of poets.[36]

While this creates the impression that Szerdahely had actually
read 'Farmer and others', the sentence is merely a verbatim but

unacknowledged borrowing from a work of Christian Heinrich Schmid. Scholars now tend to agree that Szerdahely had probably never read a single line of Shakespeare – though the evidence either way must remain inconclusive. Nevertheless it is probable enough to illustrate that the textual fidelity, the overall quality or indeed the sheer existence or non-existence of translations were not decisive factors in the formation of this literary cult. As reverence could precede knowledge and convert others just as well, translations as the transmitters of that knowledge played only a secondary role.

Most Hungarian writers of the period began to get acquainted with Shakespeare's works via translated fragments, foreign adaptations or commentaries, and very few of them went on to read the dramas in the original. Those who studied at the Reformed College of Debrecen (a stronghold of Protestant education in the eastern part of Hungary) were introduced to the world of drama by reading Johann Joachim Eschenburg's *Entwurf einer Theorie und Literatur der schönen Redekünste*, a work that saw five editions between 1783 and 1817, or the eight volumes of his *Beispielsammlung zur Theorie und Literatur der schönen Wissenschaften* (1788–95), an anthology containing some of Shakespeare's sonnets in the original and a few extracts from *Macbeth*. For some students of the college this may have been about all they ever got to know of Shakespeare, besides perhaps the occasional Hungarian performance of one of his plays. In his youth the poet Ferenc Kölcsey, author of the poem *Hymnus* which was to become the text of Hungary's national anthem, thus became acquainted with Shakespeare through those two works by Eschenburg; in addition he knew Eschenburg's *Über W. Shakespeare* (1787, 1806), Sulzer's *Allgemeine Theorie der schönen Künste*, as well as Lessing's views; later on he seems to have read some of Shakespeare's dramas in German, maybe also one or two in Hungarian, and most probably none in the original. He was one of the most learned Hungarian writers of his age, and yet he read more *about* Shakespeare than *by* him. The case of Gábor Döbrentei is one of the rare exceptions: by 1812 he had translated his first *Macbeth*, in prose but already from the original, consulting the translations of Voss, Bürger and Schiller in the process; then in 1830 he published his second *Macbeth*, this time in blank verse, together with a series of learned studies about the play and its background, which demonstrated the translator's thorough knowledge of English secondary sources as well.

He was so dedicated to the idea of conveying the play intact that he added an appendix containing the translation of all those parts of the play he had been compelled to omit from his text for the sake of decorum. He was one of those early Hungarian admirers of Shakespeare who *knew* what he was talking about. The other such exceptions included the statesman Count István Széchenyi who first read Shakespeare's plays in Schlegel's translation and only afterwards in the original; his political adversary, Lajos Kossuth, translated some parts of *Macbeth* from the original, though his contention that he had started to learn English when translating Shakespeare in prison was hardly more than a private myth to be propagated for patriotic purposes in international politics.[37]

On the whole this was more an age of praising Shakespeare than knowing his works, so the diverse functions of any translation had more to do with the requirements of a literary cult than with the spreading of knowledge. What is more, the ultimate function of translating was closely linked to the social function of the cult itself. Those Hungarian writers of the period who initiated their reading public into the ritual of Shakespeare worship wanted to exert a civilizing influence. Invariably, they sought to prove that the English reverence for their Bard was but one example among many that showed how intellectuals and their work should be respected if Hungarian culture was to be raised to the level of the most advanced countries of Europe. Those who wanted to convert their readers to Shakespeare reported not only on the quasi-religious ceremonies of Garrick's Jubilee, but also on how the English aristocracy supported the publication of his dramas, how intellectuals of humble origin were buried in Westminster Abbey, how even the lower classes in England read newspapers and books, and how the many charitable institutions relieved the hardships of the poor. All such articles implied, and most often spelled out, the exhortation that Hungary should follow suit. The nobility was often reminded of the imperative: *noblesse oblige*. The professed aim of the articles that urged Hungarians to follow the English example was to 'polish' the nation, and translating Shakespeare was one of the civilized social customs and institutions whereby this could be achieved. It was assumed that translation could cultivate the vernacular and enrich its literature, and thus contribute to the cultural prosperity and fame of the nation. Its ultimate mission was to spread enlightenment and revive a national ethos, two values thought to be indispensable to survival. For such purposes, again, translations had to be beautiful rather than faithful. Intended as works of art in their own right rather than replicas of Shakespeare's originals, the Hungarian translations in the period fulfilled the function required of them and provided texts for a literary cult.

THE AGE OF MYTH-MAKING: RELIGIOUS LANGUAGE AS JUSTIFICATION FOR THE RITUAL

The language of praise in the Hungarian reception of Shakespeare is no less enthusiastic before the 1840s than afterwards, yet the change is all-pervasive and crucial. The rhetoric of appraisal during the first six decades (from the 1770s to the late 1830s) also abounds in superlatives, but its vocabulary, analogies and apologetic arguments are borrowed almost haphazardly from diverse realms of life and only sporadically from the transcendental sphere.[38] From (approximately) the early 1840s the extolling of Shakespeare is couched in a much more consistent, almost homogeneous language dominated by religious allusions. Whether we read the reflections of a Hungarian visitor in Stratford, reviews by theatre critics about contemporary performances or versified eulogies by lesser poets, we are witnessing the appearance of a new and yet familiar idiom that looks like the triumphant though indirect and quasi-religious surfacing of a deep-rooted urge to deify and worship.

The sacralization of the discourse about Shakespeare

In this idiom it is natural to soar from down-to-earth biographical data to the region of the divine; as Bertalan Szemere remarked in 1840, only the cradle and coffin of Shakespeare belong to Stratford, 'his glory is shared by humanity which thereby feels itself related to Gods', and his work is 'almost a divine revelation'.[39] The word 'almost' indicates the inhibiting reflex of the truly religious minded before making a blasphemous equation, but this kind of caution is soon abandoned. Sometimes it is a tactful mixing of Christian motives and classical mythology that is meant to indicate a different realm where blasphemy is out of the question. In 1841 József Bajza, one of the leading critics of the period, voiced his dissatisfaction with the actors of a *Hamlet* performance by

urging them to learn their parts as carefully as if they were performing a majestic ritual, 'with sacred awe and fearful reverence
offering the ripest fruits of their diligence on the altar of the
Graces'.[40] The boundary between Shakespeare and God is still
respected when a critic writing about a performance of *Macbeth*
in 1843 quotes the famous saying of Alexandre Dumas that Shakespeare created more than anybody except God;[41] the same boundary is obliterated in 1847 when Emil Ábrányi calls Shakespeare
'the second son of God, apparently sent to the Earth to explain a
created world otherwise mute'.[42] In the same year the great Romantic poet, Sándor Petőfi (1823–49), comments on the *Richard III* of
the National Theatre with a similar idea, softened by the humorous pseudo-naivety of an apocryphal cosmogony: 'The world used
to be imperfect before Shakespeare, so God, when creating him,
said: here you are, folks, if you doubted my existence and greatness, don't doubt them any longer!'[43] (Such exclamations about
Shakespeare's divine mission have their parallels in several countries of nineteenth-century Europe; in his notes Dostoevsky called
Shakespeare 'a prophet sent by God to reveal to us the mystery
of man, of the human soul'.[44]) Another critic, Gusztáv Zerffi,
adapted a praise of Goethe by Heine when he declared that the
universe wanted to know what it looked like and therefore created
Shakespeare.[45] Still in 1847 a second-rate but popular poet of the
age, Sándor Vachott, wrote an epigram exhorting the new Noah
to take Shakespeare's divine works into his ark so that the generations born after the flood could see what the world was like.[46]
On the eve of the 1848 revolution the famous actor, Gábor Egressy,
later aptly called 'the Garrick of Hungary' and 'the priest worthy of Shakespeare, the idol of his life',[47] wrote an article titled
'The freedom of art' in which he mentioned Shakespeare's 'divine
spirit'; he also published an eloquent 'Proposal for spiritual naturalization' arguing that those who would naturalize Shakespeare
'should be chosen by the Lord'; in 1853 he added that Shakespeare could create from almost nothing, and his plays were a
veritable source of long life and health for body and soul.[48] The
old Pál Szemere, poet and theorist, a revered survivor of the first
Romantic generation, wrote a cycle of didactic poems, *Költészet*
(Poetry, 1851) surveying ecstatically the immense world created
by the immortal poet, hoping to see the birth of his Hungarian
descendants, and closing the last piece of the cycle with the
solemnly liturgical 'And now *laudetur*, Shakespeare, amen!'[49]

It is no mere coincidence that the two most famous, much-quoted and often confused aphorisms of the Hungarian Shakespeare lore were coined in the 1840s by two outstanding Romantic poets, Mihály Vörösmarty (1800–55) and Sándor Petőfi, and both were accepted as authoritative symbolic endorsements of the new (non-verifiable) use of language. Vörösmarty's way to Shakespeare led through all the stages of his home culture: first (in the 1820s) he read the plays in German translation; then, having learned English, he perused the original texts; finally he translated *Julius Caesar* and *King Lear*. Yet his significance is due to more than his *Dramaturgiai töredékek* (Dramaturgical Fragments) where 'he filled the highfalutin empty clichés about Shakespeare's art with concrete substance'.[50] His exemplary status was earned rather by *not* having discarded the hyperbolical phrases and transcendental allusions of his contemporaries. It is precisely because his reputation as a poet was unquestionable and his critical texts displayed the results of independent studies that contemporary readers must have found his praise of Shakespeare earned: when he called Shakespeare's mind 'extraordinary' and mentioned him as 'the boundless master of thoughts and feelings' (1837) or simply as 'immortal' (1838), his idiom was taken at its face value as judgement. The same happened to the famous sentence in his review of an 1841 performance of *Hamlet*: admitting that to translate this play was one of the most difficult tasks, he nevertheless exhorted his contemporary poets to attempt it because 'it must be declared unhesitatingly that a good translation of Shakespeare is worth at least one half of the richest national literature'.[51] What Vörösmarty wanted to say is clear from his letters: he thought that Hungarian literature was far from being among the richest and was still lagging behind the more advanced Western nations, therefore the translation of Shakespeare's works was more badly needed here than elsewhere to foster development. Of course he did not mean the phrase 'worth at least one half' to be taken seriously as exact numerical estimation, and he would have been surprised had he lived long enough to read all those pedantically calculating arguments for or against what later critics thought of as his *thesis*. Vörösmarty's contemporaries were probably nearer to his intended meaning when they quoted the end of his sentence as an adulatory formula with no claim to exact verifiability; possibly it was this use of the proverb-like assertion that inspired Petőfi to formulate its twin axiom. Commenting on a performance of

Richard III in 1847, at the climax of a rapturous paragraph he declared: 'Shakespeare himself is half the created world.'[52] This sentence, unlike that of Vörösmarty, transcends the boundaries of comparative *literary* judgements, replacing the notion of (half of a) national literature with (half of) the created world, and substituting 'worth' with the unqualified 'is'. This new proverbial saying was to be quoted over and over again but it could not be treated as an utterance within the critical use of language: it clearly belonged to the cultic realm. Pedantically positivist scholars may have tried hard to infer quasi-mathematical formulae and quasi-biological laws from Vörösmarty's dictum as late as 1917 ('the value of any nation's literature grows in proportion with the fertilizing influence exerted by the transplantation of Shakespeare'[53]) but nobody could be as unimaginative as to take Petőfi's axiom at its face value and to attempt its verification by seeking to measure half the created world. The status of this assertion was somewhat enigmatic, puzzling and fascinating in its context: Petőfi's previous sentences argued that his admiring similes were not exaggerating, but it was also in this review that he elaborated the light-hearted yet half-serious account of why God sent Shakespeare to the Earth. Moreover, 'teremtés', the Hungarian word Petőfi used for 'the created world', can also mean the act of (primarily divine) creation, hence the associations evoked by the new proverb were inseparable from the transcendental. All these textual strategies made readers aware of something unusual in criticism. Probably it was due to Petőfi's cultic use of language that the editor of the periodical *Életképek* published the review with a note warning the reader that it was 'the first such attempt of our young poet's fiery soul' and was 'entirely different' from another article (published together with Petőfi's) on the same topic by the periodical's 'regular' critic; in the next issue yet another critic differentiated his own sober opinion from Petőfi's 'very poetic' and 'devoutly approving' comments.[54] Later critics called Petőfi's review 'a hymn of praise written in prose', or 'the greatest hymn to Shakespeare in Hungarian', or 'not a review proper but a dithyramb, the product of poetic enthusiasm and imagination, instead of judging reason'.[55] But the poetic quality of Petőfi's article was not its most characteristic novelty; more importantly, it belonged to the new, quasi-religious idiom.

The underlying pattern of religious analogies becomes even more manifest if we compare this new idiom of the 1840s with

that of the 1850s and 1860s: all the relevant innovations are con-
solidated, no part of the system is left unconfirmed, earlier
asystemic improvisations are left by the wayside, and the prevailing whole is accepted as the ruling paradigm. When József
Székely, poet, writer and journalist, confirmed in 1852 that Shakespeare had justly been considered 'the great creative genius' whose
'miraculous' superiority is acknowledged even by the inarticu-
late, he resolved the seeming paradox by disclosing its ultimate
explanation: Shakespeare stands in the very centre of dramatic
poetry 'as a genius radiating divine revelation' and therefore all
those had been right 'who had called his works the Bible of the
world comprising the entire universe and mankind as in a mirror'.[56]
Also in 1852 Shakespeare's creative power was praised in the same
vein by another lesser writer, Imre Vahot, in his short history of
the theatre.[57] All through his career the critic and scholar Ferenc
Toldy (1805–75), traditionally called the father of Hungarian literary
historiography, adopted the same attitude to the author of this
'indispensable canon of poetry' and 'poetic cosmos' (1860).[58] Even
the dominantly analytical and technical discourse of János Arany,
the acknowledged ultimate authority among Shakespeare translators working on the first complete edition, soared to sacralizing
analogies at times, such as when he told his son that Shakespeare's
talent could be justly characterized by what a psalm sings about
God: 'Thou art great, my Lord, in the great, and thou art great
in the small.'[59] Following the logic of this religious paradigm it
comes as no surprise that a tercentenary ode by the Shakespeare
translator Károly Szász, later bishop in the Reformed Church and
supervisor of its revised translation of the Bible, would compare
Stratford to the birthplace of Jesus in Bethlehem and would elaborate the analogy between Shakespeare's miraculous creative power
and the divine miracle of resurrecting the dead.[60] Shakespeare
was not the first author to be awarded a supernatural epithet in
Hungarian, but such a coherent set of transcendental analogies
had never before been given to any other writer.

The symbolic act performed by this coherent set of transcendental analogies is no less than *deification*. It is no mere coincidence that the verb itself also pops up at the beginning of this
period, related to Shakespeare and in a tone of endorsement,
with no pejorative overtones. In an article titled 'Élet és művészet'
(Life and Art) Ferenc Pulszky (writer, critic and journalist, later
politician) exhorted Hungarian authors in 1841 to depict the life

of their country as Shakespeare (and Scott) depicted theirs, because 'then our compatriots would deify them with exuberant joy'.[61] The system of deifying verbal acts elaborates the archetypal analogy of Romantic poetics, the Coleridgean view, inspired by German philosophy, that the workings of the imagination when governing human perception is 'a repetition in the finite mind of the eternal act of creation in the infinite I AM', and the dissolving, unifying, idealizing and thus re-creating process of the poet is another modified variant of this sublime self-manifestation;[62] but the system as a whole owes its acceptance to much more than a Romantic metaphor taken literally. Only the entire ritual acquired during the previous age of initiation can explain the self-confident application of the deifying parallel to all the details of a quasi-theology: Shakespeare, like God, can create out of nothing, he can resurrect the dead, his work is like divine revelation, the Bible of the world and the canon of poetry, his birthplace is like that of Jesus, he is the second son of God, his coming has cosmogonical and eschatological significance as he was sent to earth to prove the existence of the creator and to explain the created world. Some elements of this paradigm are fitted in their respective places in a light-hearted manner but deep down they are always meant half-seriously as well; the occasionally humorous tone is but a tactful rhetorical device meant to secure the acceptance of otherwise daring or blasphemous claims. (Sometimes we find an assertion risked only jokingly by one author but maintained seriously by another.) It is only within this paradigm and because of its ultimately serious intent that a contemporary poet could apply a solemn liturgical phrase to Shakespeare and insert it in his ode without distancing modification. The influence of quasi-religious language is so pervasive that any residue of secular praise becomes isolated and extremely elaborate, lacking the support of a latent system, like the simile of Imre Vahot in 1841: 'Shakespeare's giant ghost stands like the colossus of Rhodes, under which the other dramas of the Christian world try to sail against the wind like heavy mercantile ships that are shaking tremendously but proceed little and often suffer shipwreck horrifyingly by hitting the base of the colossus.'[63] Although such attempts at using a secular language of praise are sporadically made in the period, they are superseded by the religious idiom that could rely on a well-known body of shared knowledge and its highly respectful associations. In this idiom no allusion needed further explanation and the implied aim to foster a devout attitude could be made obvious by using only a few words that evoke the latent system.

The constitution of a shared body of religious analogies had a lasting effect on Shakespeare criticism for a long time to come, and in unguarded moments the entire allegory was to return in its full Romantic splendour, anachronistically, perhaps atavistically, revealing an undiminished awareness of its biblical allusions. A fully-fledged and most instructive specimen of this can be found in a prose prologue written by the novelist Ferenc Móra in 1917 to a performance of *Hamlet* in the Szeged Town Theatre. In this rapturous text, characteristically titled *The Miracle*, Móra claimed that the word 'divination' had never been applied with such justification to a human being as to Shakespeare whose soul must have witnessed mighty thunderstorms unprecedented since the Genesis. As God created man for the Earth, he created people for literature, he performed a divine task, and performed it divinely: as God breathed life into any lumps of clay, he breathed it into any lumps of miscellaneous tales, and whatever he touched, even the most soulless material stood up and walked. The analogy of divine creation provided Móra with the potentially apologetic idea that it was the divine in Shakespeare that entitled him to transcend human morality: he was amoral like nature, his sun would shine on the good and the wicked alike, in the crater of his soul there was a volcano of every vice and virtue and he would distribute it among his creations with God's abundance and a child's devotion. The central analogy also implied the notion of unfathomable solitude: nobody can ever tell how Shakespeare learned all his mastery, how he proceeded in his work, how he felt in his euphoric or desperate moments, just as nobody had ever seen the tears or smiles of the Creator. Taken seriously, the attitude of religious humility suggested by the system of analogies precluded the possibility of explaining, let alone criticizing, Shakespeare's work; as was to be expected, Móra realized that the miraculous is, by definition, beyond human reason. 'I can give no explanation, I can only be a humble confessor of the Miracle called Shakespeare.'[64] Whether the twentieth-century author knew the Romantic antecedents of his allegory or not, the motivation is the same, and what he unwittingly presented was a belated summary of the topoi used in the quasi-religious Romantic discourse about Shakespeare.

Cast in a Romantic mould: the sacred, the aesthetic, the patriotic

The triumphant spread of this new quasi-religious language in mid-nineteenth century Shakespeare criticism was facilitated by something more general than its dovetailing with the ritual forms of a literary cult: contemporary Hungarian aesthetics was based on a functional analogy between art and religion. The psychological functions of art and religion were considered rather similar, often defined with the very same words, and the solemn rhetoric employed was usually meant to elevate the status of art to that of religion. (This manoeuvre implied that religion was considered the highest and most ultimate value.) For Pál Gyulai (in 1855) poetry was not only an infinite reservoir of joy but also 'a second divine revelation that reconciles us to the great disharmonies of life'; for János Arany (in 1860) poetry ought to provide 'propitiation'; for the novelist Zsigmond Kemény (in 1853) it is a universally applicable aesthetic norm that 'by the end of a work of art poetic justice should propitiate us'; for the philosopher and critic János Erdélyi (in 1852–3) the function of art is to propitiate, and (in 1862) poetry has 'a mission to console the world'; for the critic Ágost Greguss (in 1870) the spleen and disharmony of the age calls for art, 'the noblest tranquillizer, whose soothing, pacifying and propitiating effect equals the beneficence of religion'.[65] (These mid-century ideals, once formulated, were to die hard: in a late (1887) exposition of his views on aesthetics and morality the ageing Pál Gyulai exhorted his readers to accept art as a gift from heaven that was meant to ennoble and console us.[66]) According to this consensus the object of art is to reveal the higher (supernatural) mission of man; as the linguist and historian Pál Hunfalvy put it in 1840, an awareness of this would 'console, consecrate, elevate; hence Homer's immortality and Shakespeare's eternal life'.[67] This majestic conception of art naturally attracted a mixed terminology of aesthetics and religion; even as staunch an adherent of technical expertise in criticism as János Arany resorted to phrases like 'heavenly poetry', 'literary confession' or 'aesthetic creed'.[68] The verbal deification of Shakespeare in the language of mid-nineteenth-century Hungarian criticism would have looked much more surprising and much less easily acceptable without the new contemporary custom of juxtaposing the artistic and the religious.

Mixing or juxtaposing, however, are not the same as substituting: this group of authors, once aptly called the Hungarian Victorians,[69] for all their affinities with Victorian attitudes would not have applauded Matthew Arnold's prediction that 'mankind will discover that we have to turn to poetry to interpret life for us, to console us, to sustain us'.[70] Although some pious later critics were to castigate Arany's own poetry for a misconceived order of priority, for having subordinated religious ideas to aesthetic purposes and for letting poetic concerns usurp the central place that should have been reserved for the word of God, such reversal of traditional priorities was definitely not a conscious aim of either Arany or his major contemporaries. Their commitment to religion was still too strong to allow its programmatic replacement by art, and their need to keep religion intact led to renewed attempts to avert its convergence with art. A typical example of such worried separations is the caveat of János Erdélyi, reviewing (in 1859) a lesser contemporary poet: 'Although art often borrows inspiration and sacraments from religion, and religion in turn borrows ornaments and pomp from art, both have respective realms of their own.' Erdélyi emphasizes that whereas the essence of religion is internal spirituality, that of art is the internal made external, therefore the poems reviewed are to be blamed for their 'exaggerated use of the sacred', which is a mistake because 'poetry requires the beautiful, not the sacred, and the latter as such has nothing to do with the beautiful, unless as its component'.[71] Another aspect of the same difference is defined by limiting the legitimate sphere of critical activity: Erdélyi maintains that matters of the heart, like religion, can be scrutinized by God only; man ought to confine his censures to matters of the head.[72] Further along the same line a later distinction is heralded by Ferenc Salamon who reminds his fellow-critics in 1856 that their main concern should be to examine the way religious sentiments are expressed and not to evaluate those sentiments themselves, because the latter could illuminate the personal convictions of the artist rather than his art.[73] Although in such cases it is often difficult to tell whether it is art or religion that is defended against the other, their separate identities are preserved even when mixed metaphors or analogies are employed. (For example, in rapturous moments Gyulai would call art a second revelation or a divine instrument to console man, but he also maintains that the purpose of art lies in itself.[74] At the birth of the myth-making idiom in Hungarian Shakespeare criticism the ideal of art was endowed with quasi-religious functions but without giving up the Kantian autonomy of its aesthetic essence.

It was in this context that propitiation emerged as the central norm of literary criticism, relying on (and sometimes vaguely unifying) diverse ancient traditions of theology and aesthetics, like St Paul's reinterpretation of ritual propitiation and Aristotle's entirely different notion of reconcilement through catharsis. 'Kiengesztelődés', the Hungarian concept of propitiation, is sometimes used in mid-nineteenth-century Shakespeare criticism with a purely religious meaning (in 1841 Vörösmarty explains that Hamlet postpones the killing of Claudius because 'prayer would propitiate for the sins one committed'[75]) but more often in a sense referring to the psychology of reception, or wavering ambiguously between the two meanings. The great historical difference between key concepts were often blurred: in 1841 Dániel Gondol, later the translator of *Romeo and Juliet*, remarked in an essay that the ancient notion of fate meant the same as the Christian concept of providence or the idea of eternal justice in art, but he added that whereas 'for the Greeks the prerequisite of propitiation was something external, like the burying of Polyneikes in *Antigone*', in the dramas of the Christian era 'it is the character itself that makes its own punishment or reward and this propitiates us, too'. In *Julius Caesar* this latter type of propitiation is exemplified by Brutus's character that was too great and passionate not to clash with accepted moral norms and had to fall because any other ending would have hurt the feelings of the audience; in *Hamlet* or *Romeo and Juliet* our sorrow for the fall of the main characters 'is propitiated by the consoling thought that such beautiful characters could not have survived in such debased circumstances'.[76] In 1847 Petőfi maintains that Richard III was given the possibility of a final battle to prove his determination 'and thus after a revolting life achieve at least a death that is heroic and therefore propitiating'.[77] In 1850 the playwright Károly Obernyik made a comparison between the fate of Aeschylus's Orestes and that of Hamlet and found the latter more satisfactory because whereas in the former the final propitiation is forced and artificial (the audience cannot believe that Orestes can be anything but unhappy after his double torment), 'we find consolation in Hamlet's death as that of somebody suffering from a burdensome illness'.[78]

In such cases the concept of propitiation was used in diverse senses but always in a context integrating religious, moral and aesthetic considerations as well as a different (non-verifiable) use of verbal and ritual praise. The intellectual climate that surrounded the norm of propitiation and the whole paradigm of quasi-transcendental symbols in Shakespeare criticism was not only Romantic in origin, but it was also determined by the psychic needs of the historical period after the 1848–9 revolution. Reading the personal correspondence of critics one can find many proofs of the view that after the surrender in 1849, from the savagely cruel immediate retaliation and all through the oppressive 1850s (aptly labelled the Age of Absolutism by later historians) or even afterwards up to the 1867 compromise with Austria, the great psychological problem of Hungarian intellectuals was how to overcome a sense of hopelessness and find an antidote to pessimism.[79] In such a situation Hungarian literati could not afford to give up traditional sources of moral strength, be they forms of Christianity, a revival of stoicism or the national ethos of passive resistance. The critic and essayist Antal Csengery, trying to keep up his morale amid disastrous circumstances in 1855, exhorts Pál Gyulai: 'Try to be calm; stoicism is needed in our age, we have to be able to endure a great deal.' He adds that Eötvös's great philosophical treatise on the dominant ideas of the nineteenth century can be perused by Hungarian readers as medicine against *Weltschmerz*.[80] Writing to a grumbling friend in 1859, János Arany recommends the biblical wisdom of *vanitatum vanitas* as a remedy for suffering souls, advising him to occupy himself physically or mentally by constant activity; later (1863) in an editorial note he is probably generalizing his personal experiences when he mentions the universal human need of a refuge to regain strength.[81] Similarly, as late as 1872 Ágost Greguss seems to sum up the lesson learned by the survivors of this difficult period when he testifies to our need, in this 'imperfect and unjust' world, for a perfect and just alternative, and hails religion, art, science and morality because 'all the four lift us from this finite and tormenting world into an infinite and happy one'.[82] Creations of the human mind were ranked according to their strengthening potential, and literary works were expected to boost the reader's morale; in criticism the textual strategies of a pre-structuralist methodology were always complemented with an affective orientation checking and evaluating the impact on the reader. Typical of this concern is the remark of Pál Gyulai, reviewing a volume of second-rate ballads and romances: in the flood of soft lyrical poems published at the time he welcomed this collection of epic poems because

> we would like to be cured of our paralysis, to draw inspiration and strength from this realm of actions and events for a renewed life of useful public activity, and to make our sunken hearts rise again with the help of objective poetry to a more elevated point where the busy transactions of a wider horizon would dispell our misty daydreams, to exorcise our demons, and propitiate our disharmonies.[83]

No merely anthropological analysis of the mid-nineteenth century Hungarian cult of Shakespeare could explain its psychological motives without taking into account the needs generated by the specific historical circumstances: in order to console and give strength, literature after 1849 was expected not only to interpret life but to justify it, and the ensuing ideal of literature had a quasi-religious function that harmonized with the new quasi-religious idiom of the discourse about Shakespeare.

The triumphant spread of the new idiom was facilitated by another specific historical development in the first half of the nineteenth century: the intertwining of literary, religious and patriotic values. Although at first sight this convergence of main priorities may seem to have had its parallel in the English alliance of the Bard, the Patron Saint (St George) and the King, the genesis of their unity had been different in Hungary and its result was more romantic than Victorian in spirit. To be a Hungarian writer was considered as early as the turn of the eighteenth and nineteenth centuries something both sacred and patriotic. The diary of Ferenc Schedel, then a young would-be poet in his teens, recorded the improvised but solemn initiation ritual whereby he was (as it were) ordained by Benedek Virág, an old priest and poet living in saintly poverty: Schedel and another young poet, József Bajza, were asked to swear that they would devote their entire lives to the cause of national literature, then the old man kissed them and they felt they had been officially admitted to the body of writers. The young poet, later to become Ferenc Toldy, the first modern historian of Hungarian literature, remembered this episode till his own old age and never ceased to be moved by its memory; his young friend became a distinguished literary critic and a fearful champion of the idea that aristocratic birth is no prerogative in the republic of letters.[84] The life of the great reformer of Hungarian literary language, Ferenc Kazinczy (1759–1831), was often referred to (both in his lifetime and especially after his death) as some kind of patriotic martyrdom, an offering on the altar of his country; at the nationwide celebrations of his centenary in 1859 many orators and panegyrists used a vocabulary of sainthood, and several compared him explicitly or implicitly to Christ dying for us on the cross. Although Hungarian Romantic poetry was lacking in purely religious themes, its major patriotic poems imply a role of the poet analogous with the prophet, the *vates* (seer) or the high priest of the nation. (One could argue that religious poetry proper was precluded by a patriotic poetry that integrated religious motives and became the archetype of all poetry in Hungary: once poetry as such became implicitly religious, no place remained for a separate religious poetry.) The famous *Hymn* by Ferenc Kölcsey, later accepted as the text of the national anthem and learned by heart in childhood by many generations, is a prayer imploring God to be merciful and help the nation amid its vicissitudes; here the implied role of the poet is that of the advocate speaking on behalf of the nation in front of the transcendental judge, admitting the past sins of the community and trying to appeal for propitiation. This function of the poet is analogous with that attributed to the Paraclete[85] in the first epistle of John: 'And if any man sin, we have an advocate with the Father, Jesus Christ the righteous: And he is the propitiation for our sins: and not for our's only, but also for *the sins of* the whole world' (I John 2: 1–2). The moral responsibility of the representative poet is often defined in religious terms in early nineteenth-century Hungarian literature, usually personified by biblical figures who conveyed divine orders to their community. Such devices identifying the patriotic with the religious as the dominant ethos transformed any manifestations of literary patronage into laudable acts promoting a good (national) cause; it was Count Széchenyi, the generous founder of the Hungarian Academy and the romantic moving spirit of early nineteenth-century Hungarian culture, who inspired a nationwide 'cultus' of literary patronage.[86] (Characteristically, when the translator of Macbeth, Gábor Döbrentei, sent him a complimentary copy of his work in 1830, the Count read it on board his ship *Desdemona*, and replied in a letter immediately, thanking the translator for his work and encouraging his further efforts.) The ensuing attitude to literature implied a sense of duty, of obligatory patronage (*noblesse oblige*), which was needed at the time but it was also duly criticized for precluding a more intimate and spontaneous relation to literary works. In retrospect one can sympathize with dissenting voices like that of Zsigmond Kemény in 1853, who castigated the Maecenas-like patronage for its lack of real affection, for its dutiful taxpayer mentality and for its willingness 'to give rather than to enjoy'.[87] Similarly, in the political pamphlet *Önbírálat* (*Self-criticism*), published cautiously under a pseudonym abroad (in Leipzig), the poet János Vajda made the point in 1862 that whereas for the German-speaking population literature is 'an indispensable spiritual need', for Hungarians 'at best it is a matter of patronage'.[88] There was a grain of truth in these objections, though no need could ever be felt indispensable by any community without having learned the habit of satisfying it, and Hungarian culture is indebted to the Romantic cult of Shakespeare for disseminating an ethos of literary patronage and thus paving the way for more spiritual responses to art.

The masterly combination of transcendental and national elements in the persuasive rhetoric that tried to ensure a sufficient number of subscribers can be best exemplified by the advertisement written by Emília Lemouton in 1845 to herald her own translations of Shakespeare. The wording is all the more symptomatic because the translator, no more than 18 years old at the time, was ready to absorb contemporary ideals with a youthful enthusiasm and could not help echoing their latent ideological message. Her aim was, admittedly, to 'defend' Hungarian literature from being pilloried, 'alas', as the only one among all educated nations that failed to naturalize Shakespeare, the author who created more than anybody except God. She humbly declared her talent little and inadequate for this enormous task yet hoped to achieve success partly 'because of the strength to be drawn from the sense of duty of a patriotic girl' and partly because of the unequalled excellence of the Hungarian language which is 'more abundant, flexible and sublime' than any of those Western languages that attempted to reproduce the plays. As we are reading this not from a secret diary of its author but from a public attempt to recruit subscribers, Lemouton's references to God, to the cultural obligations of a European nation, to her own patriotic duty and to the asset of possessing a wonderful vernacular can be interpreted as parts of a skilful appeal to the basic assumptions and fundamental values of her readership. In the 1840s the list could not be complete without a sympathetic reference to the lower classes: as expected, the translator explains her decision to translate Shakespeare in prose from an aim not only to preserve both the sublime and the casual of the original but to make it more accessible 'for all classes of our country'. The metaphorical culmination of the argument manages to present her whole task as a quasi-religious patriotic act: 'Whatever degree of success meets my endeavour, I will be amply rewarded if [. . .] my humble offering on the altar of my homeland and education will not be rejected.'[89] Although the five mediocre translations Emília Lemouton could eventually complete were scathingly reviewed, the condescending attitude of some contemporary and later authors cannot be fully justified, and even the self-serving argument of her advertisement deserved a sympathetic hearing. After all she explicitly called her planned series of translations a temporary second best that should be discarded as soon as greater talents produce better ones, and her much criticized decision to render the plays in prose was in accordance with several contemporary German or French examples and with the declared preference of major Hungarian critics from József Bajza (1842) to Ferenc Toldy (1860). Moreover, even the clichés she used for advertising purposes were much more than sheer lip-service when they emphatically (and sincerely) endorsed good causes like the spread of literary patronage, the cultivation of the vernacular, the European integration of Hungarian culture and the lessening of cultural inequalities between classes. Even her sacralizing and patriotic vocabulary, so characteristic of the age, had the positive side effect of emphasizing the importance of literature, though primarily its importance lay as an instrument of patriotic and ideological purposes. Besides, the contemporary reviews of Lemouton's translations used the same language: as she translated so as to bring offerings to the altar of her country, one of her critics predicted that the time will come for translations worthy of 'the immortal Britisher', but those will no longer lack 'the divine fire' the warmth of which can be felt in every word of Shakespeare.[90] The objection is not fundamental but technical: literature can well be an offering on a patriotic altar but the latter is no good without a divine fire.

Bridging the gap between authorial prestige and audience behaviour

The widespread acceptance of the new sacralizing idiom in the discourse about Shakespeare was also connected to the historical phase of the Hungarian theatre, especially (and somewhat paradoxically) to the relative inexperience of a newly formed theatre-going audience. If one reads the contemporary accounts of Shakespeare performances it is easy to notice a recurring theme: critics in the 1840s often remarked that the behaviour of the audience betrayed their lack of understanding. After a performance of *Othello* in 1842 József Bajza tried to explain the phenomenon that in the Hungarian theatre in Pest 'Shakespeare is not appreciated as he would deserve it', and made the point that to understand the deep psychology of the plays 'very considerate and thoughtful spectators are required', and that it takes 'a well educated audience to realize that in some respects world literature has nothing comparable to Shakespeare'. Yet the critic had often witnessed that in Hungary 'the most tragic scenes of Shakespeare evoke not fear or pity but laughter in the multitude', and the only explanation he can give for this 'symptom' is that these scenes 'were completely misconstrued or not understood at all'. On the other hand the critic discerns two types within the admirers of Shakespeare: those who respect him because they read his plays and know his work from firsthand experience, and those 'who respect him to follow reported opinion and to look *connoisseurs*'.[91] What the critic is describing here is a characteristically intermediary phase in the development and integration of an audience: whereas its lower and wider strata have not yet acquired the preliminary training to understand (on an elementary level) the intended meanings of a performance, its upper strata were already hindered by another kind of preliminary knowledge that preformed any personal judgement and precluded nonconformist opinion. In the same year Imre Vahot laments the contrast between the behaviour of Hungarian theatre-goers and that of a 'really educated audience', like the spectators who filled the Viennese Burgtheater and 'who followed the performance with the greatest possible attention and congeniality', responding to its plot 'like a big, flaming, fighting heart in which Lear's vicissitudes evoke the greatly unified noble emotions of fear, pity, co-suffering, and sympathy'. The Hungarian critic was deeply impressed when noticing that here even men shed tears, and found it difficult to decide whether Lear or the audience itself was the greater tragic hero.[92] The full house of the Burgtheater was envied by the Hungarian visitor for good reason: at home, writing about a production of *Romeo and Juliet* in 1844 another critic, Andor Vas, celebrated 'the heavenly apparition' that 'a Shakespeare play was performed and yet the theatre was filled!'[93] In the following year the same critic resented that *Henry IV* (*Part 1*) was performed with the omission of quite a few serious scenes, degrading a historical drama to 'the amphibian realm of tragicomedy', and blames those responsible for the cuts because it was due to 'their error that such a masterpiece could not please some parts of the audience, especially those who lack the necessary education to understand high Shakespearean beauty'.[94] Also in 1845 János Erdélyi reported from Paris on the wonderful acting of Macready and the admiring press reviews, adding enviously that 'people go to the theatre as usual, but like schoolchildren, with a book in hand, reading Mr Robertson's translation parallel with the acting', ready to sacrifice half their enjoyment for understanding the text.[95] In 1846 a theatre critic felt compelled to apologize for the Hungarian audience of Shakespeare. He tried not to blame 'the spectators who frequent these plays in small numbers and are bored most of the time', defended their lack of enthusiasm by pointing to the right of every age to have a taste of its own; similarly, he did his best not to blame the actors either: after all they had little time to prepare for their all too frequently shifting roles and therefore could not possibly carry away an audience 'not keen on deeper study anyway'.[96]

On comparison and analysis such scattered remarks of many contemporary theatre critics fall into an interesting pattern, revealing the psychological implications of this intermediary phase in audience behaviour, the civilizing efforts of criticism and some of the the indirect social factors that perpetuate a literary cult. When a leading critic like Bajza pillories the audience for its lack of education just because it laughs instead of showing pity, or when he confidently emphasizes that only a very educated audience would understand the incomparable greatness of Shakespeare, he not only encourages the spectators to educate themselves and thereby learn the appropriate ways of responding to a play, but he implicitly threatens to stigmatize as uneducated everybody who would respond to a scene in a different way from that suggested as the only proper one and who would thus not testify to the Bard's incomparable greatness. If we imagine somebody not yet able to understand why pity is the only proper response to a certain scene, the probable solution for such a person, afraid to be stigmatized as uncouth, was to learn (by imitation) the behaviour of his or her betters. But this would easily lead to the other type of behaviour Bajza dismissed, the hypocritical conformity of those who respected Shakespeare because of his fame and only so as to pose as connoisseurs. To display the reactions of fear, pity or amusement at the right moments became Bajza's norm of *the* proper response to Shakespeare's plays; the same norm of the one and only adequate response was used by Vahot when he reminded his readers of the ideal Viennese spectators who followed the emotional vicissitudes of Lear with the uniform sympathy of one enormous heart. Both critics based their norm on the assumption that in a properly educated audience a work of art can and should evoke one and the same proper response (governed by its only right interpretation), and both assumed that the cultural function of criticism was to teach the backward how to avoid a shameful display of their ignorance and bad manners. Accordingly, from time to time contemporary critics actually scolded the audience for what they considered improper behaviour and the reproach was not altogether ineffective: in a performance of *Othello* in 1852 the protagonist was applauded after each scene with an unruly ovation that required him to come out several times, disrupting and disintegrating the play; this triggered off a series of angry and menacing articles in the press against the 'noisy and often immature yelling from the balcony'. Writing about the next performance, that of *Henry IV (Part 1)*, Antal Csengery was pleased to point out that the audience was probably reformed by the castigation, because it behaved decently, with muted enjoyment, yet displaying a susceptibility to Shakespearean beauties.[97] One can infer, perhaps, that both the *faux pas* and the subsequent docility of the audience were due to the intermediary educational phase of many of its members: it is in this phase of development that the relative newcomers of a cultural practice are neither confident enough to shake off the expectations of the initiate nor intimidated enough not to have unguarded moments when they fail to imitate. If Antal Csengery was right to suppose that the change of behaviour was prompted by reproachful articles, then those reformed were reading the papers and must have been familiar with the sacralizing idiom of the contemporary Hungarian discourse about Shakespeare. You should be careful not to behave indecently at a performance of something written by *the second son of God*.

A glimpse at the behaviour of later Shakespeare audiences in Hungary illustrates the results of this inextricable interrelation of educating and intimidating. When writing a series of reviews about the Shakespeare cycle of the National Theatre in 1923 Zsigmond Móricz characterized the audience and the formation process of its behaviour with the shrewd psychological sense of a major novelist:

> One and a half thousand people, softened by a century of education, misinterpretation, exhortation, suggestion, the terror of scholars, poets, writers, so much so that now they put their heads with perfect docility into the yoke of the Shakespeare religion, and come to the theatre with profound devotion like fanatics to the worship of God, and they laugh where they should, are moved where they should, and sleep where they should.[98]

What Móricz depicts as a docile and uniform behavioural pattern conditioned by the *yoke* of a quasi-religion is exactly what Bajza had in mind in the 1840s as the desirable ultimate object of theatrical education: to be able to give the only appropriate emotional response to each event on the stage, whether by laughter, tears or yawning. (To demonstrate boredom at the right time has always been the hallmark of a well-groomed snob.) Móricz must have read most of Bajza's arguments (in 1903 it was on Bajza's polemics that he wrote one of his earliest studies[99]), and seems to remind the Hungarian critical tradition of the darker side of their cultural impact. By repeating the aptly ambivalent 'where they should' and by juxtaposing *education* and *softening* as synonyms, or making a parallel of *misinterpretation* and *terror*, Móricz reveals his view that to civilize is to submit and suppress, and that the dictatorial side effects of conveying cultural values may stifle nonconformist spontaneity. Yet the little episode that prompted Móricz's scathing remark is worth recalling because it left a margin of hope and made the implied evaluation of the nineteenth-century critical tradition less pessimistic. Due to some technical error at the performance of *Twelfth Night* the curtain fell right after the beginning of a scene, so the scene had to be repeated but the same *malheur* happened again and the audience burst into laughter. Móricz was delighted with what he considered a miraculous residue of spontaneous behaviour left intact by domesticating terror, and he praised the audience for its courage to forget about snobbish expectations of incessant high seriousness. 'Yet the greater miracle is not that the audience could laugh with such sweet sincerity at the accident that was to profanate the sacred place, but that it could fully appreciate the three hundred years old stage comedy itself.'[100] Móricz could have added that his own personal development also testified to the possibility of shaking off the yoke before it would have left him bereft of the ability to stand up: in retrospect he admitted that Shakespeare used to be the greatest 'idol' for him,[101] yet he became independent enough to analyse audience behaviour at Shakespeare performances.

Dissenting voices: anti-romantic demythicizing

In the mid-nineteenth century the dilemma of whether to conform or risk dissent was not confined to relative newcomers to the theatre. It affected the culturally more advanced, and there were critics who fought equally fiercely against the opposite extremes of idolatrous apology and ignorant refusal. After the fiasco (in 1855) of the National Theatre's performance of *White and Red Roses*, Edmund Kean's adaptation of *Henry VI*, the critical response was divided between gloating over the fall of a classic author in front of a few bored spectators and arguing ingeniously to redeem the play at all costs. It was against both of these stances that Ferenc Salamon directed his double-edged argument: 'To judge the value of a great poet's work by the size or mood of the audience is just as wrong as to admire the great spirit of the poet even when we see blemishes in a work that was made even more flawed by the interference of alien hands.' Having distanced himself from both false extremes Salamon went on to give an example of what he considered the right critical method: he analysed the play, then characterized the prevailing taste of his own day, coming to the conclusion that the play's failure was necessary and unavoidable because in an age of trifling emotions there can be no room for a real tragedy revealing human greatness.[102] This was a carefully balanced statement, yet with a subtly apologetic slant,

unlike that of the similarly divided yet more resolutely demythicizing Pál Gyulai who felt idolatry to have been the more
harmful of the two dangers. In his review of a performance (in
1865) of *The Winter's Tale* he labelled the scornful dismissal of a
great playwright (when misunderstood or left unread) more
grotesque than a disproportionately devout admiration can ever
be; nevertheless it was his attack against the latter that sounded
more fierce here, probably because he found this phenomenon
more prevalent than the other. He was annoyed by those devotees of both the Hungarian and the European cult of Shakespeare
who deemed every play by the Bard a masterpiece, every line
some profound wisdom, and his very shortcomings worthy of
adoration. Gyulai labelled this attitude 'ridiculous idolatry' and
maintained that the perfection accessible to man can never be
absolute, and even the greatest artist is exposed to changing circumstances that make his work uneven. 'Just like in the world of
morality, absolute perfection will always remain a mere ideal in
the realm of art; we can talk about human perfection only, that
is, a greater number of good features.'[103] Though this definition
seems to imply the notion of relative perfection, probably a contradiction in terms, it reasserted the ultimate difference between
the transcendental and the human, firmly planting Shakespeare
in the latter sphere. Not that Gyulai entirely abstained from apologetic arguments; like his fellow-critic, he used subtle devices to
blame errors on external forces (for example, most of the flaws
are due to the play's subject, the excellences are the playwright's
own), but he dared to refer to *The Winter's Tale* as one of the
second-rate or third-rate plays of its author,[104] clearly implying
that Shakespeare *had* works of lesser value.

Both Salamon and Gyulai represented what we might call the
anti-romantic trend in criticism, and from their demythicizing
perspective even Shakespeare's revered plays were products of
human efforts, therefore necessarily imperfect and by no means
beyond criticism. The sober methodology of this mid-nineteenth-
century trend in opposition to the sacralizing quasi-religious
discourse about Shakespeare was based on the twin devices of
comparison and analysis. The move looks innocent but the
idoloclastic tendency of its simple implications is radical enough:
once compared, Shakespeare can no longer be taken as incomparable; once analysed, his work can no longer transcend the
reach of human reason. A typical example of this down-to-earth

approach is the way Károly Obernyik treated *Hamlet* in 1850: he accepted Shakespeare's greatness but explicitly refused to follow those who treated Shakespeare as 'an eternal exception to the Horatian rule of *nil admirari*'; he maintained that to say anything new and substantial about *Hamlet* a comparative analysis was needed between *Hamlet* and the Orestes trilogy by Aeschylus. His final conclusion was so balanced ('whilst *Hamlet* can claim more of the narrative and philosophical beauties, the tragedies of Aeschylus are dramaturgically impressive, well-motivated and impeccably consistent') that he felt it necessary to refute possible accusations of irreverence.[105] The anti-romantic edge of such arguments was especially tangible when they were formulated by authors who could remember this dilemma of quasi-religious worship or demythicizing criticism from their youth back in the age of Romanticism. They knew that the Romantic cult of genius entailed not only the analogy between the workings of poetic imagination and the divine act of creation but also the assumption that there could be inexplicable and unique masterpieces beyond any conventional strictures. They also felt that whereas this romantic conception and its sacralizing discourse would enhance the dignity of art, to admit the moral and aesthetic imperfections of all human efforts would allow a more dignified function to criticism. Paradoxically, when the young Ferenc Toldy, the devoted champion of Vörösmarty's romantic poetry in the 1820s, found himself in a critical polemic with the old Kazinczy in 1831, his own no-nonsense cast of mind opted for the more this-worldly of the two perspectives: admirable as the human spirit would be 'as an abstract entity', entering a flesh-and-blood person it can no longer be infinite, its flight cannot be free any more, and its activity will be 'frail, erroneous, and imperfect'. So to call any author 'greater than all created minds' is sheer idolatry, and 'I expell from the realm of criticism all such deifications as well as the enthusiastic claims that Homer, Shakespeare, Goethe, or Byron should be called incomparable minds.'[106]

From the mid-century the proneness to idolatry was also castigated as a romantic flaw in what critics called the national character. The growing prestige of János Arany made him an authority more and more difficult to contest (as early as 1857 Pál Hunfalvy wondered whether he could contradict Arany's views on prosody without becoming ridiculous[107]), although he himself was far from accepting any notion of unquestionable authority and found the notion and prerogatives of genius especially harmful when extended beyond a few exceptional authors. Neoclassicist in aesthetics, he kept emphasizing the moral and artistic imperfection of individual achievement, he thought that even the work of a genius is often marred by ignoring the study of principles and traditions, and he pointed out that the majority of authors, including himself, could not produce anything worthwhile by sheer instinct.[108] In spite of his anti-romantic and self-critical stance, however, when he published a collection of his poems in 1856 a reviewer made the point that only Goethe could have written a review worthy of Arany's poems and it would be ridiculous for any critic to teach such a poet instead of learning from him.[109] Ágost Greguss retorted that such an idolatrous attitude, whether to the great (Romantic) poets of the past or to their (different) successor, had always been irresponsible and harmful. (It may be more than mere coincidence that Greguss, who had spent ten months in prison in his youth for his participation in the 1848 revolution, in later life became an advocate of sober judgement.) 'Hungarians have been prone to idolize and easily go from one extreme to the other. Vörösmarty was idolized in his day, then Petőfi, now it seems to be Arany's turn. [. . .] Let's not encourage the idolatrous inclination of our good nation.' As a remedy he urged that the head should be allowed to rule over the heart, no authority should be accepted without having been subjected to scrutiny, and its acceptance should mean a reasonable degree of respect, not 'blind worship'.[110] Committed to rational measures, Greguss wanted to remain this side idolatry in Shakespeare's case as well. Having translated *Measure for Measure* (1866) and *Timon of Athens* (1867), he gave a series of lectures on the Bard in 1870, and insisted on examining the works in their historical context because 'otherwise we would attribute to him the advantages of his age and nation (as his idolaters do) or make him responsible for the errors of his age and nation (as Voltaire did)'. This was meant to cut both ways but the lectures themselves fought more vehemently against bardolatry than against debunking, so much so that the anonymous article that summed them up was published with the title 'Shakespeare bálványozása ellen' ('Against the idolaters of Shakespeare').[111]

The same (asymmetrically) divided loyalty informs his book *Shakespere pályája* (Shakespeare's Career). Commissioned by the Academy to complement the first complete Hungarian translation of Shakespeare's works, the work deserves special attention as the first Hungarian monograph on Shakespeare. (The volumes of that series came out from 1864 to 1878, while Greguss's work was published in 1880 as the first (and only) volume of a two-part monograph *Shakespeare élete és pályája* (*Shakespeare's Life and Works*) he could not complete because of his death in 1882.) Greguss's approach to his subject was characteristic of an author who had studied at the University of Halle and become acquainted with both Hegel's notion of historical development and Johann Eduard Erdmann's reconciliation of science and religion. He began his text quoting a historicizing idea from James Anthony Froude's history of England (Shakespeare's plays are the products of many generations that paved their way), precluding the possibility of treating Shakespeare as a miracle. Greguss interpreted Froude's statement as a variant of Taine's principle which he thought exaggerated in its original (Tainean) wording but true in essence: nothing can be adequately depicted unless in its natural environment. Greguss's method seems to combine positivist principles with the essentialist epistemology characteristic of mid-nineteenth-century Hungarian criticism. He maintained that Shakespeare, seen as the child of English Renaissance, should no longer be praised or blamed for attributes of his age, but presented 'in his reality'; in this way we could also discern how he used material taken from his predecessors and judge his achievement 'justly'.[112] All through the book Gustav Rümelin, whose *Shakespeare-studien* (1866) sought to disenchant his contemporaries from the cult in a coolly positivist manner is frequently quoted.[113] Greguss coupled Rümelin with Voltaire as examples of a hostile bias, and in the majority of cases he defended Shakespeare[114] and even his cult, but not without reservations and generally with more sympathy for the sceptics than for the enthusiasts. 'The Shakespeare cult (and who would disapprove of it if complemented with an unbiased insight?) does not cease to exist in the poet's country and it is to be hoped that it will continue forever.' He deemed the spread of the cult in England from the second decade of the nineteenth century excessive because critics lavished exaggerated praise on the Bard from every conceivable angle, 'they find nothing objectionable in him any more', and 'a blind and boundless admiration had become fashionable', a veritable 'mental epidemic' that originated in Germany and infected the English, producing its gravest symptoms in Coleridge's works. 'For him Shakespeare was infallible, so much so that spotting a real error in *Coriolanus* he naively expressed his hope that one day he would be wise enough to realize that the seeming imperfection was a profound beauty.'[115]

The dismissal of Coleridge's apologetic strategies (the very device I compared to theodicy) reveals Greguss's anti-romantic stance; the same tendency made him prefer those French critics who passed more balanced judgements than Victor Hugo who 'admires Shakespeare and whose book is sheer deification'. Of the Germans Greguss preferred Goethe (who could respect Shakespeare without unjustly belittling French poetry) to Schlegel and Tieck, 'the founders of a veritable Shakespeare-worship in Germany' that made the Bard the paragon of not only art but philosophy as well. He found the works of Rümelin and Humbert good antidotes to such adoration: 'Although they had a certain bias against the movement, their wholesome moderating effect has already been proved and makes us hope that the overflowing German cult of Shakespeare would withdraw to its river-bed like in England and France.'[116] As could be expected, Greguss commented on cases of myth-making, relic-worship and pilgrimage in a detached and sceptical way but without malice, condescension or cheap debunking.[117] All he can say about the Reverend Gastrell's controversial deed, usually the occasion for indignant diatribes against sacrilege, is that in this incident the Reverend 'could not be accused of exaggerated piety'.[118] He keeps a similar distance from 'the legion of worshippers' who 'revere Shakespeare's works as the depository of all the good, true, and beautiful' and read them, 'like the Bible', for guidance in various matters including the political and the ethical.[119] Greguss's reluctance to be carried away is that of a scholar representing a dignified Academy. Only in the closing paragraph and especially in its eloquent final sentence do we find him rising to pathos, arguing that Shakespeare's commitment to transcendental values and social responsibility makes his works the much needed remedy for a corrupt and confused new generation.[120] Thus the first institutionally approved book-length pronouncement on Shakespeare gave an anti-romantic criticism of his deification but referred to his art as great, morally impeccable and a reliable pillar of society. Shakespeare's undisputed authority was still needed, therefore it was preserved and appropriated, but without the (now embarrassing) quasi-religious idiom and paraphernalia of his Romantic cult.

THE AGE OF INSTITUTIONALIZATION: THE SHAKESPEARE COMMITTEE AND THE PRICE OF AUTHORIZATION

As we have seen, the appropriation of Shakespeare in Hungary started with a curious paradox: respect preceded practically any firsthand experience of the object respected. Long before they could gain access to Shakespeare's texts, late eighteenth-century Hungarian writers learned both the secular and the quasi-religious forms of reverence, from Garrick's Jubilee to literary pilgrimages, by which the British paid tribute to a playwright extolled by other European authorities as well. This phase of ritual initiation lasted from the 1770s to the end of the 1830s and was followed by a period of verbal deification in the 1840s and 1850s. To provide a terminological equivalent of (and justification for) the ritual, the language of Shakespeare criticism adopted religious metaphors culminating in the romantic analogy between the creative genius of Shakespeare and the creator of the world. By the time Hungarian writers established their first institutional Shakespeare Committee (1860), and joined forces to translate and publish their first complete edition of Shakespeare (1864–78), the new task was to *domesticate* Shakespeare in both main senses of the word: to *naturalize* a foreign author by transferring his work into a domestic cultural context, and, more specifically, to *tame* the author as it were, to render his work harmless (ideologically) by assimilating it into the prevailing set of values. In order to legitimate Shakespeare a thorough moral revision seemed necessary. In mid-nineteenth-century Hungarian culture this was achieved partly by renegotiating the principles of literary translation (with subtle ways of removing the scandalous) and partly by inventing apologetic strategies in Shakespeare criticism to prove that there was very little, if anything, in the plays that, once reinterpreted and appropriated, could violate the ethical norms of the day.

When Anasztáz Tomori, the generous patron of the first complete Hungarian edition of Shakespeare's works, offered his financial support in 1860, he commissioned the Kisfaludy Society, the leading literary society of the period, 'to supervise the ensuing translations' and promised 200 Austrian forints for each translation, a fee to be paid to the translator 'as soon as the honourable Society declare his work acceptable'.[121] The first Hungarian Shakespeare Committee that the Society promptly established (four years earlier than the Deutsche Shakespeare Gesellschaft was founded in Weimar) was made responsible for providing the criteria of *acceptability*. Although its members included authors as diverse as the poet and critic János Arany, the novelist Mór Jókai, the playwright Ede Szigligeti, and the translator Károly Szász, they all felt the need to renegotiate not only the principles of literary translations but also the relationship between moral and aesthetic norms.

It was not for the first time that they felt the pressure of contemporary expectations. They knew that the great task of producing the first complete Shakespeare was overshadowed by the menacing imperative that required literature to be cleansed of all impurities. When translating *King John* as early as 1859, János Arany was worried about the reception of the play and discussed the issue in his correspondence with his friend Károly Szász: 'How peculiar! I wonder how the shy Hungarian audience would respond to the first act that one cannot even smooth over because it is indecorum through and through.' We learn that he had just been visited by the novelist Zsigmond Kemény, who tentatively suggested the elimination of some 200 lines of Shakespeare's *oeuvre* to make it acceptable for 'the salons' as well. 'I respect the salons', commented the translator indignantly, 'but should the first *complete* Shakespeare be *mutilated?*' Besides, the problem could not be solved by excising 200 lines either, continues Arany, or the whole first act of *King John* would fall victim to prudery, not to speak of *Measure for Measure*.[122] The reply of Károly Szász, himself a minister and later bishop in the Reformed Church, reveals no trace of prudery. He fully agrees with his friend and militantly opposes the idea of omitting any part, even one single line, of Shakespeare's text: 'I do respect decorum but in such cases I find it ridiculous; it is like when the Pope in Rome ordered shirts, trousers (maybe even crinolines) for the naked sculptures of the Vatican to prevent nature from scandalizing the spectators.'[123]

By the time Arany presented the unanimous verdict of the Shakespeare Committee to the assembly of the Kisfaludy Society on 25 October 1860 he was able to couch the exposition of this delicate problem and its proposed solution in terms that reveal a firm commitment to fighting for freedom. He admits that the question could be asked whether they should allow Shakespeare's text, 'as it is, with its bawdy, sometimes obscene parts to pass into the hands of the Hungarian reader', but he formulates the ultimate dilemma with a persuasive rhetoric that eloquently endorses the claim for the translator's independence: 'What is at

stake is whether we want a complete Shakespeare or a mutilated, lacunal, castrated edition.' The horrifying associations of
mutilated and *castrated* (originally addressed to the all-male assembly
of the Society) highlight the frightful kind of lacunae suggested.
However, Arany managed both to suppress the overtly sexual
implications of his terminology and to heighten subconscious
castration anxiety further by quickly adding that the full preser-
vation of decorum would require 'such mutilation of some plays
that they would cease to be drama altogether'. The ensuing propo-
sition itself, tempered by tactical skill, was able to get away with
a vague and minimal promise of taming the occasional wildness:
'It is so important now, when we want to publish Shakespeare,
not to publish the work with gaps, that the Committee would
not like to vote for a mutilated edition.' The final conclusion thus
heralded, the Committee advised the Society to follow the example
of other nations, most notably the Germans, in 'commissioning a
translation of Shakespeare's work in its entirety, without mutila-
tions, instructing the translators to render, wherever they can do
it without damaging the play, the most bawdy parts in a milder
fashion, and thus, as far as it is possible, prevent scandal'.[124] This
little masterpiece of rhetoric worked wonders. The freedom it
claimed was not unlimited, but by defending the inviolable integrity
of the plays, it ruled out the possibility of substantial cuts or any
changes of plot; and it succeeded in authorizing the translators
themselves to preserve as much of the original text as possible, or
to decide how little, if at all, they wanted to domesticate Shakespeare.

The problem the first Hungarian Shakespeare Committee had
to solve was not simply that of verbal decorum or mere etiquette.
The responsibility its members shared was due to an issue that
cut deeper than the assumed shyness of certain audiences, or
the difference (and contest) between the taste of the salons and
that of the lower classes, or even the much debated question of
whether a woman as ferocious as Lady Macbeth was conceivable
at all. (As to the latter question, in 1830 a Hungarian translator
of *Macbeth* gave an affirmative answer, admittedly based on 'vivid
experience'![125]) The ultimate task of the Committee as an authoritative body was to redefine the limits of aesthetic and moral
acceptability before disseminating newly translated texts that were
to join the Hungarian literary canon as representatives of the
highest European culture. The aesthetic acceptability, indeed
excellence, of Shakespeare's plays was no longer challenged in

mid-nineteenth-century Hungarian culture: by that time the neo-classicist objections had been silenced, mainly by quoting Euro-pean critical authorities. Critics still discussed the aesthetic hierarchy *within* the Shakespeare canon, but the exemplary status of his whole poetic accomplishment was taken for granted. The moral debate, however, was still unsettled. The Committee had to miti-gate the fear, voiced by earlier Hungarian commentators on Shake-speare, that some scenes, acts or indeed whole plays were likely to exert a subtly demoralizing effect on the audience.

A case in point was the famous scene in *Richard III* in which Richard, at the very coffin of Henry VI whom he had murdered, is asking Anne to marry him, arguing with an eloquence so shrewd, seductive and impertinent that it cannot be resisted. Analysing the psychology of this scene in 1843, the critic Imre Henszlmann considered it the most daring poetic endeavour of all times, because Richard's wooing manages not only to overcome Anne's moral reservations but carries away the audience as well. Listening to his deceitful words, he remarks:

> It seems almost natural to us that the woman will yield to his requests, and no matter that we know him better than Anne does, we are nevertheless compelled to forget his crimes for a while when he gives her his sword pretending that he relies on the sheer justice of his cause and allowing her to choose between believing him or killing him.[126]

Henszlmann is far from censoring this scene for its demoralizing side effects, but he is sufficiently perplexed by them to express his admiration with overtones of a bad conscience. The same scene is praised in similar terms but more passionately and with even fewer reservations several years later (1847) by Sándor Petőfi, for whom 'nothing greater or more daring had ever been written by Shakespeare, and even to attempt it by anybody else would have been desperate madness, since it could not have been accom-plished but by his boundless and omnipotent creative power.' Petőfi is overawed by the magisterial psychology and craftsman-ship whereby something wellnigh unbelievable is made plaus-ible. His enthusiasm uncurbed by moral considerations, he extols the scene as 'unequalled in greatness'.[127]

What these different views of Henszlmann and Petőfi have in common is that neither of the two commentators felt it a critic's duty to denounce the insidiously demoralizing effect as evil and dangerous. This is all the more remarkable because neither of them would have subscribed to the view maintained by the critic Jenő Péterfy towards the end of the century that our tragic sentiment is *always* governed by purely aesthetic (as opposed to ethical) considerations and *that is why* 'we follow Richard III without any moral misgivings, enchanted by this extraordinary man, and when this monster falls, the tragic value of his fall is due to his extraordinariness', and not to 'ethical considerations' or 'human justice done'.[128] Henszlmann and Petőfi were *not yet* concerned with the threat of demoralization, Péterfy was *no longer* concerned with it, but between them the Shakespeare Committee, the first Hungarian institution devoted to disseminating Shakespeare's work, could not afford to ignore this problem. In an age when the aesthetic norms of Hungarian literary criticism were usually supplemented with ethical criteria, to authorize the plays as highly valued texts of the Hungarian canon required tacit or explicit moral approbation as well.

The task of smoothing away the most bawdy phrases could be left to the translators, but defending the plays against possible charges of basic immorality required apologetic critical strategies. Mid-nineteenth-century Hungarian criticism tried to rescue Shakespeare in two ways: either by proving that the lack of poetic justice does not amount to immorality or by arguing that poetic justice is not lacking at all. Something like the first of these rescue operations is performed by the critic Ferenc Salamon, who seems to have deplored the excessive paraphernalia of poetic justice; he was glad to see that in *Henry VI* angelic self-sacrifice and devilish intrigue are not contrasted, virtue is not rewarded and vice is not punished in a horrifying manner to please the latent sadism of the audience. Writing in 1855 he appreciated that Shakespeare had been no didactic champion of any doctrine, be it socialism or the emancipation of women, and that the playwright had confined himself to animating individuals with natural emotions and passions.[129] This approval of plays that defy the requirements of explicit poetic justice dovetails with Salamon's opinion, expressed when writing about a performance of *The Comedy of Errors* in 1863, that Shakespeare's straightforward representation of the natural can never be immoral unless we see it through the spectacles of a new, corrupt and decadent age in which the place of morality is often usurped by etiquette, an age when the sophisticated indecency and covert immorality of contemporary French drama look *comme il faut* and preferable to Shakespeare's honesty.[130] This argument is not far from the second type of apologetic strategy, the one that manages to find a moral message in the plays. A similar line of defence was fortified by Ágost Greguss in 1864 when the National Theatre celebrated the third centenary of Shakespeare's birth by performing *A Midsummer-Night's Dream*;

> It reveals the profound understanding and delicate moral sense of the poet [. . .] that he is only playing with the unruly fairies, that he never mentions them with reverence or approval, moreover, that he depicts this folk [. . .] as rather naughty and spiritually subhuman, whereas he displays true and warm sympathy for the craftsmen through the praise they receive from Theseus, the mouthpiece of the poet himself.[131]

The two critics praise totally different Shakespeares, but the functions of their diverse apologetic strategies are similar: they justify aesthetic excellence in a manner that precludes the charge of immorality. Moreover, both apologetic strategies are essentially secular, demonstrating that the plays do not clash with explicit aesthetic and moral norms. Unlike the elaborate metaphorical deification of Shakespeare in early nineteenth-century Hungarian criticism, with its hymnic praises of the Bard as 'God's second son' who was sent to Earth to explain the Creation and to prove the omnipotence of the Almighty, neither of the two mid-nineteenth-century apologies argue that Shakespeare's divine, absolute and unfathomable perfection is by definition incomparable and beyond criticism. The literary criticism of the period is full of warnings against the idolatry of authors, and Shakespeare is no exception. For the most vigorous critic of the period, Pál Gyulai, no human greatness could ever be absolute. Writing about a performance of *The Winter's Tale* in 1865 he remarked scornfully that 'there are ridiculous members of the Shakespeare cult who find something profound even in his simplest lines and who idolize even his shortcomings'. This is no less grotesque, the critic adds, than the snobbish and condescending behaviour of those who sneer at Shakespeare's less famous plays without trying to understand them.[132] Although the centenary performance of *A Midsummer-Night's Dream* in 1864 was supplemented by a dumb show of Shakespeare's apotheosis, the critics of the period abstained from quasi-religious glorification and resorted to entirely secular methods of analysis, comparison and differentiation even when they sought to defend the Bard.

It is not until the end of the century that we encounter again such a priori vindications one might call literary theodicy. 'I would sooner blame my own eyes than find flaws in any play by Shakespeare', observed a Hungarian critic in defending *King John* against the verdict of his German colleagues in 1892; 'all his plays are revelations', and any imperfections one might discover in them are due either to his unavoidable concessions to an uncouth age or to the inevitable weaknesses of acting.[133] The transcendent implications of this apology would be spelled out more clearly at the turn of the century. When the second Hungarian Shakespeare Committee, founded in 1907, successfully appealed to the government for financial support, the morals of the plays were no longer considered dubious. In 1910 *Magyar Shakespeare-Tár*, the official periodical of the Committee, published 'Shakespeare és a Biblia' ('Shakespeare and the Bible'), a pious study by Arthur Yolland, a naturalized Hungarian citizen and professor of English at the University of Budapest. Demonstrating that many phrases and ideas of the plays originate in the Bible, Yolland argued that in the alarming moral decay of the new age Shakespeare's message is the safest bulwark of true morality. Unlike the subversive and corrupting hedonism of modern art, the paper concluded, Shakespeare's plays reveal the workings and triumph of Providence.[134] In 1917 the novelist Ferenc Móra provided an enthusiastic prologue, entitled characteristically 'The Miracle', to a performance of *Hamlet*, and revived the romantic analogy between Shakespeare's creative methods and God's very act of creating the world. Moreover, the prologue developed the simile into an allegorical system of correspondences in which instances of dramatic amorality were easily explained away as manifestations of a divine wisdom far beyond our capacity to understand. As God breathed life into any lump of clay, Shakespeare accepted and mysteriously resurrected any old story. Here Shakespeare's sun would 'shine on the good and the wicked alike', and from the crater of his soul he would distribute all the vices and virtues among his creations, 'with God's abundance and a child's piety'.[135] The morals of *this* Shakespeare could not be challenged any more. The work of domestication completed, a new sacralization began, evoking devout and deferential attitudes soon to be followed by fiercely iconoclastic reactions.

4

The European Context: Typological Problems of Dissemination

TOWARDS A SOCIOLOGICAL TYPOLOGY OF LITERARY CULTS

The Romantic appropriations of Shakespeare in England and in Hungary are different in many ways, and both differ from their counterparts in other European countries, but all of them belong to the same broad paradigm: they are instances of quasi-religious cult-formation around a lay figure, in the realm of literature, at a relatively late stage of civilization. It is within this paradigm that their resemblances and differences fall into a typological pattern analogous with that of religious cults. To understand the quasi-religious, therefore, one should locate the religious: the system of basic concepts in the sociology of religion indirectly reveals the ultimate failure of the analogy and helps to outline the unique types of *literary* cult-formation.

Ever since Max Weber introduced and his disciple Ernst Troeltsch elaborated the opposition between the concepts of church and sect, scholars have been trying to refine the criteria of both. *Sects* have been differentiated from churches by their withdrawal from the world and their defiance against the institutions and values of the society that surrounds them. Their attitudes are isolationist, their stance is exclusive, new members can join them voluntarily but only after an illuminating conversion experience, a sudden reorientation interpreted as a second birth that requires a new, strictly ethical, often ascetic way of life. As opposed to them, *churches* acquire their members and relate to society in a totally different way: one can be born a member of a church, churches provide formalized means of divine grace, churches have hierarchies and dogmas of their own, they can include the entire population or seek to convert everybody, and they are liable to make a compromise with the institutions and values of the society. Distinct from both of these formations, religious *cults* share some characteristics with each. They resemble sects in keeping a distance from the mainstream religion of contemporary society, but unlike sects, they are not schismatic. Sects usually abandon the religion that gave birth to them because they consider themselves the only true adherents to the old faith in its intact purity; cults, on the other hand, have no parent religion in their environment – they are either diasporic representatives of an alien religion or they are home-bred innovations with no continuous genealogical ancestry. However, we can separate two main subtypes of religious cults according to their respective prehistories: it may have been derived from an earlier transplantation of some foreign tradition or from an entirely endogenous development. Thus cults invariably represent something new and unusual, though their novelty may be of different origin, and eventually they may be institutionalized as one of the established churches or *the* church, giving birth to sects that turn against them.[1]

If we accept the additional concept of a *religious movement* applying to an organized group when it seeks to be institutionalized and wishes 'to cause or prevent change in a system of beliefs, values, symbols, and practices concerned with providing supernaturally based general compensators',[2] then we can discern a further difference between sect and cult, one that may help to locate literary cults within the broader paradigm comprising the quasi-religious as well. Whereas sects are by definition religious movements because they always split off from religious traditions to restore former religious ideals, cults do not necessarily grow into fully-fledged religious movements, they may lack an elaborate theology of their own and need not establish religious institutions either. Sociologists of religion recently discerned two types of cults that had not evolved into religious movements: *audience cults* and *client cults*. Audience cults are the least organized among all cults; from time to time members gather to listen to a lecture of some (usually occult) topic, and at such occasions they sell printed matter and souvenirs, but most of the time they disseminate (via posted brochures and mass-communication) their pseudo-scientific tenets (from astrology to flying saucers), usually achieving no deep and life-long commitment. The disseminators and participants of the client cults have a short-term relation, like that of healer and patient, counsellor and client; the disseminators tend to be more organized than their clients, and the latter often keep their denominational affiliations as well. Whereas the cults that evolve into religious movements promise general compensation for the goods not or scarcely available on earth (a doctrinal characteristic of major religions), audience cults do not promise significant later rewards and give little more than the pleasant thrill of social entertainment, and client cults (like psychoanalysis) offer more valuable but narrowly specific goods, like the healing of neurosis, not comparable to eternal life or the meaningful illumination of earthly existence.[3] This broad, if somewhat schematic, system of religious and quasi-religious formations helps us to discern those features of the Shakespeare cult that cannot be reconciled with any of the types mentioned, and enables us to define the essential criteria of the type so far missing from the system: the artistic, more specifically the literary cult.

Viewed within the broad system that comprises both the religious and the quasi-religious, the first remarkable thing to notice is that the Shakespeare cult unites some characteristics of churches, sects and cults. Just as churches, and unlike sects and cults, its relation to its cultural environment (whether in England or in Hungary) has never been hostile or antagonistic. By mutual adjustment and appropriation it managed to permeate most of the major institutions: the dissemination of *respectful* knowledge about Shakespeare was not confined to theatres, books and the press, but was facilitated by schools (in Hungary first at the level of higher education in the late eighteenth century, then slowly coming down to lower levels as well). By the early nineteenth century it became one of the hallmarks of an educated gentleman to know the high cultural status of Shakespeare and the quasi-religious discourse and ritual considered adequate to his greatness. A later church-like feature is that the Shakespeare cult generates and regenerates institutions of its own, Shakespeare clubs, committees and societies, with a quasi-priesthood (separated from the laymen) interpreting Shakespeare apologetically to make his supposed message morally acceptable and to acquire a fully legitimized place among the established institutions of society, more and more in alliance with political and ecclesiastical authorities. It is distinctly church-like to commission a body of experts with the task of morally checking, authorizing, translating and disseminating the basic texts. After a pre-church period of adapting the texts to the prevailing set of aesthetic and moral norms of the day, institutional approbation was secured by theodicy-like apologetic interpretations that tended to blame any potential flaws on external circumstances or the human limitations of recipients and transmitters. Having been justified by all means, the full text and the superhuman prestige of its author can be appropriated for national purposes or by literary movements.

Another church-like feature is that membership is not the privilege of one class but can be obtained by (almost) the whole cross-section of society, just as the missionary zeal of the disseminators which seeks to convert people from (nearly) all walks of life, though by different means. (When in 1923 Zsigmond Móricz wrote about a century of ardent missionary work that tried to convert people to the 'Shakespeare religion', the wording of his thesis revealed that he had the procedures of a church in mind.) Like churches, the Romantic cult of Shakespeare had dogmas of its own, especially about the unfathomable perfection of the plays and the quasi-transcendent omniscience of their author, and critics were expected to assent to them and to explain away anything incompatible with them, preferably with explicit gestures of self-humiliation. Church-like hierarchy is not far to seek either: after an early period with a charismatic founder and a few devoted apostles surrounded by a loose and undivided community of devotees, a process of differentation began resulting in an institutional hierarchy of responsible experts (organizers, translators, scholars, actors, directors). As regards the other-worldly compensation churches promise their members, the Shakespeare cult offers something vaguely similar even to that: its members could hope to receive not only something this-worldly ushered in as one of the most cherished cultural values of mankind but also something that deserves a quasi-religious discourse and ritual, something claimed to be a second divine revelation illuminating the meaning of life. On the whole the Shakespeare cult is too large-scale to be contained within the narrower walls of a sect or a traditional cult: as a social formation it is too comprehensive, its institutions are too well organized and thoroughly legitimized, its membership is too hierarchical, its ideology too universal, its readiness to make a compromise with the state too consistent.

DIFFERENT TYPES OF CULT FORMATION:
ENGLAND AND HUNGARY

Yet it is not exactly the quasi-religious analogue of the religious church, and has some features in common with religious sects and cults as well. In England the genesis of the Shakespeare cult had a period, the middle third of the eighteenth century, when its adherents tried to exempt Shakespeare's plays from aesthetic requirements that works of other authors were still expected to fulfil. In *this* period members of the Shakespeare cult were as defiantly opposing the aesthetic and moral norms of their environment as a schismatic sect would defy the soulless system of norms propagated by the institutionalized mainstream church. Although occasionally we find European examples of the sudden (sect-like) conversion experience that prompts somebody to join the fold of the Shakespeare cult, the usual process (repeated over and over again ever since the late eighteenth century) is entirely different: it is the steady and almost imperceptible influence of the environment in early childhood that prepares us to accept the implied contention that Shakespeare deserves quasi-religious verbal and ritual forms of reverence. It is this early psychological preparation that subsequently makes it possible for somebody to encounter something Shakespearean with the elevating sense of a metaphysical experience, and such later convulsions tend to confirm the half-conscious early commitment made in childhood. The minority consciousness so characteristic of sects has no equivalent in the Shakespeare cult, at least among its mainstream manifestations, although some of its schismatic sects, like the Baconian or the Oxfordian, show a familiar pride of being persecuted for the true faith,[4] and those (like Tolstoy and his sporadic followers in several countries) who oppose the cult as a whole show the defiant attitude of a handful of stubborn atheists ready to face any repercussions for picking a quarrel with a mighty state and its dominant religion.

Compared to the system of religious and quasi-religious cults the Shakespeare cult shows features of both main subtypes: its novelty may come from an endogenous development or from the early transplantation of a tradition from foreign countries. In England it grew out of endogenous innovation, though not wholly without adapting ancient religious traditions (we saw the connection between the Biblical *yobel* and the 1769 Jubilee) or the humanist glorification of great authors; in Hungary it was transplanted from England and Germany, so much so that the verbal and ritual forms of adoration had been learned before the objects of adoration (the actual texts) were available. Diversified in the course of its development, the Hungarian cult of Shakespeare started as a transplanted religious cult, then it was more and more institutionalized and turned into something like an established church, giving birth to fundamentalist sects that fought for what they invariably called the 'real' Shakespeare against the 'distorted' images rejected as unworthy of the Bard. Although the notion of healing is related to the Aristotelian theory of theatrical catharsis in practically all its subsequent interpretations, and occasional metaphors associate the encounter with Shakespeare's works with a miraculous recovery from some crippling malady (like the young Goethe's comparing himself after having read a Shakespeare play for the first time to a blind man whose eyesight has been suddenly restored by a magic hand[5]), the Shakespeare cult hardly resembles the client cults. It resembles much more an unusually well-organized audience cult in which the audience gathers not for the sake of occult lectures but for performances in the theatre. It is even more cult-like than the average audience cult because experiencing a performance in a community is like taking part in a ritual, a communal re-enactment of a well-known and meaningful sequence of symbolic actions;[6] knowing the plot of the most notable Shakespeare plays enables the spectators to view the unfolding of predictable events with familiar words, a cultural ritual hallowed by a dim awareness of the religious origin of drama and by the quasi-religious discourse about Shakespeare.

Sociologists found that members of audience cults have no strong and lasting faith but the willing suspension of disbelief Coleridge once called poetic faith; we found something similar in quite a few cases, for example in the self-confessed emotional motivation of Washington Irving's affectionately ironical pilgrimage to Stratford. Most Hungarian participants of the cult, however, have been motivated by something much stronger than such self-generated and flickering dedication; their commitment has been strong and lasting, intertwined with patriotic and religious ideals. Inasmuch as the Hungarian can be considered a special kind of client cult, to study its genesis, workings and effects may be useful for the sociologists of religion who admit to having but a dim and scanty knowledge about its role in religious innovation and its recruiting methods.[7]

The typological difference between the English and the Hungarian cults of Shakespeare cannot be reduced to that of endogenous innovation and acclimatized transplantation; their respective geneses follow different models of cult-formation. In the light of recently systematized ethnographic data sociologists discern three models of cult formation that we can use here as a basis for comparison: the old *psychopathology model,* the later added *entrepreneur model* and the *subculture evolution model.* According to the psychopathology model the formation of a cult is a new cultural response to a personal and social crisis: the founder suffers from a mental disease that inspires a novel kind of vision offering a hitherto unknown compensation first for his own malady, then for people tormented by a similar disease and ready to unite in a cult that relieves their pain. In terms of the entrepreneur model the essence of the cult is business-like: like an entrepreneur hoping to make profit, its founder appears on the market with a new kind of compensation packaged and wrapped as attractively as any other new product would be; having found his brand of commodity after long apprentice-years in former cults and much experimentation, in the end his own cult begins to flourish and repays all his invested efforts not only with material goods, but also with glory, power and entertainment. According to both the psychopathology and the entrepreneur models it is individual innovation that triggers off cult formation; the subculture evolution model is unique in its emphasis on interdependence and mutual influence within a group of equals. It assumes a step-by-step cult formation of disadvantaged people without a leader: realizing their common failure to seize rare or non-existing goods they invent compensations for themselves and through the interchange and mutual processing of these a more and more coherent group is defined, a new entity separated from its environment to evolve into a new religious cult that subsequently supplies its material needs and recruits its members by drawing on the resources of the society outside.[8]

In the light of these three models (heuristic ideal types rather than actual entities) the genesis of the English Shakespeare cult differs from the Hungarian in following the entrepreneur model and owing its ritual largely to the inspiration of a founder. Although Garrick's opponents (both then and later) were unjustly exaggerating when they reduced the motivation of his apostolic work to vanity and greed, it would be pointless to deny that the great actor organized the 1769 Jubilee and its theatrical aftermath not only to teach a nation how to worship the glorious Bard but also to enhance his own fame and the income of his Drury Lane theatre. Although there was an obviously mundane calculation at work in the business-like behaviour of lesser figures as well, such as Thomas Sharp, the founder of the relic industry in Stratford, or of Mary Hornby, the notoriously self-aggrandizing warden of the birthplace in the early nineteenth century, not to speak of their numerous descendants in later ages, the scale and inventiveness of Garrick's business mentality was not to be surpassed. His Shakespeare Jubilee was aptly called 'his marketing masterpiece' and there is no doubt that he belonged (with Josiah Wedgwood and William Hogarth) to 'the most astute eighteenth-century entrepreneurs of culture', but for me the relevance of this observation is not that his 'marketing claims' were deceitful (though it is true that Shakespeare did not need him to be rescued from oblivion, and that in the prologue to his adaptation of *The Winter's Tale* he promised 'To lose no *Drop* of that immortal Man' and yet he omitted three acts[9]). Similarly, it is fair to see Garrick's Jubilee, together with the opening of Boydell's Gallery and the Ireland forgeries, as 'the prime examples of the process whereby in the latter part of the eighteenth century Shakespeare became commercialized and was made into a commodity', and to mention those 'who saw through the avaricious self-interest of the entrepreneurs'.[10] Yet, of course, there was more to the Jubilee than the self-advancement of a vain and ambitious actor: it demonstrated that a playwright can be treated as a god and his birthplace a shrine for pilgrims,[11] and that the transcendental epithets applied to him are not embarrassing symptoms of spilt religion, not even casual and, at best, pardonable effusions of naive enthusiasm, but parts of a coherent, well-founded and acceptable discourse dovetailing with a similarly elaborate system of symbolic actions. Garrick as a skilful entrepreneur was epoch-making by dint of codifying a cultural transfer. Whatever his marketing aims and interests were, he organized the most decisive ritual event that confirmed the propriety of a quasi-religious verbal and behavioural pattern[12] applied to a secular writer. It was his Jubilee and its lasting effect (enhanced by his subsequent stage version at Drury Lane) that made the entrepreneur model prevail at the foundation and formation of this literary cult in England.

As opposed to this the transplantation of the cult into Hungarian soil was much less the singular act of a charismatic leader than the result of renewed efforts by a community of devotees for whom the cult of Shakespeare was not an enterprise but a cause. Moreover, it was a *common* cause: though inseparable from indirect self-expression it reflected the common patriotic desire to inspire Hungarian literature and polish the nation. Far from promising significant commercial success, in Hungary the cult of Shakespeare did not pay back before the mid-nineteenth century and often called for a financial sacrifice; even the first complete Hungarian Shakespeare (1864–78) was only made possible by a Maecenas figure. Yet the general compensation characteristic of all the three models is clearly discernible: since political expansion was impossible and the yoke of foreign powers often unshakeable, cultural conquest remained the only substitute whereby to restore national self-esteem. No wonder that the early import of the Shakespeare cult in (what was thought to be) the competition of European nations became a cultural issue of great pride and prestige. Thus, unlike the English cult of Shakespeare that developed according to the entrepreneur model, in Hungary the genesis of the Shakespeare cult tended to follow the subculture evolution model. A similar observation had already been made, though with resort to a somewhat mystical explanation, in a 1909 history of Shakespeare's Hungarian reception referring to the 1830s: 'Initially the Shakespeare cult in Hungary was not due to the apostolic efforts of a literary centre, but was conceived in several souls at the same time due to the immediate impact of Shakespeare's genius.'[13] It is true that here the cult was not initiated by any literary centre, and the observation rightly points towards a kind of community model; but assuming the immediate and simultaneous impact of genius reveals that the scholar was carried away by the myth-making idiom itself and is ready to ignore his own data about the transplantation of the cult in Hungary. Far from a mystical, immediate and simultaneous conception in many souls, it was by adapting foreign (mainly English and German) patterns of behaviour that the Hungarian cult of Shakespeare was conceived, and its most characteristic features are connected with this mediation.

Thus even a first glance at the respective geneses of the English and Hungarian Shakespeare cults highlights differences that preclude any dream about a universally applicable model of cult formation and makes us realize that even the typology worked out by sociologists of religion will not suffice. What the researcher is confronted with in mid- and late-eighteenth-century England can justly be termed the conception of the cult, its manifestations in literary criticism were aptly called the genesis of idolatry,[14] and its development had always been considerably influenced by factors calling for the entrepreneur model; in Hungary it began with an initiation into an adopted ritual, so its genesis at home is already the exodus of its foreign predecessor. This literary cult is already old enough to wander when it enters Hungarian cultural life, and there it begins to work and function according to the subculture evolution model of cult formation, or rather (if I can risk forging a more general term for the purpose) to the *community model* because it is assimilated in the mainstream culture too easily to be called a *sub*culture. Their paradoxically different phases of development at the very beginning leads to a further difference later on: in Hungary the adoption of ritual praise preceded the thorough study of Shakespeare's works, and in the second period the ritual was given a retrospective justification by a myth-making quasi-religious discourse. So in Hungary, unlike in England in the late seventeenth and early eighteenth centuries, there was no initial pre-cultic phase when Shakespeare's works would have been judged impartially by the same norms as applied to any other drama. As soon as Shakespeare's name was mentioned at all in university courses, like in the aesthetic lectures of György Alajos Szerdahely in the late 1770s and 1780s, he was mentioned as exceptionally great, together with a recommendatory account of the reverent and apologetic treatment he was given in England.[15] True, eventually Shakespeare was to emerge in late eighteenth-century England as an incomparable figure who deserves a theodicy-like apologetic criticism, but this had been preceded by a period when his works could be both compared to those of others and criticized no less severely than any other play; in Hungary it wasn't until the 1920s and 1930s that Shakespeare could be exposed to such genuinely egalitarian treatment, and even this late period was too idoloclastic not to be determined, if inversely, by the psychology of the cult. These rebellious idoloclastic gestures were no less totally preoccupied with their object than the most fervently idolatrous manifestations had been, and their respective (opposite) biases showed striking psychological similarities. Until the period of secularization (roughly from the 1950s) a relatively unbiased examination of the plays had been rare and had to be disguised as admiration; even the scholarly discourse of the nineteenth and early twentieth centuries was not exempt from the tacit aim to vindicate the omnipotence of Shakespeare and explain away any possible evidence indicating the contrary. The omission of the pre-cultic phase made a difference no common denominator could eliminate. Curious as it may sound, it is exactly because the Hungarian cult of Shakespeare started its life as a transplantation of the English (and partly the German) that they belong to different types.

THE CULTIC PRE-FORMATION OF LITERARY RECEPTION

Our common beginnings not only recede into the past, they also stay with us, and our individual developments often reveal atavistic repetitions of the *grand recit*. The distinct birthmark of the Hungarian cult was the paradoxical sequence of learning to revere the Bard before getting to know his works, and this birthmark appears on diverse individuals of subsequent generations. Not that there was something uniquely Hungarian about this; on the contrary, in cultures as diverse as Germany and Russia Shakespeare was glorified before being thoroughly read. 'His name was a password before his works came to be known, his "Genius" was a court of appeal (*Berufungsinstanz*) before his art was to be thoroughly studied,' as Günther Erken rightly maintains about the beginnings of the Shakespeare reception in Germany, although he erroneously couples this point with the traditional (and blatantly exaggerated) claim to the uniqueness of that story, with the assertion that 'in no other country of the continent had Shakespeare acquired as paradigmatic a meaning as in Germany'.[16] Yu. D. Levin's research on the beginnings of Shakespeare's reception in Russia also revealed that in the eighteenth century Shakespeare was initially mentioned in a way that reflected an awareness of his greatness without any reliable knowledge of his work.[17] (The very beginning of the Russian reception is symptomatic: when an article in the *Comments on the St Petersburg News* mentioned 'excellent Hamletic and Othellonian comedies' as early as in 1731, 'excellent' was probably all the information received about the plays in question, because the article was taken over from a foreign source and 'it is quite obvious that neither the translator nor the reading public had the slightest idea of what the reference meant'.[18]) As we have seen, the early Hungarian reception, especially between the 1770s and 1830s, followed a similar sequence of initiation: reverence preceded knowledge. Initially even the most prominent writers had but scanty, second-hand and unreliable information about his works, though they were already aware of the high esteem the author was held in all over Europe, especially in England and Germany. Though representative rather than unique, the hermeneutics of the Hungarian case is nevertheless worth recapitulating.

. The ritual of initiation is roughly the same for each generation: they first acquire the social practice of quasi-religious worship and then they get acquainted with the works, acquiring a knowledge that is always mediated to some extent and is usually pre-formed by cultic expectations, whether in a devoutly myth-making or rebelliously demythicizing fashion. Analysing the Hungarian documents of the last two centuries one can draw a conclusion that supports Cassirer's thesis (that relied both on Hegel's philosophy of religion and empirical explorations of myth) that it is not the cult that is added later to an already existing myth, but it is the myth that is invented as a retrospective interpretation of an already existing cult, and mythical interpretation grows out of the efforts to find the meaning of (and reasons for) cultic behaviour.[19] Although it does not follow that the exponents of the ritual explanation of myth are right when they claim that ritual always and by necessity precedes myth and *causes* its birth, in the case of the Hungarian cult of Shakespeare something similar happened and even the causal connection can be established. With a slight (heuristic) exaggeration one could say that when the Hungarian readers learned from articles how devoutly the civilized English treated the objects made of Shakespeare's mulberry tree, or when Szerdahely's pupils learned from their professor that the proper way of evaluating Shakespeare's plays is to make the quality of their best parts representative of the whole and attribute any flaw to the imperfect eye of the recipient, such readers had to conclude that Shakespeare must be a kind of supernatural being to be worshipped and not to be criticized. The conclusion may have remained subconscious, but its latent logic is omnipresent underneath the religious allusions and sacralizing idiom of the new discourse: Shakespeare *must have been endowed* with God-like creative power *because* in England, that is on a pinnacle of European civilization, he had been worshipped like a god. The implied reasoning resembles those ritual theories of myth which maintain that myths are invented to interpret ritual, to justify social customs and to confirm belief, and their lives are prolonged for the sake of these functions.[20]

The initial peculiarity of the Shakespeare cult, the learning process in which an adopted reverential attitude and its imitable forms of praise preceded any close acquaintance with its object entails interesting epistemological consequences. Instead of paving the way for evaluation, understanding is already *pre-formed* by evaluation, that is it cannot help selecting data that are compatible with the adopted judgement and that would confirm the semi-conscious commitment that had already been made to preserve it. No wonder that some Hungarian writers had been aware of the subtle compulsion to conform to reverential attitudes and experienced how difficult, if not impossible, it can be to remove the obligatory spectacles and see with their own eyes. The cultural pre-formation of all understanding and evaluating is never something we can shake off, but in the case of Shakespeare our childhood experiences of reverential patterns of behaviour are retained in our memories with unusual stubbornness, and conditioned reflexes die especially hard.

The truth of this observation is confirmed by the example of Lázár Petrichevich Horváth, whose admiration for Shakespeare originated in the respectful words he had heard about Shakespeare in his childhood, at the beginning of the nineteenth century, when he himself, a mere seven-year-old boy, had yet 'no idea what kind of animal Shakespeare was'.[21] And the same preformation of personal experience is still conspicuous at the end of the century when Pál Rakodczay was dissatisfied with previous interpretations of *Hamlet* and argued for more independent approaches, unwittingly demonstrating the still inevitable failure of such attempts. 'It would be interesting to know how many people see and enjoy *Hamlet* with their own eyes,' he wondered, adding that 'we have got accustomed to the comfortable belief in the traditional so much that most people know the commentaries of *Hamlet* better than the play itself.' The mediation of pompous criticism and bombastic acting precluded any exploration of Hamlet's 'real' character, so Rakodczay declared himself to be determined to forget whatever he had read about this subject and to confine his opinion to what he could see with his own 'pious' and 'simple' eyes, since 'there is no need for spectacles to see the vault of Shakespeare and its golden fires'.[22] Symptomatically, the indignant commentator is unaware of the self-contradiction inherent in his argument: seeking to explore 'the play itself' or the protagonist's 'real character' he attempts a feat no less than getting to know the Kantian *Ding an sich*, but this essential knowledge, however unbiased he tries to be when discarding his much criticized traditional spectacles, must lead to the discovery of a vault sprinkled with golden fires, that is something splendid, exquisite and immensely valuable (especially because in the nineteenth century 'boltozat', the Hungarian word for vault, was also used for the vault of the sky, a well-known symbol of heaven). As could be expected, Rakodczay easily finds and describes Hamlet's 'real' character and concludes that *Hamlet* (implicitly one of the golden fires) is 'a masterpiece of world literature', unwittingly revealing that his attempt to interpret Shakespeare differently was subconsciously pre-formed by the good old essentialist assumptions of a lay epistemology and the widespread consensus about Shakespeare's superhuman greatness.

More or less the same trap of pre-formed judgement waited for those twentieth-century Hungarian commentators who deliberately tried to forget all their previous knowledge about Shakespeare and find his ultimate features. Although the great novelist, Zsigmond Móricz, was subsequently praised by another writer for attempting 'to wipe clean the table of his brain', for trying to remove all his previous knowledge and adopted judgements about Shakespeare, and for being determined to comment on the Shakespeare cycle of the National Theatre (in 1923) as if it were his very first encounter with the plays,[23] the experiment, with all its valuable results, was doomed to failure. After the late eighteenth-century initiation into the ritual of the Shakespeare cult and the subsequent Romantic period of mythicization all such efforts to restore the innocence of a first encounter were but naive and nostalgic dreams, useful as metaphorical exhortations to search for new insights but deceptive when taken literally as programmatic statements. Chateaubriand's attempt, in 1836, to put aside the classical reading glass (*lunette classique*) to get a clearer image of the whole may have led to relative success, but in an ultimate sense it was doomed to failure.[24] And it is worth noting that the enthusiastic Hungarian translator and propagator, in 1838, of Chateaubriand's enthusiastic views on Shakespeare was the same

Lázár Petrichevich Horváth who had been induced in his childhood to revere Shakespeare long before he knew 'what kind of animal' the bearer of that respected name was.

To study the cultic pre-formation of individual judgement highlights the subtle and otherwise often imperceptible means by which previously acquired second-hand knowledge colours our presumably actual experiences. The predetermined processes of learning one can examine in the personal accounts of how people in the nineteenth century *came to know* 'Shakespeare' (in this sense the name itself is a term of appraisal learned from predecessors long before one could check the implied judgement) testify to the validity of Husserl's phenomenological thesis about the omnipresence of 'pre-knowledge'. Research in this field justifies his tenet that we can have no primary or pure experience of an object, no first encounter that would convey to us *only* the actual content of direct and immediate acts of perception. What Husserl considered the inevitable characteristic of all experience, namely that it contains, by necessity, a certain secondary knowledge about the object, that is it always includes knowledge about such features that have not yet become manifest,[25] could be empirically illustrated and to a great extent decisively verified by a great many psychological data taken from this research. There is ample evidence that what we get here is always mediated experience, inseparable from inherited knowledge, whether it is chanelled through straight inheritence or via elicited reaction, or both. What the individual can get to know here is never fully intact from social processing, and what we consider *the* object here is but a reified aspect, the last snapshot about the flux of intermingled traditional and newly conceived beliefs about what the object should be. Usually what we experience is a seamless unity of inherited opinion and personal experience, but sometimes we are aware of a divided loyalty that justifies Wittgenstein's observation about the occasional divergence of how (*as what*) we are expected to see something, and how (*as what*) we actually see it.[26] These moments are but minor hitches in the otherwise smooth and imperceptible pre-formation of literary experience, and such inner conflicts are rarely as dramatic as in the great idoloclasts (like Tolstoy or the Hungarian Lajos Nagy), but all such discrepancies indicate the all-pervading presence of past opinions in our present judgements.

It applies not only to Englishmen that (as Henry Crawford says in *Mansfield Park*) one gets acquainted with Shakespeare without knowing how, yet by studying personal recollections a common tendency seems to emerge. All that Shakespeare's name means for us is acquired by an individual through a learning process that has no clear-cut periods but can be divided into three approximate (and overlapping) phases. It starts with the semi-conscious adoption of evaluative judgements prepared by the community; then follows a search for possible explanations to justify (or, rarely, to refute) the adopted judgements, and this second phase leads to actual sensual experiences of the plays. But at any moment of this process the individual's consciousness is in full contact with the cultural prehistory of the entire society, a prehistory embedded in the last consensus and tenaciously striving to prevail. The study of the Shakespeare cult provides many interesting concrete illustrations to the general phenomenological thesis (though nowadays it may sound little more than a worn-out commonplace) that the actual individual experience is a momentary synthesis of a latent communal prehistory, and our present knowledge is greatly determined by the judgements of others in the past. To examine the cultic context of Shakespeare's reception is like finding the proper magnifying lense that turns whatever the nineteenth-century commentators thought to be the thing itself (the play itself, the character of the protagonist, etc.) into a construct unwittingly made by reifying an interpretation prescribed by inherited and highly reverential expectations. This magnifying lens makes visible all those features that originate in the apologetic processing of everything Shakespearean, showing us an enlarged picture about our indirect ways of understanding, at the inevitable moment of cultic preformation.

Yet *some* kind of preformation would be unavoidable without the cult as well, and not only because Husserl's general phenomenological thesis about perception is applicable here. The traditional ways of teaching literature in higher education has always contained an early phase of making the student aware of the whole scheme, whether chronological, spatial or both, of literary works before (and sometimes instead of) getting acquainted with most of the works themselves. The essence of the survey course of English literature taught at the beginning of the twentieth century at Edinburgh University, an archetypal institution of traditional scholarly training and famous for its high academic standards, was 'the provision of information about the course of

English literature over the centuries', and the student who attended these compulsory lectures 'could write a knowledgeable answer on, say, the development of verse satire in England before Dryden, talking about Marston, Hall and others, whom he had never read and was not expected to have read'.[27] The obvious shortcomings and latent advantages of such an indirect approach to a subject via second-hand knowledge are not easy to ascertain but its heavy reliance on a map of learning charted by previous explorers clearly indicates that the Shakespeare cult is not the only processing of information which makes us adopt the judgement of our predecessors about things we have not yet had the opportunity to see for ourselves. What is more, when in the course of traditional survey lectures the students 'had been *told* about [. . .] attitudes and movements' of literary history, they 'knew about them as objective historical facts',[28] which means that their knowledge was not much less built on *belief* in prestigious hearsay (taken for facts) than the pseudo-knowledge of the Hungarian child at the beginning of the nineteenth century who heard his parents talk *respectfully* about Shakespeare before he could test their opinion by personal experience or indeed (admittedly) could have had any idea about who on earth Shakespeare had been.[29] The essential similarity of the two situations can be illustrated by their common denominator: when the late eighteenth-century Hungarian professor of aesthetics, allegedly not having read any of Shakespeare's plays himself, illustrated Shakespeare's *miraculous* abilities in his lectures by repeating a reference (plagiarized from an unnamed German authority) to an awe-inspiring statement of 'Richard Farmer and others',[30] the students were expected to believe the transmitted opinion (three times removed from its origin) at least until they had an opportunity, if at all, to test it for themselves. A contemporary student who read this reference in the professor's seemingly erudite textbook, written in Latin, was in no position to doubt, let alone challenge, Shakespeare's distinguished status in the literary canon. If we imagine this student confronted with an adaptation of (say) a *Hamlet* based on a German text itself an adaptation of a previous adaptation,[31] or (somewhat later) with a performance of a few popular scenes of a Shakespeare play coupled with some other fragments taken from other plays,[32] it is clear that in most cases the intimidating verdict of authority had to be accepted without a possibility to test it by any first-hand experience of the relevant works.

Shakespeare's canonical status can be safeguarded by cultic procedures and historical narrations in parallel ways, and assent to it is likely to become a criterion of social acceptability. The substitution of personal experience with narrated history was (and to some extent has remained) a customary means of protecting and preserving the canon, especially when learning literary history was not optional but obligatory. To put it bluntly, whatever is required for examinations is thereby a prerequisite for advancement, though this social function alone can never be a sufficient justification for any material taught. In this respect teaching methods in diverse European countries had been surprisingly similar for a long time after the promotion of national literature into a subject to be taught at secondary schools and universities. When Ferenc Toldy published his comprehensive history of Hungarian letters in 1865, he urged the teachers of his country to use it as an aid to instruction in the following way: they should first read out a passage, then explain its technical terms, and if needed read a relevant literary work asking the students to point to those of its features that justify the characterization and judgement read in the passage.[33] Though Toldy advocated this method as a preliminary exercise to pave the way for independent readings and evaluations of literary works later in adult life, he also considered it a prerequisite for successful examinations, and it is clear that it implied and actually required the acceptance and undisputed vindication of pre-formed judgement. The Scottish parallel is even more unambiguous: as a distinguished ex-student of Edinburgh, David Daiches remarked that it was from his experience at that university that he 'had learned to distrust the vast information-giving lecture course and the view that a student could pass all his examinations from lecture notes without having read the literary works he was discussing'. Although he admitted the benefit of acquiring a sense of the past through learning a chronologically prearranged sequence of authors, works and movements, he found that the gain was far outweighed by the fixation of 'wrong habits of mind about literature', and the wrong expectation that in three years the student could learn all about the entire history of English literature, which in fact produced only 'a kind of dictionary-knowledge, bound to be largely second-hand and to involve a great waste of time spent reading about second-rate literature in secondary sources'. To liberate students from the blind obedience to a superimposed canon and as a corrective to the Edinburgh method Daiches instigated an English studies course at the University of Sussex which did not 'prescribe an orthodox reading list of "great books" beyond which the student must not stray', emphasized that the relative greatness of books is a matter of differing opinions, pointed to the especially wide range of interesting minor works in English literature, urged students to explore the richness of literature far beyond the limited realm of a few canonized classics and to discover their own favourite alternative works 'off the beaten track', and proposed to test the genuine understanding of poetry via final examinations that contained a practical criticism paper modelled on I. A. Richards's Cambridge tradition, that is making the students date, characterize and evaluate anonymous texts.[34] But in spite of these or similar efforts, the educational pre-formation of literary opinion can never be entirely eliminated; the new scheme of teaching literature at Sussex, with its ideal of 'an independent student, helped to discover not only new knowledge but himself, becoming increasingly self-reliant (and self-critical) as he becomes more knowledgeable',[35] may have been designed to substitute the traditional share of indirect knowledge in university education with personally discovered primary knowledge, and it may have succeeded to a great extent, but a residue of the old method turned out to be indispensable. To *start* with personal experience would be too late here anyway; students are aware of Shakespeare's high canonical (and cultic) status long before their first year at a university.

THE SHIFTING EMPHASES OF RECEPTIVITY AND RESISTANCE: SOME TYPES OF THE SHAKESPEARE CULT IN EUROPE

The fact that due to their diverging geneses the Hungarian cult of Shakespeare belongs to a different type than the English does not mean that cults formed by other than endogeneous development are all derivative in the same way and fall into the same type of imported cults. The more we analyse the details, the less we would accept the unified scheme a positivist scholar, Arthur Weber, once proposed as equally applicable to the history of the Shakespeare cult in Germany, France and Hungary. According to this scheme these cults took the same three steps: first, the period of 'spontaneous imitation and inspiration' when Shakespeare exerts an influence on writers and inspires original works; second, the period of dissemination when those inspired writers translate the plays, making them available for the wider public; third, when they are taken to the solemn halls of scholarship to be submitted to thorough analyses.[36] In the light of our data about the Hungarian cult, however, this scheme cannot stand up to close scrutiny, because the reading public (not very wide in the late eighteenth century) learned about the admirable Shakespeare's fame and foreign worship at the same time as (or sooner than) the writers themselves came to be inspired by him to write original works. The history of Shakespeare in Hungary was much more aptly distinguished (by an outstanding literary historian of the same period, Frigyes Riedl) from both his German and his French reception. The French intellectual climate fostered other kinds of literary tradition: the classical spirit, 'with its preference for logical order, for rationalism, for a moderate and carefully disciplined imagination, made it difficult for the new English drama to get recognition', a similar obstacle was the great French school of drama both in theory and practice, and Voltaire himself, some of whose plays were influenced by Shakespeare, coupled his adoration with more and more hostility. In Germany, as Riedl points out, Shakespeare's reception was initially retarded by some factors, namely by a preoccupation with metaphysics, by pietism and by the influence of French culture, yet the enthusiastic reports of Lessing, Herder and Goethe paved his way and eventually made him a German 'spiritual colony' and 'textbook item'.[37] (Riedl's version and its account of initial German resistance is all the more important because most references to the history of Shakespeare in Germany emphasize the incomparably early beginnings of the highly reverential appropriation of *unser Shakespeare*, and to some extent even the 1978 edition of the representative *Shakespeare-Handbuch* prolongs this view, asserting that 'from the very beginning the German reception of Shakespeare tended towards idolatry'.[38])

One should resist a simplified contrast of French resistance versus German acceptance for other reasons as well. In France the adherence to the neoclassical ideals of the home tradition was not necessarily incompatible with a distinctly cultic worship of Shakespeare; Jean-François Ducis' thoroughly Frenchified adaptation of *Hamlet* for the stage, first performed in 1769 and persisting till the first decades of the nineteenth century, 'was influenced more by Corneille, Racine, and Voltaire than by Shakespeare', yet in his study Ducis adorned the bust of Shakespeare with a wreath each year on the poet's birthday, an occasion he called the *fête de Sainte-Guillaume*.[39] On the other hand, recent research, especially that of Werner Habicht, convincingly demonstrates that the splendid account of the Bard's German *nostrification* and its decisive role in the awakening of a national identity was itself a nineteenth-century cultural myth woven at the cost of suppressing evidence of former controversies and ignoring or obliterating all traces of ambivalence towards 'unser Shakespeare'. In order to consider the early discovery and appropriation of Shakespeare by Lessing, Herder and the *Sturm und Drang* as some kind of 'spiritual prefiguration of the Franco-Prussian wars', and eventually a triumphant liberation from the yoke of French classicism, this self-serving national myth had to ignore not only that 'it was via France that many eighteenth-century Germans first came to know about the Bard – even before Lessing', but also the dichotomy of paying lip-service to Shakespeare's quintessentially Germanic spirit and thoroughly adapting his plays 'to suit the sensibilities and intellectual horizons of German middle-class audiences'.[40] (One could also point to mid-eighteenth-century German examples of half-hearted apology: some critics found an excuse for Shakespeare's deviation from French norms yet they lacked the confidence to *justify* Shakespeare or to discard those norms altogether.[41]) A similar ambivalence haunted the theatrical career of the Schlegel-Tieck translation: much as the romantics 'insisted on performances faithful to the original texts', their own translations were challenged by rival nineteenth-century translations, by the works of those who 'envisaged performances compatible with current stage conditions and audience expectations, and for this reason rejected the subtleties, stylistic irregularities and obscurities that had resulted from Schlegel's too close rendering of the English original, and offered more polished versions instead'. Moreover, the Schlegel-Tieck translations were hardly ever performed without first having been shaped 'into more or less heavily adapted stage versions' by theatre practicians.[42]

As regards the opposition to the German cult of Shakespeare in the Romantic age, the evidence of which came to be suppressed by the national myth, let it suffice to mention Christian Dietrich Grabbe's pamphlet (*Über die Shakspearo-Manie*, 1827). Himself a playwright eager to emulate and surpass Shakespeare, in this pamphlet Grabbe sought to free German drama from an influence he felt overpowering. He asked three subversive questions: where did the fashionable admiration of Shakespeare ('zur fashion gewordene Bewunderung Shakspeares') come from; does Shakespeare deserve it; and where does it lead the German theatre? The answers were meant to disclose the shady side the maniacs ('Shakspearo-Manisten') and deifiers ('Shakespeare-Vergötterer') would have preferred to ignore: the artistic flaws in the plays, the incoherence of the Romantic criticism so enthusiastic about Shakespeare's art, the politically undesirable ideals inherent in the extolling of lethargic heroes like Hamlet.[43] We find later examples of sporadic and sometimes fierce resistance in both cultures, occasionally applying the same labels of disparagement like 'mania' or 'superstition' to the cult of Shakespeare; in this instance let it suffice to mention Gustav Rümelin's *Shakespearestudien* (1866), Roderich Benedix's book (*Die Shakespearemanie. Zur Abwehr*, 1872) urging us to demythicize Shakespeare and Georges Pellissier's *Shakespeare et la Superstition Shakespearienne* (1914). Though Rümelin was subsequently accused of dilettantism and his critique of Shakespeare was soon answered by reformulation in apologetic terms (Shakespeare's weaknesses had been unavoidable concessions to his primitive audience), his disenchanting treatment (epitomized in its former title, *Shakespearestudien eines Realisten*, changed after its first serialized publication in 1964–5) was typical of those advocating a down-to-earth approach instead of the soaring praise inspired by the Romantic tradition.

It is worth noting that unlike in France and even in Germany, there was no patriotic resistance to Shakespeare in Hungary; here no writer thought that Shakespeare's acceptance would jeopardize the genuine identity of national culture.[44] On the contrary, the naturalization of this author (preferably to be done before any other nation) had always been a matter of patriotic pride, something to boast of, an indisputable indication of a nation's legitimate claim to full membership in the European community of nations. At the tercentenary of the poet's death the chairman of the Shakespeare Committee, Albert Berzeviczy discovered a spiritual affiliation, mutual attraction, indeed a family tie between the playwright's poetry and the Hungarian 'national soul', a striking similarity between his history plays and the medieval history, legislation and constitutional development of Hungary, factors 'rooted in the nature of the Hungarian race'. With so well-disposed a national character it is no wonder, he concluded with great satisfaction, that we find but a few nations that naturalized Shakespeare sooner than the Hungarians did, or few that produced more valuable Shakespeare scholarship, and 'we are well ahead in this competition, with so many behind us'.[45] If one surveys such outbursts of national pride over the Hungarian appropriation of the Bard, with all their differences in argument and rhetoric they have one distinct feature in common: what they praise as the chief cultural virtue is invariably the quick readiness to accept, and what they imply as the corresponding vice is a stubborn will to resist. This preference for cultural adaptability rather than defensive self-assertion pervades other proud and much-repeated claims of Hungarian literature as well; for centuries poets extolled the unsurpassable capability of the Hungarian language to reproduce antique or alien verse forms in translation, taking for granted that such import is always valuable. Late eighteenth-century Hungarian writers programmatically declared their eagerness to assimilate the values of foreign literatures, an idea often supported with the claim that to translate is no less original a contribution to culture than to write works of their own. This prevailing assumption is all the more important because in the mid-nineteenth century several literary works thematized the dilemma between European-style cultural modernization and old ethnic values, usually ending on a balanced note of harmonious reconciliation. (Far from the recent national inferiority complex so justly castigated nowadays by some leading Hungarian writers.[46]) 'The Hungarian spirit [...] had been quick to adopt new ideas and trends, great innovations and inventions throughout the early centuries,' as Károly Vadnay remarked with characteristic pride at the turn of the century, enumerating examples of cultural import, including some that took place long before the appropriation of Shakespeare.[47] The typological place of the Hungarian cult of Shakespeare is inseparable from the all-pervading ethos of this cultural ideology.

The typological differences separating the Hungarian cult of Shakespeare from its German and French counterparts are essential and help us understand why other East European countries differ in their attitudes to Shakespeare. Although to a considerable extent it was the desire to imitate and, more importantly, to emulate the German model (considered second only to the English) that instigated the respectful appropriation of Shakespeare in Hungary, there was no initial reaction in that country whatsoever. As regards the divergence from the French road to Shakespeare, the parting of the ways is even more abrupt and decisive: though a residue of Voltaire's ambivalent praise and latent hostility is embedded in Bessenyei's early appeal to his compatriots to read Shakespeare, there is hardly any sign of traditional French-like reluctance later on, at least until the (sporadic) idoloclastic reaction after the First World War. (The mid-nineteenth-century dilemma, voiced by several critics, between German or French cultural orientation was decided mostly in favour of the German, and after 1867 this was further confirmed by its more easily accessible language in the Austro-Hungarian Monarchy, so much so that towards the end of the century French culture was regarded as a desirable antidote to the overwhelming German influence. At its foundation in 1895 Eötvös College, the new stronghold of higher educaton, was modelled on the École Normale Supérieure with the professed aim to counterbalance the threat of German cultural domination.) The differences between Central and East European countries are partly due to their different proportions of English, German and French cultural influences and partly to other local factors, but they invariably refute the opinion, held by some scholars for a long time, that all these smaller countries followed roughly the same pattern in their appropriation of Shakespeare. We can accept that for the peoples between the Baltic and the Black Seas at the turn of the eighteenth and nineteenth centuries Shakespeare represented an inspiring symbol of national self-awakening, a spiritual ally in their fight for political independence and distinct cultural identity; we can also accept that they all felt and resented their backwardness, castigated themselves for lagging behind the leading West European nations and wanted to catch up with them by reforming their language and by translating foreign, mainly Western literature with a special emphasis on Shakespeare. But it is not equally true and requires widely differing qualifications to say that 'these literatures are bereft of their national characters by their commitment to foreign ideals, till the mid-nineteenth century when the inspiration of folk poetry helps them to discover themselves and create modern literatures.'[48] Their temporary readiness to abandon their national character was so different in intensity that we cannot speak about a uniform disposition to accept foreign ideals; moreover, as the essential attitude motivating cultic behaviour is an *unconditional* devotion, the more reluctant and qualified a nation's devotion, the further it is from the pure, archetypal literary cult, hence they all belong to diverse subtypes. The differing strengths of their traditional commitment to an inherited cultural stock and to already acclimatized foreign transplants differently moderated their enthusiasm for Shakespeare, and the confrontation helped them realize their unique cultural features and reassure the national identity to which Shakespeare had to be adjusted. Whereas in Hungary the voice of *qualified* admiration hardly survived Bessenyei's clearly Voltairean adjectives ('effrayant', 'sublime', 'terrible', 'majestueuse') and hostile opinions had been practically muted until the 1920s, some of her more reluctant neighbours tended to reiterate their diverse priorities before allowing them be reconciled with Shakespeare. True, Hungary is 'similar to the other Central East European countries in considering Shakespeare almost a national classic',[49] but in those other countries it was not invariably nor necessarily the cult that secured for him a distinguished place in the national canon, so the Hungarian cult of Shakespeare cannot be simply labelled 'East Central European' because that would blur and obliterate too many important differences (just as 'Western' cannot be a meaningful common denominator for Shakespeare cults as diverse as, say, the English and the French) for the sake of foregrounding, rather vaguely, their geographical origin. But it would be no less erroneous to agree with the scholar who saw in the Hungarian cult of Shakespeare the ultimate evidence of Hungary's historical role as 'the final bastion defending Western Christianity and the common European cultural heritage', and explicitly argued that 'there had never been a cult of Shakespeare East of the Carpathian mountains, so it would be futile to search for one.'[50] Of course if you abstain from research as futile, it is unlikely that you would find anything that would refute the assumption.

To illustrate how long an initial reluctance can last (and in a sense how productive it can be) the Polish story is a good example. English comedians played some of Shakespeare's dramas in Poland as early as the early seventeenth century, and although these performances exerted an influence on the beginnings of Polish secular drama, the century following the invasion (in 1655) of the Swedish King Charles X was not favourable for its development, and when the great epoch commenced with the accession to the throne of Stanisław August Poniatowski in 1764, it was dominated by *French* taste. The romantic inclinations of the awakening national drama were attracted to the Shakespearean stage, but when the writers grouping around the first public theatre in Warsaw (Franciszek Bohomolec, Franciszek Zabłocki, Prince Adam Czartoryski) made this explicit and Czartoryski published a laudatory article about Shakespeare in *Monitor*, they soon came to realize how difficult it was to defend Shakespeare against the wrath of their neoclassicist opposition. The forerunners of Polish national drama were inspired by an author who was labelled a mere barbarian by Voltaire's Polish adherents. It is the strength of this neoclassicist influence that explains why, when the father of the Polish theatre, Wojciech Bogusławski, translated *Hamlet* and it was performed in Lvov in 1797, it was not only based on the German text of Friedrich Ludwig Schröder but Bogusławski adapted it to the requirements of French taste, removing everything violent and making the audience feel comfortable with a happy ending. In his preface Bogusławski attempted to justify this interference by calling it necessary in an enlightened age, otherwise the five-hour-long original would destroy all the conventions of drama and kill the interest of the audience, its low characters and repulsive scenes would debase the magnificence of tragedy, and its putting to death guilty and innocent alike would have no moral whatsoever. He admitted that this work of Shakespeare's genius had beauties of its own but he made his objections too explicit not to imply that only such a thoroughly adapted Shakespeare should be accepted as worthy of the Polish stage.

In spite of this divided loyalty this period is not without cultic phenomena. However, not all apologetic arguments are cultic in spirit. There is no trace of theodicy-like defence in the article written in the *Monitor* (1766, No. 65) by Bishop Ignacy Krasicki (under the pseudonym Teatralski): against those accusing Shakespeare of having violated the rule of the three unities he resorted to the sober analytical counter-arguments of Samuel Johnson's 1765 *Preface*. The same applies to the memoirs of Stanisław August Poniatowski, written in French, and defending the rich historical and local colours of Shakespeare's irregular art against the solemn and pompous monotony of French tragedy. It is much nearer to an essentially cultic apology that for Princess Izabella Czartoryska whatever seemed vulgar, uncouth or impossible in those otherwise admirable plays must have been due not to the author but his age. The argument dovetailed with her cultic devotion: after 1784 she created an English garden in which there were separate shrines to commemorate Polish and foreign writers; in the latter there was a miniature portrait of Shakespeare together with cherished relics, not only a splinter from the mulberry tree but also an entire chair of the Bard she had bought at the Stratford birthplace in 1790 for 20 guineas together with a certificate proving its genuineness. It is difficult to resist the temptation to dismiss this extravagance with the usual sarcastic remarks of later commentators (for instance, she became 'enamoured [. . .] of the chair on which the Matchless Bard had pressed his sacred posterior'[51]), but we should resist it because even the most extreme manifestations of her devotion fall into a consistent pattern revealing the transfers and substitutions by which a Catholic religiosity regulates the quasireligious worship of a secular writer. The princess also treasured a piece of stone from the Verona grave of Romeo and Juliet, and when count Jan Tarnowski returned from his Italian journey in 1806 she received from him two invaluable presents: a painting about the tomb of the immortal lovers and (probably the most precious of relics) a little bone from their bodies! It is clearly the cult of saints and their relics that corresponded to her apologetic arguments that blamed Shakespeare's age for anything below perfection in the plays.

Favourable as the nineteenth-century Polish literary scene had been to Shakespeare, it was no less the site of resistance than that of acceptance. At the end of the 1820s the Romantic wave had risen together with Shakespeare but its opposition was quick to reinforce the river-bed of the mainstream home culture to prevent its overflow. Characteristically, when in 1828 the great Romantic poet Adam Mickiewicz exhorted his fellow-poets to create the hitherto missing modern historical drama in Polish literature by adapting Shakespeare, he implied the need for adjusting the work of the British poet to Polish national requirements. The rising Polish national drama (Mickiewicz, Aleksander Fredro, Julius Słowacki) and the late nineteenth-century Polish novel (first and foremost Henryk Sienkiewicz) were inspired by *their* Shakespeare. Yet neoclassicist hostility survived in the critical writings of Kazimierz Stadnicki, who flatly refused to ackowledge Shakespeare's divergent merits. Even more significant was the resistance of those who detected materialist priorities in Shakespeare's works and condemned them for their lack of Catholic values. This Catholic wing of the critical opposition enlisted Jozef Szujiski (though his drama *Jerzy Lubormirski* owed a lot to *Hamlet*) and the poet Zygmunt Krasiński, both of whom deplored Romanticism as unethical individualism and moral relativism. Krasiński castigated Shakespeare for his apparent lack of faith in human existence, for his scattered and disparate fragmentariness instead of the coherence of a higher unity, for a magisterial account of disharmony instead of striving for universal harmony, and for his lack of a spiritual dimension that could have been achieved only by the Christian hope of redemption. (Far from precluding real tragedy, in the eyes of Krasiński only the hope of redemption could actually *warrant* a profound sense of the tragic.) Ultimately neither the neoclassicist nor the Catholic objections could prevent Shakespeare's acclimatization in Poland, but due to the Polish balance of resistance and receptivity an unusually thorough negotiation of conflicting values was needed, which led to a tradition of interesting reinterpretations including such later achievements as those of Stanisław Wyspianski or Jan Kott, and such large-scale Shakespeare festivals as that of 1946–7.[52] The Polish reception of Shakespeare has always been coupled with vigorous reassertions of Polish cultural priorities.

As in Poland, in Russia Shakespeare had to face the initial resistance of the disciples of French neoclassicism, though that was not the only obstacle to be overcome. After the early performances of German troupes the first significant event was the *Hamlet*-adaptation, written in 1748 and performed in 1750, of Aleksandr Sumarokov (1718–77). The author of neoclassicist tragedies and comedies and the director of the first permanent theatre in the country, Sumarokov probably used the French translation of La Place, a radically transformed version[53] he tried to make acceptable by substantial further alterations: he substituted the Ghost with a dream, supplied the main characters with confidants (Hamlet can confide in Armance, Ophelia in Flémina, and she also has a nurse called Ratuda) and made substantial changes in the plot: Polonius and Claudius are planning to kill Gertrude and Hamlet, then Polonius would like Claudius to marry Ophelia, but Hamlet manages to escape from his assassins and finally he appears triumphantly in front of the cheering people. The play obediently keeps the rule of the three unities, instructively foregrounds the conflict of emotion and duty and educates the audience with a lavish collection of wise sayings; all in all its author was proud of the fact that his play barely resembled Shakespeare's original. (Nowadays this would be a dangerous statement because in some circles of translation studies neither translations nor adaptations are allowed to be judged by such antediluvian terms as 'faithful'; nevertheless we should not ignore or deny that some translators or adaptors of the past consciously tried *not* to be faithful.) We must bear these alterations in mind when we recollect that Sumarokov's play was published in six editions in the 1780s: the success was that of a neoclassicist adaptation almost beyond recognizability. And although Sumarokov's pioneering work was followed by other translations and adaptations, including *The Merry Wives of Windsor* adapted in 1786 by Tsarina Catherine the Great herself, 'they bore very little resemblance to the English originals'; moreover, in the first decade of the next century Russian translations were based on the neoclassicist French adaptations by Jean-François Ducis, and even in the 1820s, when Shakespeare was known only to the intellectual elite in Russia, his plays were staged 'in versions made from Ducis' adaptations translated at the beginning of the century'.[54] On the other hand, the first translators working from the originals (from the late 1820s onwards) tried to render the texts literally but this very effort led to heavy-handed versions tiresome to read and unsuitable for staging. It is significant that in spite of all the adjustment Shakespeare 'did not become popular in these early Russian versions, his plays were slighted in preference to French neoclassicist plays for a long time, and his stories were alien to a public that would have preferred to see its own national themes on the stage'.[55] In early nineteenth-century Russian criticism French neoclassicist strictures of Shakespeare were soon confronted with German romantic praise, yet even this confrontation was based more on borrowed arguments than on profound and personal knowledge of the original plays.

Pushkin is the great and epoch-making exception. Between 1820 and 1824 he was liberated from Byron's influence by Shakespeare; in 1824 he declared that he held Shakespeare (and Goethe) in higher esteem than the Bible. Encouraged by Shakespeare's example his *Boris Godunov* (1825) discarded the rule of the three unities and the eighteenth-century requirements of decorum for the sake of creating a rich and vivid world. Pushkin admittedly wrote his play 'according to the system of our Father Shakespeare',

and his own enormous impact on Russian literature helped the
naturalization of that father, yet one cannot but agree with the
comment that in the tradition of Russian historical drama instigated by *Boris Godunov* 'Shakespeare's impact manifested itself
not in a direct way, but at a second hand.'[56] The degree to which
it was a characteristically russified poet who gained admittance
is indicated by the appearance of distinctly Russian alter egos of
Shakespearean characters: Nikolai Leskov's *Provincial Lady Macbeth*
(1865), Turgenev's *Hamlet of Shchigri District* (1849) and *The King
Lear of the Steppes* (1870). In his essay 'Hamlet and Don Quijote:
the two eternal human types' (1860) it was the Russian character
Turgenev meant to chastise in a wavering, egotistical and paralysed Hamlet as opposed to a resolute Don Quixote. It was after
such a strongly self-centred way of national appropriation that
Tolstoy's passionately conservative and Christian attack on Shakespeare was launched at the turn of the century ('Shakespeare
and the drama', 1906), though privately he had formulated its
mutinous views some fifty years earlier. (It is a telling observation that in mid-nineteenth-century Russia sceptical or subversive comments on Shakespeare were mostly confined to private
diaries and letters, and it was rare that someone, like Chernysevsky
in 1855, publicly protested against the blind veneration of the
playwright.[57]) Translated into English (1907) Tolstoy's pamphlet
was much debated in Europe, and its hostile interpretation of
the Shakespeare cult as 'mania', 'blind worship', 'spiritual epidemic' and 'mass-psychosis' incited mutinous ideas in Hungary
as well,[58] but it was *Russian* culture which Tolstoy meant to defend
against what he feared to be the dangerous culmination of an
immoral and irreligious tradition of European drama. Although
one cannot accept the unfounded and misleading statement that
'Shakespeare has never exerted a significant impact on Russian
literature,'[59] the impact has always been formed as much by resistance as by acceptance, and its significance owes more to the
former than to the latter.

These European Shakespeare cults are all derivative when compared to the English, yet they can be divided into two main groups
according to whether it was the German or the French taste that
prevailed at their respective beginnings. The German-type attitude to Shakespeare (adopted, for example, in Hungary) was
essentially reverential and after a brief hesitation gave up the
idea of open, whole-scale and programmatic resistance, allowed

only sporadic individual dissent, and yet resorted to a thorough, if tacit, adaptation of the plays to suit the needs of the home culture. The French-type attitude implied a lasting and more explicit reluctance to accept cultural self-submission, and even when it was the most penetrable it fostered openly self-asserting ways of adaptation. To distinguish the two zones of interest Hungary is a good case in point because in that country French cultural influence had never been strong and lasting enough to instigate a neoclassicist rejection of Shakespeare, and the affinity to (and love-hate with) German culture made even the sense of cultural rivalry lead only to a desire to emulate (and outdo) the German worship of Shakespeare. Germany was considered the earliest continental nation to be initiated into the cult of Shakespeare and the prime model for cultural appropriation; when the Hungarian press notified its readers that the great Romantic poet, Mihály Vörösmarty was working on his translation of Shakespeare's *Julius Caesar*, the chief recommendation was the remark that in the new text 'our beautiful language often seems to render the unique features of the great Englishman's original more felicitously than the abundant German language does'.[60] Although Vörösmarty had translated Shakespeare's original, the success of his translation was to be evaluated by German parallels.

To realize the typological difference between a German or French cultural influence is not the same as accepting any ready-made value judgement about them without taking into account the whole range of their respective cultural consequences. We have to scrutinize, for example, the once popular Hungarian opinion, expounded by a scholar in 1917, that 'we have to be grateful to fate for having chosen the German literature, not the French, for our guide in the cult of Shakespeare' and thus 'the British giant spirit could win an easy victory over the minds and hearts' and his conquest of Hungarian culture could be 'a veritable march of triumph'. On the other hand, what could any nation learn from a French literature that was 'too small-mindedly envious to understand Shakespeare's real greatness, and could not make her disciple, Russian literature, understand it either'? So, in Russia, Shakespeare 'had to struggle with the indifference, jealousy, and misunderstandings of even those most educated.'[61] This opinion, prompted by the assumption that only unconditional acceptance can be fruitful, is not only grossly unfair, attributing ignoble motives to entire cultures, but it also confuses strongly self-assertive appropriations with a complete lack of understanding, and ignores (and thereby precludes) the possibility of cultural enrichment by elicited reaction. (Besides, the sweeping generalization overlooks those diatribes in mid-nineteenth-century Hungarian criticism which were directed *against* the overwhelming influence of the German theatre and implied a preference for French taste – an alternative also too complex in its far-reaching consequences to allow a facile evaluation.) It is imperative that we take a closer look at the social and cultural impacts of literary cults in general before we attempt to evaluate the role of the Shakespeare cult in any European country.

5

The Postponed Question of Judgement:
Functions and Values Reconsidered

Returning to the bracketed problem of comprehensive evaluation a review of historical functions may help us steer a reasonable course between the crude and unargued extremes of considering any cult either the solemn symbol of humanism or the blinding epidemic of superstition. To start with the reassessment of well-known little facts, it is a commonplace, yet rarely taken seriously enough for any conclusions, that the development of Stratford owes a great deal to its quasi-pilgrim tradition. When David Garrick exhorted the town's officials in 1770 to provide for a decent pavement, keep the town clean and well lit to make this 'Holy-land' more attractive for visitors,[1] he appealed to their loyalty to the Bard but he could just as well have appealed to their economic interest. Though the Rotunda of the Garrick Jubilee was demolished after the event, and the Great Pavilion was likewise removed after the tercentenary festival, the cultic attitude confirmed by such celebrations implied a cultural commitment that could be relied upon when the town needed funds for building theatres, libraries or galleries. Perhaps partly due to the Protestant mentality, prominent visitors to Stratford from Garrick's time to the late nineteenth century had often voiced their wish to see the reverence of Shakespeare turned into something useful, and even amid soaring Romantic praise we find orators pointing out that adoration should also serve some rational ends. (There is nothing surprising, let alone self-contradictory, in this; whether we accept Max Weber's starting point that at the birth of religion even the most archaic forms of magic were meant to serve earthly purposes in a rather rational, if erroneous, way,[2] or we prefer to take heed of Wittgenstein's caveat and beware of too direct equations of ritualistic actions and the rational ends attributed to them by later interpreters of different cultural backgrounds,[3] no ritual ceremony would preclude the possibility of simultaneous or indirect practical benefits.) To feel the intricate closeness of intertwined traditions let it suffice to remind ourselves of one example: on 23 April 1827, at the beginning of a three-day celebration, when the Muses of tragedy and comedy ornamented Shakespeare's bust with a wreath of bayleaves and an occasional poem gave voice to the hope that Stratford would become a training arena for young histrionic talents, the members of the Shakespeare Club marched to New Place to lay down the cornerstone of a small permanent theatre. That theatre was opened at the end of the same year; first it was called the Shakespearean Theatre, later the Royal Shakespearean Theatre and finally the Theatre Royal, and amid all sorts of vicissitudes it survived until 1872. The cornerstone was laid as a quasi-ritual embedded in a cultic event, yet the theatre was meant to serve a distinctly secular cultural purpose, though named in a more and more monarchical fashion, and was situated in a town visited by quasi-pilgrims who would make the greater part of the audience: how can we separate cult and culture, the quasi-religious and the secular, the spiritual and the political? And the tradition of theatre-building in Stratford followed this unified pattern of cult and culture: the next theatre, a surprising 'modern Gothic' building at the hallowed site of Garrick's Rotunda, was built after the nationwide fundraising appeal of the Shakespeare Memorial Association, and opened its gates on 23 April 1879, the first day of a two-week Shakespeare Festival, with a performance of *Much Ado about Nothing* and an ode written for the occasion by John Westland Marston. This theatre could entertain 800 spectators, and was designed to serve diverse cultural ends: it included a library (mainly of dramatic literature) and a fine art gallery (chiefly of Shakespearean paintings), and the building was suitable for concerts and public lectures. The spectacular cultural and economic development of Stratford would have been impossible without the cultic tradition of pilgrimage, relics and jubilee-type anniversaries, and no grumble about the commercial shallowness of tourism should make us forget this.

In Hungary no theatre was built in honour of Shakespeare but cultural development was spurred on by the energies and enthusiasm of his literary cult. In the late eighteenth century when the Hungarian press first disseminated news about how the British paid tribute to their Bard, the ultimate purpose of the articles was to improve the nation by following the British example, to make familiar both the custom of ritual celebrations of writers and the implied idea of meritocracy. The growing prestige of the writer, irrespective of his birth, rank or class, was no less important a benefit of this dissemination than the improvement of the vernacular literary idiom by translations, the acquisition of more and more civilized theatre-going habits, or the importation of such financial aids to publishing as advertisements and subscriptions. For the first half century of Shakespeare's appropriation there was no permanent theatre building for Hungarian acting in the country, and learning about the British ways of reverence (with the implied notion of how great and important a playwright can be) helped the formation of a mentality that eventually made the building of theatres financially rewarding. Surveying the history of the Shakespeare industry two scholars remarked that out of 20 visitors to Stratford who go to see a Shakespeare play there 19 would never bother to see one at home;[4] even such exaggerated assumptions contain a grain of truth in the (potential) implication that a touristic quasi-pilgrimage to a cultic place may lead to the gradual acquisition of cultural habits. Analysing the behaviour of the spectators at the Shakespeare cycle of the Hungarian National Theatre in 1911 the novelist Zoltán Ambrus observed that the mixed audience may have been prompted to come to the theatre by exalted advertisements, but its curiosity, once awakened, could be channelled towards any other noble cultural objects.[5] One of the indirect effects of late eighteenth- and early nineteenth-century initiation into the cult of Shakespeare was that it made the idea of the theatre more attractive; the director of a Hungarian troupe in the late nineteenth century found that to perform Shakespeare was a financially rewarding endeavour not only in the capital but in more backward parts of the country as well.[6] Without the sacralizing idiom of nineteenth-century Shakespeare criticism it would have been much more difficult, if not impossible, for Shakespeare studies ever to establish a periodical of its own or to achieve the status of importance that attracted the financial support of the Ministry of Religion and Education for collecting a Shakespeare library within the University Library in Budapest. The financial support needed for translating and publishing Shakespeare's works (and, indirectly, the works of other foreign classics) would have been much more difficult to secure without the prestige suggested by cultic ritual and praise. When (in 1848) Gábor Egressy, the Hungarian Garrick, proposed that the translation of Shakespeare's works should be officially financed from national sources, he could make his appeal more emphatic by arguing that Shakespeare's *oeuvre* was a 'fairy cupboard' miraculously containing everything needed: 'eternal' literature, 'the only true and unchangeable' laws of aesthetics, a 'sound, pure, and cultivated' taste, splendid histrionic art and prophetic wisdom.[7] The Maecenas of the first complete Hungarian edition, Anasztáz Tomori, was an admirer of the great Romantic poet Vörösmarty who had learned to adore Shakespeare from the sacralizing discourse of his youth, long before he inherited the great fortune that enabled him to promote the cause of Shakespeare's translation. The ethos of making a sacrifice for naturalizing Shakespeare, either in financial terms or by dedicating a part of one's life to the task, became part of the more general commitment to the cause of literature, especially at the turn of the eighteenth and nineteenth centuries when it was couched in terms both patriotic and religious: you had to bring your offerings to the altar of your fatherland. The cult of Shakespeare played an important role in the merging of literary, patriotic and religious values, and this enhanced the possibilities of cultural growth. In Hungary the aura of Shakespeare's name has preserved something of this threefold tradition, its impact makes the new (and often lavish) editions of his works financially possible, and explains, partly at least, why the performances of several of his plays outnumber those of the most illustrious plays of the Hungarian canon.

This is not to say that the impact of the Shakespeare cult has always been wholesome, especially on *criticism*. Coleridge's somewhat enigmatic statement that only a reverential criticism can be congenial to Shakespeare (and thus hope to understand his work) is true in many ways but the danger of a critical self-paralysis caused by unconditional reverence should not be ignored or underestimated. In its own time Coleridge's thesis was wholesome, because immediately after the age of neoclassicist norms only a reverential attitude could secure a sympathetic hearing for an author of irregular plays, and the reverence Coleridge required was meant as a necessary but not sufficient condition of sound criticism. Even the most apologetic assumptions of

Coleridge (like the idea that whatever seems to be incoherent in Shakespeare's plays ought to be scrutinized further because it *must be* part of a perfect and premeditated whole) were meant to encourage study, critical analysis and painstaking exploration, rather than to authorize sheer irrational adoration. True, reverence, and especially that of a cultic kind, not only fostered some genres and activities of criticism and scholarship but also hindered some others. But the positive side is not to be underestimated, especially in those critical genres which are closely related to philology in the classical sense: bibliography, textual criticism and background studies. As the common aim of these disciplines is to restore a faded original, to retrieve and transmit an ever-receding cultural heritage, their activity is meant to be essentially re-cognitive, re-productive, re-constructive,[8] and this aim, whatever its implied theoretical problems may be, strengthens the basically cultic disposition of preserving and thus revering even the most minute details once they are related to a writer.

The characteristic attitude of philological restoration is similar to a cult of the text: the scholar is both a humble worshipper and a high priest who has to protect every word of the writer; hence, as was pointed out, the cult of the Bard has something in common with the cult of the word, making 'bardolatry' and 'wordolatry' converge and strengthen each other.[9] This joining of forces was not detrimental to the methodology of Shakespeare scholarship and on the whole it encouraged the development of philology in general, even if one has to accept the conclusions of an excellent study ('"Shakespeare can do no wrong": bardolatry and scholarship') proving that editors of scholarly editions felt it obliga-tory to counterbalance or explain away any inconsistencies of the plays in their subtly but obsessively apologetic footnotes.[10] Such observations were bound to embarrass the scholarly world and seem to justify the supposition of a sympathetic reviewer that the impact of the same scholar's previous book-length efforts, the four subsequent volumes of Kristian Smidt's *Unconformities* (1982, 1986, 1989, 1993), 'to make criticism acknowledge its cultic bias' was mercilessly muted by 'the critical institution's suppression of self-awareness', due to the institution's vested interest in a dissociation of itself as serious and relevant from the cultic as banal and peripheral.[11] But Smidt's examples of apologetic footnotes also show that the urge to ameliorate did not go as far as totally eliminating the flaws by tampering with the text or keeping silent about them. Even the most piously cultic reverence of Shakespeare could not undermine scholarship altogether, and in the long run its wholesome cultural effects prevailed over its harmful side effects. The great indebtedness of textual criticism to the epoch-making paper of Walter Wilson Greg, *The Rationale of Copy-Text*, is inseparable from Greg's pioneering textual studies of Shakespeare's plays; in fact his analyses of the textual problems of those plays were instrumental in his generalizations about editorial methods. And he could not have devoted so much attention to the textual minutiae of those texts if Shakespeare had not been considered so indisputably important as an author of wellnigh superhuman dimensions; it is no mere coincidence that the impact of Shakespeare studies on textual scholarship can be compared to that of the Bible.

In countries where Shakespeare had to be translated it was not the editing of the originals that could benefit from the emotional energies and textual strategies of the cult, but the scholarly and literary activities of translation. In Hungary, for example, those who advocated shy or prudish omissions had to face the indignation of devoted admirers of the playwright who argued that in the case of such a God-like author only a complete, genuine and unadulterated translation would do. The conventions and auxiliary genres of translations (like the critical revision and written assessment of a translation before it is finalized for publication) took their present-day shape amid the preparations for the first complete Hungarian edition of Shakespeare (published between 1864 and 1878); similarly, from the mid-nineteenth century onwards diverse sorts of positivist research, whether the tracing of biographical connections, genetic explorations of topoi, or minute background studies, owe their development, partly but considerably, to Shakespeare scholarship. True, the result of this kind of research was sometimes banal, and as late as in 1916 Mihály Babits, the translator of *The Tempest*, was probably right in his scathing criticism of the rather shallow yearbook published by the Shakespeare Committee to celebrate the tercentenary of the playwright's death. He found the entire collection of studies empty, verbose and futile, and deplored this institutional 'cult of mediocre philology' as unworthy of the spirit of its subject, especially because the editors ignored the newly relevant aspects of Shakespeare's *oeuvre*, excluded young talent both from the volume and the Committee, and kept silent about the pressing need for some new translations.[12] In spite of the 'sclerosis' of cultic scholarship that was to be observed by several later scholars,[13] no wholesale condemnation of cult-inspired philology can be justified. Although the worship of Shakespeare intensified the positivist accumulation of miscellaneous little facts about him, and it implied a messianic belief in the coming of a scholar for whom everything would fall into a pattern and eventually make sense, the results of that accumulation and belief, for example the data hoarded and revised in the periodical *Magyar Shakespeare-Tár* (*Hungarian Shakespeare Store*) at the beginning of the twentieth century are still worth knowing and Hungarian Shakespeare scholarship can ignore them only at its own peril. József Bayer's monograph *Shakespeare drámái hazánkban* (*Shakespeare's Plays in Our Country*), published in 1909 in two volumes, is rich in data about the history of Shakespeare's reception in Hungary, and although Bayer himself was hardly the scholar who had been expected to come and provide a comprehensive pattern, his reverence for everything Shakespearean stimulated him to write a thoroughly positivist book that survived the heyday of the subsequent *Geistesgeschichte*, then survived the decline of any *grand recit*, and has remained indispensable to this very day.

However, the cultic attitude does more harm than good in those genres of criticism which rely more heavily on independent interpretation and evaluation. The institutional demand for apologetic interpretation has always been difficult to resist, and the temptation to resort to self-serving, circular arguments that serve 'the idolatry of collective self-projection' formed habits of mind just as dangerous as they do today.[14] Ever since the late eighteenth century when György Alajos Szerdahely warned his students that confronted with a play of the great Shakespeare critics were expected to keep silent about its flaws and extend the beauties of some parts to the whole, Hungarian commentators of Shakespeare have often felt an invisible wall blocking the way to free and unbiased judgement. Characteristically, as a professor of aesthetics Szerdahely had no intention to subvert this apologetic convention, although his terse description reveals that he was fully aware of the manipulation in the critical process: the critic was bound to choose such methods and strategies that were likely to yield the required ameliorative judgement. Yet this pre-formation of procedures to secure a result within the expected was not necessarily prejudication, that is premature judgement without a due examination of evidence, neither did it preclude any mention of flaws as unwelcome and embarrassing nuisances; on the contrary, it often led to the critic's increased inventiveness and dexterity in negotiating inconsistencies, in highlighting the pros and cons of a delicate issue, and, well, in finding the saving grace in the teeth of aesthetic or moral heresies discovered in the plays. As the sacralizing idiom of Romantic Shakespeare criticism was to be substituted by the empirically verifiable evidence of poetic greatness, there was a need to legitimize the quasi-transcendental significance of this author by secular and down-to-earth methods; thus even the withdrawal symptoms of the post-romantic critical discourse had a stimulating effect as well. Moreover, the acquired reflex of giving an author or a work the benefit of the doubt before jumping to condemnatory conclusions led to a wholesome habit, even if we rarely treat lesser authors the same way and hardly ever give them such sympathetic hearings before passing judgement on their work. And at this point one could abandon the agnostic's aloof tower and admit that the need to find ameliorating evidence was not wasted on an unworthy author. However, all these mitigations of the curtailments of critical freedom cannot amount here to a full vindication of the cultic influence.

The range of cultural effects cannot be complete without the tacit encouragement that the sheer example of the Shakespeare cult gave to a proliferation of cultic elements in cultural life. As the early nineteenth-century Hungarian articles, like the one published in 1834 in *Honművész* about the 1769 Stratford Jubilee, ended with exhortations to follow the British example ('When shall we, Hungarians, erect a splendid memorial for our Károly Kisfaludy?'[15]), one of the most important lessons European nations learned from the manifestations of the British cult of Shakespeare was the social acceptability and propriety of verbal and ritual celebrations of writers, actors, scholars or any other outstanding promoters of culture. This *ritualization of culture* was not the invention of the British cult of Shakespeare but it certainly gained considerable moral support from it. The proliferation of cultic elements, in turn, exerted a stimulating impact on culture, including scholarly benefits: for example, the relics piously accumulated in literary museums can sometimes be used by an editor as evidence for tackling a textual crux or a chronological problem. (The typewriter preserved with the furniture of a modern Hungarian poet was examined to distinguish genuine autographs from later copies.) But the possibility of a future philological application is not the only cultural potential of the reverence for literary relics. Boswell's kneeling down before the (forged) manuscripts of Shakespeare and his pious confession when kissing them was hardly separable from his desire to preserve every potentially significant morsel of Johnson's life in his great biography; similarly, the patron of the first complete Hungarian edition of Shakespeare's plays, Anasztáz Tomori, is known to have treasured the clothes of the deceased Vörösmarty, the great Romantic poet he had never ceased to adore, and one can safely assume that his fervour to preserve them was not separable from his eagerness to give financial help to the translators. The relics collected and exhibited in the Hungarian museum of histrionic art imply the significance of every little prop related to the theatre, and this significance could not have been implied had there been no cult of Shakespeare and had not his quasi-religious worship overflowed to the adoration of the great actors who personified his creations, be they David Garrick, John Philip Kemble, Gábor Egressy or Árpád Ódry. One could argue that the recent appeal to the conscience of Hungarian society to provide a home for retired actors could not have had the persuasiveness it had without the traditional cult of the theatre which unites the same trinity of literary, patriotic and religious values as the cult of Shakespeare. The statues of poets, writers and actors on the streets and in the squares of European countries owe a lot to the indirect impact of the Shakespeare cult, and their ritual inaugurations are late descendants of literary rites at least as old as Garrick's Jubilee. Celebrations of the diverse anniversaries of writers have become occasions to intermingle cultic and scholarly activities: when members of Hungarian literary or scholarly organizations make a pilgrimage to the birthplace of a poet or writer to celebrate the centenary of his or her birth, the event abounds in ritual forms of reverence, but they are usually coupled with a conference which is flexible enough to tolerate irreverently critical scrutiny as well. Occasionally one feels the tension between those participants whose piety is offended by anything short of unconditional admiration and those who feel that the ritual is stifling the spirit of true scholarship, but more often the divided loyalty of such occasions disappears in a seamless unity compatible with both purposes and dovetailing with other ritualized events of scholarly life. If one looks attentively enough at the public 'defence' of a PhD dissertation in Hungary, when the candidate has to prove his or her competence by answering the written objections of selected opponents and the improvised comments of anybody present, the whole scenario resembles a rite of passage whose essence is to test whether somebody can endure a certain amount of beating from elders before being accepted as a fully-fledged member of the community. (Little wonder that the successful 'defence' is followed by a reception that resembles a little feast.) Such rites fall into a complex pattern of literary pilgrimage, jubilee-like festivals, openings of exhibitions in literary museums, centenary conferences and so on, and if this entire ritual embroidery of our cultural life feels natural today it is due to such precedents as the Shakespeare cult that made people accustomed to the presence of quasi-religious elements in secular contexts.

Among the cultural values fostered by the Shakespeare cult special attention should be paid to the way this audience cult has always helped not only the formation of an audience but that of a community as well, providing what Turnerian anthropology would call *communitas* and *anti-structure*. As the spirit of Garrick's Jubilee had something in common with the medieval *jubilaeum* and with the Old Testament *yobel*, participation in ritual events of the Shakespeare cult has been inseparable from a transitory and hypothetical subversion of the social hierarchy and from a re-enactment of an other-worldly ideal of ultimate unity and equality in a quasi-religious context. Some of the cult's opponents maintained that it was permeating society as an epidemic from the educated upper classes down to the intimidated simpler folks who tried to imitate them, but even these hostile views implied a willy-nilly acknowledgement of social comprehensiveness and of a common denominator provided by the reference to Shakespeare in a world otherwise divided by class, wealth, education, nation or denomination. The quasi-religious (and supra-denominational) sense of *communitas* is not equally dominant in different epochs; the somewhat carnivalesque mingling of classes at the 1769 Jubilee was abandoned for the sake of a more segmented Victorian tercentenary festival in 1864 when the first week was meant to be for the well-to-do (even they were subdivided by a sophisticated hierarchy of prices and availability) and this was followed by three days for the poor, nevertheless with *similar* programmes. The early articles that tried to naturalize the

customs of the British cult of Shakespeare in Hungary under-
lined its comprehensive character; later in the nineteenth century
repeated efforts sought to make the range of participants wider
by disseminating the appropriate forms of (audience or pilgrim)
behaviour among susceptible lower classes. True, later opponents
of the cult were to criticize this teaching process as thinly veiled
acts of forced indoctrination, and indeed to learn the choreogra-
phy of appropriate audience behaviour is to conform to a uniform pattern at the cost of losing the uniqueness of individual
response, but the gain is more valuable than the loss because
those ready to learn the rules of the game can become fully legitimate participants in the ritual of a community that transcends
many social boundaries. When in his attack on the Shakespeare
cult the novelist and social critic Lajos Nagy deplored the middle classes for being impressed by the world of aristocracy presented on the stage, he added that these (or any other lower)
classes simply *cannot* be interested in the intimate life of kings,
just as no lord can be interested in the psychological problems
of his servants. But this remark unwittingly reveals that the champion of social justice ignored a valuable experience embedded in
the phenomena he was so determined to castigate: the imaginary identification of a member of any class with the problems of
those higher or lower in the social hierarchy implies a sense
of the same ultimate *communitas* as that felt by many early and
later pilgrims arriving at Stratford from different countries and
denominations. (Stratford as a denominational no man's land
for quasi-religious experiences is able to complement one's own
otherwise limited share of ritual experience the same way as the
narrow confinement of class barriers can be transcended: we must
remember the testimony of the Hungarian Calvinist who had
longed all her life to go to Stratford and kneel down at Shakespeare's grave as members of other denominations do in their
churches.[16]

The Shakespearean theatre is eminently suitable as a site of
communal experience because (as Hungarian critics of two centuries often remarked) the author's preferences are enigmatic,
sometimes unfathomable, his sympathy is rather evenly distributed among his creations, and none of his monsters are bereft of
human motivations or alienated to the point where the spectators'
imaginary identification would be impossible. The attractive amorality with which immoral characters are often treated may have

required apologetic arguments in a Hungarian criticism tormented by the somewhat Platonic worry about the demoralizing effects of artistic imitations of unethical behaviour, but the sacralizing idiom inherited from the Romantic cult of Shakespeare suggested a grandiose line of defence: the unfathomable quasi-transcendental greatness is beyond the reach of human strictures and cannot be wrong, so whenever the plays seem anything but perfect it is due to some kind of human error in their transmission. This apologetic assumption both authorized and legitimized the common identification of spectators of different origin with the entire world of this glorified author, indicating that it takes a transcendental object to create a bond of brotherhood among its worshippers. To make this bond all-inclusive, or at least comprehensive enough to include people of diverse origin, a more technical prerequisite was also needed, a mutually shared background knowledge, a familiar mythology that could unify. This was provided by the well-known figures and themes of Shakespeare's plays as a common source of reference, just as Friedrich Schlegel urged modern literature to substitute traditional myths with a unifying new mythology of its own.[17] Most of the spectators at a performance of *Romeo and Juliet* know the symbolic value of the protagonists (and the plot) beforehand, and the prologue can only remind them of the well-known ending, so their experience is more like the anticipation of a familiar ritual than a surprising adventure. This prescience of dramatic events can be willingly or halfconsciously suspended to some extent, and there is evidence that even a mid-twentieth-century Hungarian audience of *Romeo and Juliet* was subconsciously hoping in the last act that the lovers would avoid death,[18] but this suspension can never be effective enough to make room for any real surprise when the predictable does happen, and no subconscious hope can undermine the sense of participating in a familiar sequence of symbolic actions in the company of people with basically the same disposition. The price we pay for this rather widely spread new mythology, including mythicized information about Shakespeare himself, is that we have to assent to the unverified (and often unverifiable) opinion of previous generations before (or instead of) we can get access to the texts or historical documents they are about; but it is not only in a literary cult that verification is substituted with belief: a retrospective glance at traditional methods of higher education showed that survey courses at prestigious universities likewise disseminated an enormous body of second-hand information presented as historical facts for students who could not (and were not expected to) test them by personal experience. In societies divided by differences of personal prehistories the discursive, theatrical and pilgrim customs of the Shakespeare cult provide a much larger meeting house than those of the more exclusive literary cults (like those of James Joyce or Henry James[19]) which tend to recruit sophisticated people from the realm of higher education. Of course the Shakespeare cult is not the land of perfect equality, and people of different backgrounds may not get the same service here either, but on the whole the social impact of this cult has been nearer to equalizing than to polarizing, and it has helped to preserve a residue of cultural integrity for the otherwise fragmented communities of our postmodern era.

Surveying the diverse effects of the Shakespeare cult one can finally try to face the question of Pál Gyulai, asked at a tercentenary performance of *A Midsummer-Night's Dream* on 23 April 1864: how much remains of the enthusiasm of cultic celebrations in our everyday cultural work once the festivity is over? The lesson to be learned from the historical evidence of two centuries is that very much remains of it: the cult was the midwife at the birth of many cultural values and it fostered their growth more significantly than it ever hindered the development of others. The first hundred years of Shakespeare in Hungary, as a scholar aptly remarked in 1909, 'was also the history of Hungarian drama and acting, criticism and translation, the cultivation of taste and judgement';[20] after yet another century it is safe to add that all these segments of culture not only coexisted with but in many ways also benefited from the verbal and ritual forms of reverence learned from the British cult of Shakespeare. Although the adopted attitude of quasi-religious worship was inseparable from the reflexes of self-submission that tended to restrain the free exercise of judgement, this tendency rarely paralysed criticism completely and it often stimulated its reawakening or invigorated its resistence. And even the self-submitting attitude of unconditional adoration should not be thought of as superstitious from the beginning and merely harmful, because the too early dominance of a cool analytical spirit could have caused more harm than good and would not have created an intellectual climate as mild and favourable for cultural growth as the prevalence of cultic attitudes did. When trying to assess the historical effects of the

Shakespeare cult it is worth remembering that the great Hungarian poet and translator, János Arany, deplored the futile critical soberness of several medieval historians as 'scholarly naivety'. Whereas they rigorously abstained from incorporating unverified data from oral traditions, they took over no less unverifiable data from elsewhere, and could not exclude the untrue by eliminating the improbable, hence their pointless methodological austerity obliterated the traces of Hungarian folk poetry for no comparable gain. Whenever we are trying to evaluate the role played by a literary or indeed any kind of cult, Arany's final comment is an important warning not to discard something that fostered important values in the past and can be of similar service in the future: 'There is no more obstinate enemy of the naive than that rudimentary and no less naive state of mind in which an individual or a nation begins to outgrow the preoccupations of childhood, and with the missionary zeal of the converted wages war on heresies disowned not long ago, being ashamed now, in the light of reason, of the very things cherished in the past.'[21]

Notes

All translations are by the present writer unless indicated otherwise.

PREFACE

1. Originally published in *Gray's Inn Journal*, No. 12, 15 December 1753. My quotation is from Vickers (1974–9), Vol. 4, p. 93.
2. Cf. Gilley and Sheils (1994), pp. 211–14.
3. Dobson (1992), p. 6.

CHAPTER 1 THE EXPLORATION OF A LITERARY CULT: THEORETICAL ASSUMPTIONS AND METHODOLOGICAL PROBLEMS

1. Czigány 1984, pp. 217, 222.
2. Hermans, Theo: 'Report', in Delabastita and D'hulst (1993), pp. 184–6.
3. Wellek (1955–91), Vol. 1, p. 8; Wellek and Warren (1954), p. 106; Wellek (1963), p. 203.
4. Cf. Ayer (1976), pp. 150–1.
5. Szigethy (1979), pp. 60, 62, 235.
6. Anon, 'Shakespeare-innep Stratfordon 1769. Sept. 6-án', *Honművész*, Nos 9, 10, 11 (1834), pp. 66–8, 75–6, 82–4.
7. Fontenrose (1966), p. 53; Ruthven (1976), pp. 81–2.
8. Jonson (1641), quoted from Spingarn (1957), p. 19.
9. Harbage, Alfred, 'The myth of perfection', in Harbage (1966), p. 31, see also p. 37.
10. Harbage (1966), p. 38.
11. Harbage (1966), pp. 31, 38.
12. Jerrold, Douglas, 'Bajazet gag, or, the manager in search of a star', *The New Monthly Magazine* (1842), p. 189.
13. Muir (1977), pp. 92–109.
14. Taylor (1989), pp. 38–9.
15. See the persuasive argument in De Grazia (1991), pp. 222–3.
16. Dávidházi and Karafiáth (1994), pp. 11–27.
17. Marder (1963), p. 9.
18. Raleigh (1965), p. 23.
19. Kermode, Frank, 'The patience of Shakespeare', in Kermode (1971), pp. 149–63.
20. Spencer, T. J. B., 'The tyranny of Shakespeare', in Alexander (1964), pp. 169–70.
21. French (1972), pp. 1–5.

22. Jones, Emrys (1977), pp. 1–5; Baldwin (1944).
23. Szerdahely (1784), pp. 128–9.
24. Buczy (1817), p. 30.
25. Fábri and Steinert (1978), Vol. 1, pp. 123–5.
26. Turner (1978), pp. xiv, 28, 140–71, 234–7, 253.
27. Leopold (1987), pp. 290–1.
28. Cholnoky, Viktor, 'Shakspere', *Nyugat*, Vol. I (1908), p. 233.
29. Gyulai, Pál, 'Téli rege', in Gyulai (1908b), Vol. 2, pp. 192–5.
30. Gyulai, Pál, 'Szépirodalmi szemle', in Gyulai (1908a), p. 138.
31. Szabó (1965), pp. 26–52.
32. Brown and Fearon (1970), pp. 8–10.
33. Irving (1985), pp. 344–7.
34. Kilbourne, Brock, K. and Richardson, James, T., 'Cultphobia', *Thought*, Vol. LXI, No. 241 (1986), pp. 258–65.
35. Lukács, György, 'Shakespeare időszerűségének egyik vonatkozásáról', in Lukács (1970), Vol. 1, pp. 18–19.
36. Vadnay, Károly, 'A magyar Shakespeare-kiadás pártfogójáról: Emlékezés Tomorira', *A Kisfaludy-Társaság Évlapjai*, Vol. XXIX (1894–5), p. 176; Riedl (1916), p. 9.
37. Pósa (1942), p. 3.
38. Császár (1917), pp. 27–8.
39. Frazer (1921), Vol. 1, p. xxvii.
40. Stark and Bainbridge (1985), p. 171.
41. Stark and Bainbridge (1985), p. 207.
42. Turner (1978), p. 1.
43. Ruthven (1976), pp. 74–5.
44. Fontenrose (1966), pp. 18–20, 59–60.
45. Fodor and Lepore (1993), pp. 6–7, 209–10.
46. Fodor and Lepore (1993), pp. ix–x.
47. Turner (1978), pp. xiii–xiv, 1, 22.
48. Engler (1990), p. 72.
49. Babcock (1964), p. 23.
50. Irving (1985), p. 347.
51. Ábrányi (1847), p. 291.
52. Gibbon (n.d.), Vol. 1, p. 383.
53. Cf. Gibbon (1984), pp. 84–8, 92.
54. Apart from the evidences in his *Decline and Fall of the Roman Empire*, see Pocock (1985), pp. 152–6.
55. Gibbon (n.d.), Vol. 1, p. 382.
56. Gibbon (1984), p. 103.
57 Oliphant Smeaton's note in Gibbon (n.d.), Vol. 1, p. 383.
58. Frye, Northrop, 'The archetypes of literature', in Lodge (1972), p. 431.
59. Frye (1957), pp. 19, 126.
60. Huxley (1893), Vol. 4, Macmillan, pp. 287–8.
61. Bate, J. (1989), p. 22.
62. Schelling (1857), p. 140.
63. Wittgenstein, Ludwig, 'Remarks on Frazer's *Golden Bough*', in Wittgenstein (1993), pp. 119, 125, 129.

64. Richards (1976), p. 7.
65. Richards (1976), p. 8.
66. Raleigh (1965), p. 3.
67. Pocock, J. G. A., 'Gibbon's *Decline and Fall* and the world view of the late Enlightenment', in Pocock (1985), p. 152.
68. Ellwood (1986), p. 212.
69. Bayer (1909), Vol. 1, p. 126.
70. Nagy, Lajos, 'Shakespeare ellen', in Nagy (1959), Vol. 1, pp. 91–107.
71. Turner (1974), pp. 226–7; Turner (1978), pp. 26, 234.
72. Simson (1967), pp. 6–7.
73. Jusserand (1891), pp. 360–1, 406–7.
74. Turner (1978), p. 234.
75. Whitehead (1954), p. 102.

CHAPTER 2   THE GENESIS OF A RITUAL: THE SHAKESPEARE CULT IN ENGLISH ROMANTICISM

1. Gentleman (1770), Vol. 1, p. 387.
2. England (1964), p. 165.
3. See Hobsbawm and Ranger (1992).
4. England (1964), p. 5.
5. Turner (1978), pp. 35–8.
6. Contemporary newspaper clipping, unidentified. I found it in the Folger Shakespeare Library, Art Vol. d45. Garrickiana, p. 105.
7. 'Particulars of the Jubilee at Stratford', *Town and Country Magazine*, Vol. I (1769), p. 475. Cf. Bate, J. (1989), p. 32.
8. Bate, J. (1989), p. 33.
9. England (1964), p. 12.
10. England (1964); Stochholm (1964); Deelman (1964).
11. *The London Chronicle*, 9–11 May 1769. See also Garrick's reply there, 13–16 May 1769. Cf. Stochholm (1964), pp. 8–9.
12. Cradock (1826), Vol. 1, pp. 215–16.
13. The letter was published in *The Public Advertiser* on 16 September 1769. Cf. Stochholm (1964), pp. 56–7.
14. Bate, J. (1989), p. 33.
15. Shakespeare (1769), p. 7.
16. *The Public Advertiser*, 16 September 1769, p. 3, col. 1. Cf. Stochholm (1964), pp. 62–3.
17. Stochholm (1964), pp. 62–3.
18. Victor (1761–71), Vol. 3, pp. 213–14.
19. Cf. Boswell's account in *The Public Advertiser*, 16 September 1769. In Deelman's reconstruction (Deelman (1964), pp. 239–40) this belonged to the entertainments of the second evening.
20. Victor (1761–71), Vol. 3, p. 207. Cf. *The Public Advertiser*, 16 September 1769, p. 3, col. 1.
21. Cf. Deelman (1964), p. 206.
22. Deelman (1964), pp. 175–206; England (1964), pp. 43–9; Stochholm (1964), pp. 51–65; Brown and Fearon (1970), pp. 80–2.

23. Cf. Deelman (1964), pp. 213–14.
24. *The Public Advertiser*, 16 September 1769. Cf. Stochholm (1964), p. 78; Deelman (1964), p. 221.
25. Deelman (1964), p. 226.
26. Garrick (1763–4), pp. 124–55; Victor (1761–71), pp. 223–6. Cf. Stochholm (1964), pp. 91–2; Deelman (1964), pp. 230–1.
27. Cf. *Lloyd's Evening Post*, 1–4 September 1769; Dodd (1770), pp. 268–9; Wheler (1806), pp. 191–6; England (1964), pp. 57, 127–42.
28. Deelman (1964), pp. 231–3; Vickers (1974–9), Vol. 5, p. 355.
29. Garrick (1831–2), Vol. 1, p. 332; England (1964), pp. 57–8.
30. Originally in *Universal Magazine*, Vol. LV (1769), p. 159. Quoted from Schoenbaum (1991), p. 104.
31. Deelman (1964), pp. 245–6; Stochholm (1964), p. 102; Brown and Fearon (1970), pp. 85–6; Angelo (1828–30), Vol. 1, pp. 49–50; cf. Deelman (1964), p. 251; Stochholm (1964), pp. 98–100. On the masquerade see Boswell's account, *The Public Advertiser*, 16 September 1769, and an entry in his diary, Brady and Pottle (1956), p. 283; cf. Stochholm (1964), p. 97.
32. Victor (1761–71), Vol. 3, p. 229. Cf. England (1964), pp. 62, 65; Stochholm (1964), p. 103.
33. *The St James Chronicle*, 9–12 September 1769, p. 4, col. 2. Cf. Deelman (1964), p. 257; Stochholm (1964), p. 106.
34. Brady and Pottle (1956), p. 283. Cf. Deelman (1964), p. 255; Stochholm (1964), p. 105.
35. Brown and Fearon (1970), p. 92. (This letter was first published in the first edition of this book in 1939.)
36. James Boswell, 'Letter to the London Magazine', *The London Magazine*, Vol. XXXVII (1769), p. 451.
37. England (1964), pp. 3–4.
38. Turner (1978), pp. 35–8.
39. Taylor (1989), p. 120.
40. Dobson (1992), p. 216–19.
41. Dobson (1992), p. 223.
42. Dobson (1992), p. 6.
43. 'Occasional Prologue, Spoken by Mr *Garrick* at the Opening of Drury-Lane Theatre, 8 Sept. 1750', in Vickers (1974–9), Vol. 3, p. 365.
44. England (1964), pp. 85–123.
45. Dunn (1939), pp. 126, 172–3.
46. Archenholz (1791), pp. 237–8. Cf. England (1964), pp. 85–123.
47. Klaniczay, Tibor, 'A nagy személyiségek humanista kultusza a XV. században', in Klaniczay (1985), p. 45.
48. Dryden (1970), pp. 53, 56, 58, 94, 121–2, 126, 130, 132, 147, 157, 159–61, 166, 170–1, 177, 210, 215.
49. Bate, J. (1989), p. 22.
50. Marder (1963), p. 18; Babcock (1964), pp. 121–5.
51. Montagu (1970), p. 10.
52. Vickers (1974–9), Vol. 4, pp. 289–91.
53. Vickers (1974–9), Vol. 5, pp. 344–55. Cf. Wheler (1806), pp. 175–85; England (1964), pp. 251–63; Deelman (1964), pp. 138–43, 214–25.

54. See Dobson (1992), p. 7.
55. Cf. Bate, J. (1989), p. 30.
56. Originally in Ritson (1783), p. vi. Quoted from Vickers (1974–9), Vol. 6, p. 337.
57. Gentleman (1770), Vol. 1, p. 387.
58. Taylor, E. (1774); for the review see *Gentleman's Magazine*, Vol. XLV (1775), p. 90.
59. Martin Sherlock's 'A Fragment on Shakespeare. Extracted from Advice to a Young Poet' was translated from the French in 1786, but the French version was also a translation (made in 1780) of a part of the author's Italian work published in 1779. My quote is from Vickers (1974–9), Vol. 6, pp. 436–8.
60. Theobald (1970), pp. iii–v.
61. Theobald (1970), pp. 7–12.
62. Dryden, John, 'Defence of the Epilogue, or An Essay on the Dramatic Poetry of the Last Age', in Dryden (1970), pp. 121–5.
63. Theobald (1970), pp. 40–1. Cf. Seary (1990), pp. 69–70.
64. Dryden, 'Defence of the Epilogue', in Dryden (1970), p. 125.
65. Smith (1928), p. 38.
66. Jarvis (1995), p. 88.
67. De Grazia (1991).
68. De Grazia (1991), p. 145.
69. Hume (1969).
70. Morgann, Maurice, 'An Essay on the Dramatic Character of Sir John Falstaff' (1777), in Vickers (1974–9), Vol. 6, pp. 170–1.
71. Vickers (1974–9), Vol. 6, p. 165.
72. Stack, Richard, 'An Examination of an Essay on the Dramatic Character of Sir John Falstaff' (1788), in Vickers (1974–9), Vol. 6, pp. 469–79.
73. Bate, W. (1987), pp. 182, 213.
74. Montagu (1970), p. 11.
75. Coleridge (1967), Vol. 2, p. 109.
76. Prickett (1976), p. 28.
77. Coleridge (1884), pp. 232–3.
78. Coleridge (1905), pp. 307–8.
79. Babcock (1964), p. 199.
80. In his notebook 26 October 1803. Cf. Prickett (1976), pp. 82–4.
81. To Mrs Evans, 5 February 1793. Coleridge (1956), Vol. 1, p. 48.
82. To George Fricker, 4 October 1806. Coleridge (1956), Vol. 2, p. 1189.
83. Coleridge (1884), p. 273.
84. Harbage, Alfred, 'The myth of perfection', in Harbage (1966), p. 31.
85. See Brown and Fearon (1970), pp. 16–17.
86. Turner (1978), pp. 17–21.
87. Turner (1978), p. 241.
88. Turner (1978), pp. 20, 240–1.
89. Halliday (1960), pp. 41–2.
90. Quoted in Halliday (1960), pp. 67–8. Cf. Bate, J. (1989), p. 31.
91. See the full text of the letter in Brown and Fearon (1970), pp. 91–3.

92. Vickers (1974–9), Vol. 5, p. 410.
93. Marder (1963), p. 240.
94. Adams (1961), p. 185.
95. ('Recently I travelled through Stratford-upon-Avon in Warwickshire, the place where Shakespeare was born. I saw his house and sat in his chair from which people started to carve off pieces. I, too, cut off a piece for 1 shilling. I will have it mounted in rings, and distribute them, in the manner of Lorenzo-boxes, among the Jacobians and Goetheans.') Lichtenberg (1983), Vol. 1, p. 574.
96. Lichtenberg (1983), Vol. 1, pp. 262, 492–3, 534–56, 569–70, 574, 582–602.
97. On 16 September 1791. Cf. Lichtenberg (1983), Vol. 3, pp. 949–50.
98. See Irving (1985), p. 346; Halliday (1960), pp. 121–2.
99. For the whole story see Malone (1970), pp. 22–3; Ireland, S. (1970), pp. 2–5; Ireland, W. (1971); Chalmers (1971a); Chalmers (1971b); Brown and Fearon (1970), pp. 67–70; Halliday (1960), pp. 82–109; Marder (1963), pp. 218–26; Babcock (1964), pp. 23–6; Grebanier (1966).
100. Ireland, W. (1971), p. 7.
101. England (1964), pp. 79–80.
102. England (1964), p. 81.
103. Irving (1985), p. 356; 'A Letter from the Place of Shakespeare's Nativity', *British Magazine or Monthly Repository for Gentlemen and Ladies*, Vol. III (1762), p. 301, cf. Chambers (1930), Vol. 2, pp. 286–7; England (1964), pp. 74–5; Marder (1963), pp. 205–7, 236–7; Brown and Fearon (1970), pp. 49, 65–7, 72, 146–56, 160–3, 272–3, 276; Halliday (1960), pp. 122–3.
104. Wheler (1806), pp. 34, 129.
105. Wheler (1814), pp. 3–4.
106. Spencer (1964), p. 16.
107. Irving (1985), pp. 344–53.
108. Wesselényi (1925), pp. 120–7.
109. Wilson (1827), pp. xxxix.
110. Irving (1985), p. 345.
111. Jones, G. (1836), pp. 4, 8–9, 11, 15–16, 18–21, 35–6, 39–43, 45, 51–2.
112. Spencer (1964), pp. 16–17; Halliday (1960), p. 149.
113. Grinfield (1850), pp. 3–8, 10, 21, 24–6, 38, 47–8.
114. Grinfield (1850), pp. 28, 52. The article is quoted from *Edinburgh Review*, No. CLXXXI, August 1849.
115. Grinfield (1850), pp. 18–20, 24–5, 33–4, 36–7, 40–6.
116. Jones, Wainwright and Yarnold (eds) (1978), pp. 433–9; Gilley and Sheils (1994), p. 300.
117. Bellew (1863), p. 313.
118. Jephson (1864), pp. v–vi, 1–3, 18–23, 38–9, 42–3, 132–5, 183–7, 194, 196, 200–3.
119. Rónay (n.d.), pp. 37–79.
120. Turner (1985); Turner (1974), pp. 166–230.
121. Szabó (1965), pp. 26–52.
122. [Anonymous], 'The Home and Haunts of Shakespeare', *The Review of Reviews*, No. V (1892), pp. 519–20.

123. Marder (1963), p. 245.
124. Boldizsár (1965), pp. 224–5.
125. Fox (n.d.).
126. Turner (1978), p. 23.
127. Turner (1978), pp. 6–7, 33–4.
128. Cf. England (1964), pp. 67–71; Marder (1963), p. 258; Deelman (1964), pp. 291, 310.
129. Shakespeare (1827), pp. 15–34.
130. Shakespeare (1830), p. 19.
131. Cf. Marder (1963), pp. 260–1; England (1964), pp. 72, 82.
132. Cf. England (1964), pp. 71–2, 82; Marder (1963), p. 259; Halliday (1960), pp. 135–6; Rónay (1865), pp. 137–210; Knight, G. Wilson, 'St. George and the Dragon', in Knight (1967), pp. 91–111.
133. On the simultaneity of secularization and religious revival in cult formation see Stark and Bainbridge (1985), pp. 429–56.
134. Jephson (1864), pp. 184, 202.
135. Cf. Halliday (1960), pp. 154–60.
136. Marder (1963), p. 261.
137. Spencer (1964), p. 125.
138. Hunter (1864), pp. 200–10; cf. Spencer (1964), p. 126.
139. Wordsworth (1864), pp. 383–404.
140. Jephson (1864), pp. 20–21.
141. Wordsworth (1864), pp. 383–404.
142. Wordsworth (1864), pp. 383–404.
143. Wordsworth (1864), pp. 383–404.
144. Shakespeare (1864), p. 52.
145. Brown and Fearon (1970), pp. 184–5. Cf. Halliday (1960), pp. 160–1; Marder (1963), pp. 261–3.
146. See Shakespeare (1864). Cf. Halliday (1960), p. 161; Marder (1963), pp. 262–3; Cox (1865); Hunter (1864).
147. Cf. Levine (1988), pp. 13–81.
148. Hunter (1864), p. 239. Cf. Spencer (1964), p. 125.
149. *The Public Advertiser*, 16 September 1769. Cf. Stochholm (1964), p. 56.
150. Brady and Pottle (1956), pp. 294–6. Cf. Deelman (1964), pp. 171–2.

CHAPTER 3   A MIDDLE EUROPEAN CASE STUDY: THE DEVELOPMENT OF THE SHAKESPEARE CULT IN HUNGARY

1. [Anonymous,] 'Az Anglusokról némelly Jegyzések', *Mindenes Gyűjtemény*, No. 2 (1789), 2nd quarter, pp. 28–30.
2. *Mindenes Gyűjtemény*, No. 2 (1789), 2nd quarter, pp. 20–1.
3. *Mindenes Gyűjtemény*, No. 23 (1790), 3rd quarter, pp. 365–8.
4. *Mindenes Gyűjtemény*, No. 8 (1790), 4th quarter, pp. 114–19.
5. *Mindenes Gyűjtemény*, No. 13 (1790), 4th quarter, pp. 207–8.
6. *Mindenes Gyűjtemény*, No. 13 (1790), 4th quarter, p. 208; No. 14, pp. 209–11.
7. Kiss (1826), p. 750.

8. Cf. Archenholz (1791), pp. 237–8.
9. *Mindenes Gyűjtemény*, No. 14 (1790), 4th quarter, p. 211.
10. Hermans, Theo, 'Report', in Delabastita and D'hulst (1993), pp. 185–6.
11. Kermode (1983), pp. 159–60.
12. [Anonymous,] 'Shakespeárnak Jubileuma', *Mindenes Gyűjtemény*, No. 13 (1790), 4th quarter, pp. 207–8; Kiss (1826); [Anonymous,] 'Shakespeare-innep Stratfordon 1769. Sept. 6-án', *Honművész*, (1834), No. 9, pp. 66–8; No. 10, pp. 75–6; No. 11, pp. 82–4.
13. See, for example, Bessenyei (1777), p. 77; Szerdahely (1784), pp. 128–9, 179; Péczeli (1792), pp. 229–91.
14. Wesselényi (1925), pp. 120, 124, 127; Szemere (1845), Vol. 2, pp. 171, 259–60.
15. Cf. Kádár (1916); Kádár (1918); Kádár (1919–22).
16. Bayer (1911).
17. Cf. Levine (1988), pp. 13–81.
18. Döbrentei (1830), p. 267.
19. Kazinczy (1879), in Kazinczy (1960), Vol. 1, p. 74.
20. Kiséry (1996), in Klein and Dávidházi (1996), p. 32.
21. Péczeli (1792), p. 5.
22. Péczeli (1787), p. 446.
23. [Anonymous,] 'Román, 's mi jobb a' Románnál', *Mindenes Gyűjtemény*, No. 12 (1789), 2nd quarter, p. 188.
24. Marsden (1995), pp. 16–17.
25. [Anonymous], [Untitled article], *Hadi és más nevezetes történetek*, (1790), 2nd period, p. 120.
26. Bessenyei (1777), p. 77.
27. Bessenyei (1983), pp. 348–50.
28. Radnai (1889), p. 25.
29. Bailey (1964), p. 2.
30. Le Tourneur (1776–83), Vol. 1, pp. i–x.
31. Bailey (1964), p. 14.
32. Walpole (1963), p. 11.
33. Cf. Montagu (1970).
34. Bayer (1909), Vol. 1, pp. 12–14; Jánosi (1914), pp. 51–2; Solt (1965), in Kéry, Országh and Szenczi (1965), p. 11.
35. Jánosi (1914), pp. 51–2.
36. Szerdahely (1784), p. 128–9.
37. Cf. Frank, Tibor, '"Give me Shakespeare": Lajos Kossuth's English as an Instrument of International Politics', in Klein and Dávidházi (1996), pp. 47–73.
38. Cf. Maller (1984), in Maller and Ruttkay (1984), pp. 40–1.
39. Szemere (1845), Vol. 2, p. 171.
40. Szebeklébi [Bajza, József], 'Hamlet', in Bajza (1899–1901), Vol. 5, p. 239.
41. O.25 [Unidentified author], 'Macbeth', in Maller and Ruttkay (1984), p. 132.
42. Ábrányi (1847), p. 291.
43. Petőfi (1847).

218   *Notes*

44. Translated and quoted by Yu. D. Levin, in Levin (1989), p. 127.
45. Zerffi (1847).
46. Vachott (1846), p. 125.
47. Greguss (1880), p. 391; Várdai (1909), p. 214.
48. Egressy, Gábor, 'Művészet szabadsága', *Életképek*, (1848) 1st period, p. 67; Egressy (1848); Egressy (1867), pp. 182–3; cf. Greguss (1880), p. 391; cf. Várdai (1909), p. 214.
49. Szemere, P. (1890), Vol. 1, pp. 125–6.
50. Solt (1965), in Kéry, Országh and Szenczi (1965), p. 20; cf. Bayer (1909), Vol. 1, p. 36.
51. Vörösmarty, Mihály, 'Hamlet', *Athenaeum*, 28 January 1841.
52. Petőfi (1847).
53. Császár (1917), p. 7.
54. *Életképek*, 27 February 1847. See also Petőfi (1987), pp. 120–1.
55. Bayer (1909), Vol. 1, p. 57; Várdai (1909), p. 209; Császár (1925), p. 314.
56. Székely, József, 'Shakespeare', in Vahot (1852), pp. 282–3.
57. Vahot, Imre, 'A játékszín általános történetének vázlata', in Vahot (1852), pp. 55–8.
58. From the archives of Kisfaludy Society, quoted in Bayer (1909), Vol. 1, p. 105.
59. Arany (1968), p. 910.
60. Szász, Károly, *Shakespeare*. Koszorú, 8 May 1864, pp. 436–7.
61. Pulszky, Ferenc, 'Élet és művészet', *Athenaeum*, (1841), 1st period, p. 467.
62. Coleridge (1969), Vol. 1, p. 202.
63. Vahot, Imre, 'Töredékgondolatok a világköltészetről', *Athenaeum*, (1841), 1st period, p. 390.
64. Móra, Ferenc, 'A csoda', in Maller and Ruttkay (1984), p. 310.
65. Gyulai (1908a), p. 138; Arany (1968), p. 36; Kemény (1971), pp. 290–1; Erdélyi (1890), p. 516; Erdélyi (1961), p. 551; Greguss (1872), Vol. 1, pp. 165–6.
66. Gyulai (1902), Vol. 2, 248–9, 253.
67. Hunfalvy, Pál, 'Rhapsodiák', *Athenaeum*, (1840), 2nd period, p. 33.
68. Arany (1962), p. 427; Arany (1968), pp. 403–4.
69. Halász (1959), pp. 479–80; Halász (1977), pp. 304–46.
70. Arnold, 'The study of poetry' (1880), in Ricks (1972), p. 171; Buckley, Vincent, 'Matthew Arnold: poetry as religion', in Arnold (1973), pp. 150–67; Willey, Basil, 'Arnold and religion', in Allott (1975), pp. 236–58; Dávidházi, Péter, 'The importance of Matthew Arnold's Critical Theory', *Acta Litteraria*, (1978), pp. 339–50.
71. Erdélyi (1890), pp. 66, 68–9.
72. Erdélyi, János, 'A három divatlapról', *Magyar Szépirodalmi Szemle*, (1847) 2nd period, p. 12.
73. Salamon (1889), Vol. 1, pp. 85–6.
74. Gyulai (1908a), p. 138; Gyulai (1902), Vol. 2, pp. 248–9.
75. Vörösmarty, Mihály, 'Hamlet', *Athenaeum*, 28 January 1841.
76. Gondol, Dániel, 'Regény és dráma, párhuzamban', in Maller and Ruttkay (1984), pp. 107–8.
77. Petőfi (1847).

78. Obernyik, Károly, 'Hamlet', in Maller and Ruttkay (1984), p. 180.
79. Sőtér (1963), p. 229.
80. Gyulai (1961b), pp. 227, 237; Csengery (1870–84), Vol. 5, p. 309.
81. Arany (1888–9), Vol. 1, pp. 465–7, Vol. 2, p. 275; Arany (1963), p. 312.
82. Greguss (1872), Vol. 1, p. 396.
83. Gyulai (1961a), p. 53.
84. Cf. Dávidházi, Péter, '"Iszonyodnám enmagam előtt": Egy írói Oidipusz-komplexum drámája', *Holmi*, Vol. VII, No. 3 (1995), pp. 350–65, No. 4, pp. 513–25.
85. Cf. Dávidházi, Péter, 'A Hymnus paraklétoszi szerephagyománya', *Alföld*, Vol. XLVII, No. 12 (1996), pp. 66–80.
86. Cf. Toldy (1872–3), Vol. 2, p. 97.
87. Kemény (1971), p. 259.
88. Vajda (1970), pp. 55–9.
89. See the advertisement quoted in full by Czeke, Marianne, 'Lemouton Emília Shakespeare-fordítása', *Magyar Shakespeare-Tár*, Vol. VIII (1916), p. 158.
90. Károly Somfai in *Pesti Divatlap* (1845), p. 791.
91. Bajza, József, 'Shakespeare, francia színművek s az Athenaeum', in Bajza (1899–1901), Vol. 5, pp. 161–4.
92. Vahot, Imre, 'Lear király', in Maller and Ruttkay (1984), pp. 128–32.
93. Vas, Andor [real name: Hazucha, Xavéri Ferenc], 'Romeo és Júlia', *Életképek* (1844), 2nd period, p. 560.
94. Vas, Andor [real name: Hazucha, Xavéri Ferenc], 'IV. Henrik király', *Életképek* (1845), 1st period, pp. 215–16.
95. Erdélyi (1985), p. 216.
96. L. P. [unidentified], 'Hamlet', in Maller and Ruttkay (1984), pp. 142–3.
97. Csengery (1870–84), Vol. 5, p. 368.
98. Móricz (1978–84), Vol. 1, pp. 448–9.
99. Móricz (1978–84), Vol. 1, pp. 54–91.
100. Móricz (1978–84), Vol. 1, pp. 447–9.
101. Móricz (1963), p. 169; Móricz (1978–84), Vol. 1, p. 410.
102. Salamon, Ferenc, 'Shakespeare színpadunkon', in Salamon (1907), pp. 126–35.
103. Gyulai, Pál, 'Téli rege', in Gyulai (1908b), Vol. 2, pp. 192–5.
104. Gyulai, Pál, 'Téli rege', Gyulai (1908b), Vol. 2, pp. 191–9.
105. Obernyik, Károly, 'Hamlet', in Maller and Ruttkay (1984), pp. 178–81.
106. G [Toldy, Ferenc], 'Felelet Kazinczynak', in Toldy (1874), p. 326.
107. Hunfalvy, Pál, 'A' magyar nemzeti versidom', *Magyar Nyelvészet* (1857), 2nd period, p. 72.
108. Arany, János, 'Zrínyi és Tasso', in Arany (1962), pp. 438–9.
109. Salamon (1889), Vol. 1, p. 34.
110. Greguss, Ágost, 'Eszmecsere a "népiesség" ügyében', *Pesti Napló*, 22 July 1856.
111. [Anonymous], 'Shakespeare bálványozása ellen. Greguss Ágost egyetemi tanár felolvasásai nyomán', *Magyarország és a Nagyvilág*, 1 January 1871. See also Maller and Ruttkay (1984), p. 201.

112. Greguss (1880), pp. 3–6.
113. Cf. Rümelin (1866).
114. Greguss (1880), pp. 5, 228, 309–10, 322–5, 328, 367.
115. Greguss (1880), p. 360.
116. Greguss (1880), pp. 360–7.
117. Greguss (1880), pp. 62, 96, 310–11.
118. Greguss (1880), p. 96.
119. Greguss (1880), pp. 310–11.
120. Greguss (1880), pp. 62, 96, 310–311, 360–7, 405.
121. See *Magyar Shakespeare-Tár*, Vol. 1, No. 3 (1908), p. 231.
122. Arany (1888–9), Vol. 2, p. 78.
123. Arany (1888–9), Vol. 2, p. 80.
124. Arany (1966), p. 341.
125. See Maller and Ruttkay (1984), pp. 82–3.
126. Henszlmann, Imre, 'Figyelmeztetés Shakespeare Harmadik Richárdjára', in Maller and Ruttkay (1984), p. 127.
127. Petőfi (1847), p. 251.
128. Péterfy (1983), pp. 18–19.
129. Salamon (1907), Vol. 1, pp. 128–9.
130. Salamon (1907), Vol. 2, pp. 323–5.
131. Greguss, Ágost, 'Szentivánéji álom', in Greguss (1872), Vol. 2, p. 287.
132. Gyulai (1908b), Vol. 2, pp. 192–5.
133. Ignotus, 'János király', in Fábri and Steinert (1978), Vol. 1, pp. 123–5.
134. Yolland, Arthur, 'Shakespeare és a Biblia', *Magyar Shakespeare-Tár*, Vol. 3, No. 3, (1910), pp. 198–215.
135. Móra, Ferenc, 'A csoda', in Maller and Ruttkay (1984), pp. 307–12.

CHAPTER 4   THE EUROPEAN CONTEXT: TYPOLOGICAL PROBLEMS OF DISSEMINATION

1. Stark and Bainbridge (1985), p. 21; cf. Ellwood (1986), pp. 215, 220.
2. Stark and Bainbridge (1985), p. 23.
3. Stark and Bainbridge (1985), pp. 24–30, 208–13.
4. Harbage, Alfred, 'Shakespeare as culture hero', in Harbage (1966), pp. 101–19.
5. Goethe, Johann Wolfgang, 'Zum Schäkespears Tag', in Blinn (1988), Vol. 1, p. 99.
6. Knight, G. Wilson, 'Shakespeare and ritual', in Knight (1981), pp. 148–60.
7. Stark and Bainbridge (1985), p. 212.
8. Stark and Bainbridge (1985), pp. 171–88.
9. Taylor (1989), pp. 119–120.
10. Bate, J. (1989), p. 45.
11. Cf. Bate, J. (1989), pp. 30–1.
12. Cf. Willems (1979), p. 361.
13. Bayer (1909), Vol. 1, pp. 29–30.
14. Babcock (1964).

15. Szerdahely (1784), pp. 128–9, 179; see also pp. 43, 62, 68, 93.
16. Schabert (1978), pp. 717–18.
17. Levin (1988), pp. 8–16.
18. Levin (1989), p. 115.
19. Cassirer (1923–9), Vol. 2, pp. 270–2.
20. Cf. Ruthven (1976), pp. 16, 35–8; Fontenrose (1966), pp. 26–8.
21. Petrichevich Horváth, Lázár, 'Shakespeare és drámái', *Athenaeum*, 7 January 1838, pp. 19–20.
22. Rakodczay, Pál, 'Valami Hamletről', *Színészek Lapja*, Vol. XVI, No. 5 (1898), pp. 9–11.
23. Németh (1973), p. 162.
24. Cf. Bailey (1964), pp. 41–3.
25. Husserl (1972), pp. 23–45.
26. Wittgenstein (1953), p. 202.
27. Daiches, David, 'The place of English Studies in the Sussex Scheme', in Daiches (1970), p. 82.
28. Daiches, David, 'The place of English Studies in the Sussex Scheme', in Daiches (1970), p. 86.
29. Petrichevich Horváth, Lázár, 'Shakespeare és drámái', *Athenaeum*, 7 January 1838, p. 19–20.
30. Szerdahely (1784), p. 128–9.
31. Cf. Kiséry (1996), in Klein and Dávidházi (1996), p. 32.
32. Cf. Bayer (1911).
33. Toldy (1872–3), pp. 3–10.
34. Daiches, David, 'The place of English Studies in the Sussex Scheme', in Daiches (1970), pp. 88–9, 99.
35. Asa Briggs, quoted by Granville Hawkins, in Daiches (1970), p. 200.
36. Weber, Arthur, 'Shakespeare hatása a vígjátékíró Vörösmartyra', *Magyar Shakespeare-Tár*, No. 3, (1911), p. 11.
37. Riedl (1916), pp. 10–11.
38. Schabert (1978), pp. 717–18.
39. Bailey (1964), pp. 14, 17, 32–3.
40. Habicht (1994), pp. 3–6.
41. Joachimi-Dege (1907), p. 14.
42. Habicht, Werner, 'Topoi of the Shakespeare cult in Germany', in Dávidházi and Karafiáth (1994), pp. 52–3.
43. Grabbe, Christian Dietrich, 'Über die Shakspearo-Manie', in Blinn (1988), Vol. 2, pp. 207–28. On Shakespeare's influence on Grabbe's plays see, for example, Price (1932), pp. 339–41.
44. Cf. Császár (1917), pp. 252–3; Riedl (1916), pp. 10–11.
45. Berzeviczy, Albert, 'Shakespeare és a magyar nemzetlélek', *Magyar Shakespeare-Tár*, Vol. VIII (1916), pp. 1–11.
46. Esterházy, Péter, 'Európa', in Esterházy (1991), p. 234.
47. Vadnay, Károly, 'A magyar Shakespeare-kiadás pártfogójáról: Emlékezés Tomorira', *A Kisfaludy-Társaság Évlapjai*, Vol. XXIX (1896), p. 173.
48. Maller, in Maller and Ruttkay (1984), pp. 20–1.
49. Maller, in Maller and Ruttkay (1984), p. 20
50. Gál (1945), p. 115.

51. Schoenbaum (1991), p. 108.
52. Cf. Campbell and Quinn (1966), pp. 646–50; Helsztyński (1965), pp. 5–33.
53. Cf. Bailey (1964), pp. 8–11.
54. Levin (1989), pp. 115–16, 122.
55. Maller, in Maller and Ruttkay (1984), p. 21.
56. Levin (1989), pp. 118, 121.
57. Levin (1989), pp. 129–30.
58. Dávidházi (1989), pp. 226–43.
59. Császár (1917).
60. Cf. Ruttkay, Kálmán, 'Klasszikus Shakespeare-fordításaink', in Kéry, Országh and Szenczi (1965), pp. 27–8.
61. Császár (1917), pp. 33–4.

CHAPTER 5 THE POSTPONED QUESTION OF JUDGEMENT: FUNCTIONS AND VALUES RECONSIDERED

1. Cf. Brown and Fearon (1970), pp. 91–3.
2. Weber (1964), pp. 1, 7.
3. Wittgenstein, Ludwig: 'Remarks on Frazer's *Golden Bough*', in Wittgenstein (1993), pp. 119, 125, 129.
4. Brown and Fearon (1970), p. 5.
5. Ambrus, Zoltán, 'Shakespeare-ciklus', *Nyugat*, Vol. IV, No. 10 (1911), pp. 958–61.
6. Rakodczay, Pál, 'Shakespeare a vidéken', *Magyar Shakespeare-Tár*, No. 3 (1911) pp. 213–18.
7. Egressy (1877).
8. Böckh (1877), pp. 1–33.
9. Murray, Krieger, 'Shakespeare and the critic's idolatry of the word', in Evans (1976), p. 194.
10. Smidt, Kristian,'"Shakespeare can do no wrong": bardolatry and scholarship', in Dávidházi and Karafiáth (1994), pp. 11–27.
11. Charles Lock's review of Dávidházi and Karafiáth (1994), in *Literary Research*, Spring–Summer, No. 23 (1995), pp. 10–11.
12. Babits, Mihály, 'A Shakespeare-ünnephez', *Nyugat*, 16 June 1916.
13. Keresztury, Dezsö, 'Shakespeare', *Nagyvilág*, No. 3 (1964).
14. Cf. Felperin, Howard, 'Bardolatry then and now', in Marsden (1991), pp. 141–2.
15. [Anonymous,] 'Shakespeare-innep Stratfordon 1769. Sept. 6-án', *Honművész*, No. 11 (1834), pp. 82–4.
16. Szabó (1965), pp. 26–52.
17. Schlegel (1906), Vol. 2, pp. 357–63.
18. Mészöly (1972), pp. 54–5.
19. Cf. Takács, Ferenc, 'The idol diabolized: James Joyce in East European Marxist criticism', in Dávidházi and Karafiáth (1994), pp. 249–57; Rahv, Philip, 'Henry James and his cult', in Rahv (1978), pp. 93–104.
20. Bayer (1909), Vol. 1, p. 127.
21. Arany, János, 'Naiv eposzunk', in Arany (1962), pp. 270, 272–3.

Bibliography

Ábrányi, Emil, 'Drámairodalmunk 's a' szinbiráló választmány', *Életképek*, Vol. IV (1847), first period, p. 291.

Adams, John, *Diary and Autobiography of John Adams*, Vol. 3, eds Butterfield, L. H. with Faber, Leonard C. and Garrett, Wendell D. Cambridge, Mass.: The Belknap Press of Harvard University Press, 1961.

Alexander, Peter (ed.), *Studies in Shakespeare: British Academy Lectures*. London: Oxford University Press, 1964.

Allott, Kenneth (ed.), *Matthew Arnold*. London: G. Bell & Sons, 1975.

Angelo, Henry, *Reminiscences of Henry Angelo*, 2 vols. London: H. Colburn, 1828–30.

Arany, János, *Arany János levelezése író-barátaival*, 2 vols. Budapest: Ráth Mór, 1888–9.

Arany, János, *Arany János összes művei, vol. 10, Prózai művek 1, Eredeti szépprózai művek, Szépprózai fordítások, Kisebb cikkek, Tanulmányok, Iskolai jegyzetek*, ed. Keresztury, Mária. Budapest: Akadémiai, 1962.

Arany, János, *Arany János összes művei, vol. 12, Prózai művek 3, Glosszák, Szerkesztői üzenetek, Szerkesztői megjegyzések, Előfizetési felhívások*, ed. Németh, G. Béla. Budapest, 1963.

Arany, János, *Arany János összes művei, vol. 13, Hivatali iratok 1*, eds Dánielisz, Endre, Tőrös, László and Gergely, Pál. Budapest: Akadémiai, 1966.

Arany, János, *Arany János összes művei, vol. 11, Prózai művek 2, (1860–1882*, ed. Németh, G. Béla. Budapest: Akadémiai, 1968.

Archenholz, Johann Wilhelm von, *A Picture of England*, trans. from the French. Dublin: P. Bryne, 1791.

Arnold, Matthew, *Matthew Arnold: A Collection of Critical Essays*, ed. Delaura, David J. Englewood Cliffs, NJ: Prentice-Hall, 1973.

Ayer, A. J., *Language, Truth and Logic*. Harmondsworth, Middlesex: Penguin Books, 1976.

Babcock, Robert Witbeck, *The Genesis of Shakespeare Idolatry 1766–1799. A Study in English Criticism of the Late Eighteenth Century*. New York: Russel & Russel, 1964.

Bailey, Helen Phelps, *Hamlet in France From Voltaire to Laforgue*. Genève: Librairie Droz, 1964.

Bajza, József, *Bajza József összegyűjtött munkái*, 6 vols, ed. Badics, Ferenc. Budapest: Franklin-Társulat, 1899–1901.

Baldwin, T. W., *William Shakespeare's 'Small Latine and Lesse Greeke'*, 2 vols. Urbana: University of Illinois Press, 1944.

Bate, J. *Shakespearean Constitutions: Politics, Theatre, Criticism 1730–1830*. Oxford: Clarendon Press, 1989.

Bate, W. Jackson, *Coleridge*. Cambridge, Mass. and London: Harvard University Press, 1987.

Bayer, József, *Shakespeare drámái hazánkban*, 2 vols. Budapest: Franklin-Társulat, 1909.

Bayer, József, 'Egy vándorló színtársulat Shakespeare-műsora 1820–1837 közt', *Magyar Shakespeare-Tár*, Vol. IV (1911), pp. 194–212.

Bellew, J. C. M., *Shakespeare's Home at New Place, Stratford-upon-Avon*. London: Virtue Brothers & Co., 1863.

Bessenyei, Georg von [= Bessenyei, György], *Die Geschäfte der Einsamkeit*. Wien: Joseph Garold, 1777.

Bessenyei, György, *A Holmi*, ed. Bíró, Ferenc. Budapest: Akadémiai, 1983.

Blinn, Hansjürgen (ed.), *Shakespeare-Rezeption: Die Diskussion um Shakespeare in Deutschland*, 2 vols. Berlin: Erich Schmidt Verlag, 1988.

Böckh, August, *Encyklopädie und Methodologie der philologischen Wissenschaften*, ed. Bratuschek, Ernst. Leipzig: Teubner, 1877.

Boldizsár, Iván, *Zsiráffal Angliában*. Budapest: Magvető, 1965.

Brady, Frank and Pottle, Frederick A. (eds), *Boswell in Search of a Wife*. Melbourne, London, Toronto: William Heinemann, 1956.

Brown, Ivor and Fearon, George, *Amazing Monument: A Short History of the Shakespeare Industry*. Port Washington, NY and London: Kennikat Press, 1970 (first edition 1939).

Buczy, Emil, 'A' tragoedia' legfőbbje a' görögöknél 's mostani álláspontja', *Erdélyi Muzéum*, Vol. IV, No. 9. (1817).

Campbell, Oscar James and Quinn, Edward G. (eds), *A Shakespeare Encyclopaedia*. London: Methuen, 1966.

Cassirer, Ernst, *Philosophie der symbolischen Formen*, 3 vols., Berlin: Bruno Cassirer Verlag, 1923–9.

Chalmers, George, *An Apology for The Believers in the Shakespeare Papers, which were exhibited In Norfolk-Street*. New York: Augustus M. Kelley Publishers, 1971a (reprint of the London 1797 edition).

Chalmers, George, *A Supplemental Apology for the Believers in the Shakespeare Papers*. New York: Augustus M. Kelley Publishers, 1971b. (reprint of the London 1799 edition.)

Chambers, E[dmund] K[erchever], *William Shakespeare: A Study of Facts and Problems*, 2 vols. Oxford: Clarendon Press, 1930.

Coleridge, Samuel Taylor, *Aids to Reflection and The Confessions of an Inquiring Spirit*. London: George Bell & Sons, 1884.

Coleridge, Samuel Taylor, *Specimens of the Table Talk*. Edinburgh: John Grant, 1905.

Coleridge, Samuel Taylor, *Collected Letters of Samuel Taylor Coleridge*: 1785–1800; 1801–1806, ed. Griggs, Earl Leslie 2 vols., Oxford: Clarendon Press, 1956.

Coleridge, Samuel Taylor, *Shakespearean Criticism*. Ed. Raysor, Thomas Middleton, 2 vols. London: Dent, and New York: Dutton, 1967.

Coleridge, Samuel Taylor, *Biographia Literaria*, 2 vols, ed. Shawcross, J. Oxford: Oxford University Press, 1969.

Cox, James Junior, *The Tercentenary: A Retrospect*. London, 1865.

Cradock, Joseph, *Literary and Miscellaneous Memoires*, 2 vols. London: J. B. Nichols, 1826.

Császár, Elemér, *Shakespeare és a magyar költészet*, Budapest: Franklin-Társulat, 1917.

Császár, Elemér, *A magyar irodalmi kritika története a szabadságharcig*. Budapest: Pallas, 1925.

Csengery, Antal, *Csengery Antal összegyűjtött munkái*, 5 vols, Budapest: Kilián, 1870–84.

Czigány, Lóránt, *The Oxford History of Hungarian Literature: From the Earliest Times to the Present*. Oxford: Clarendon Press, 1984.

Daiches, David (ed.), *The Idea of a New University: An Experiment in Sussex*. London: André Deutsch, 1970.

Dávidházi, Péter, *'Isten másodszülöttje': A magyar Shakespeare-kultusz természetrajza*. Budapest: Gondolat, 1989.

Dávidházi, Péter and Karafiáth, Judit (eds), *Literature and Its Cults: An Anthropological Approach (La littérature et ses cultes: Approche anthropologique)*. Budapest: Argumentum, 1994.

Deelman Christian, *The Great Shakespeare Jubilee*. London: Michael Joseph, 1964.

De Grazia, Margreta, *Shakespeare Verbatim: The Reproduction of Authenticity and the 1790 Apparatus*. Oxford: Clarendon Press, 1991.

Delabastita, Dirk and D'hulst, Lieven (eds), *European Shakespeares: Translating Shakespeare in the Romantic Age*. Amsterdam and Philadelphia: John Benjamins, 1993.

Döbrentei, Gábor [translation and notes], *Shakspeare remekei. Vol. 1. Macbeth. Szomoru játék öt felvonásban. Angolból, mai eléadhatáshoz alkalmaztatva.* Pest: Wigand Ottó, 1830.

Dobson, Michael, *The Making of the National Poet: Shakespeare, Adaptation and Authorship, 1660–1769.* Oxford: Clarendon Press, 1992.

Dodd, James Solas, *Essays and Poems*. Corke: E. Swiney, 1770.

Dryden, John, *Selected Criticism*, eds Kinsley, James and Parfitt, George. Oxford: Clarendon Press, 1970.

Dunn, Esther Cloudman, *Shakespeare in America*. New York: Macmillan, 1939.

Egressy, Gábor, 'Indítvány a szellemhonosítás ügyében', *Életképek*, Vol. V, 20 February 1848.

Egressy, Gábor, *Egressy Galambos Gábor emléke: Saját műveiből síremléke javára rendezték fiai*. Pest: Emich Gusztáv, 1867.

Ellwood, Robert, 'The several meanings of "cult"', *Thought*, Vol. LXI, No. 241 (1986).

England, Martha Winburn, *Garrick's Jubilee*. Columbus: Ohio State University Press, 1964.

Engler, Balz, *Poetry and Community*. Tübingen: Stauffenburg Verlag, 1990.

Erdélyi, János, *Tanulmányok*. Budapest: Franklin-Társulat, 1890.

Erdélyi, János, *Erdélyi, János válogatott művei*, ed. Lukácsy, Sándor, Budapest: Szépirodalmi, 1961.

Erdélyi, János, *Úti levelek, naplók*, ed. Erdélyi, T. Ilona, Budapest: Gondolat, 1985.

Esterházy, Péter, *A halacska csodálatos élete*. Budapest: Magvető, 1991.

Evans, G. B. (ed.), *Shakespeare: Aspects of Influence*. Cambridge, Mass. and London: Harvard University Press, 1976.

Fábri, Anna and Steinert, Ágota (eds), *A Hét. Politikai és irodalmi szemle. 1890–1899, 1900–1907. Válogatás*, 2 vols. Budapest: Magvető, 1978.

Fodor, Jerry and Lepore, Ernest, *Holism: A Shopper's Guide*. Oxford, UK and Cambridge, Mass.: Blackwell Publishers, 1993.

Fontenrose, Joseph, *The Ritual Theory of Myth*. Berkeley and Los Angeles: University of California Press, 1966.

Foulkes, Richard, *The Shakespeare Tercentenary of 1864*. London: The Society for Theatre Research, 1984.

Fox, Levi (ed.), *The Shakespeare Birthday Book*. Norwich: Cotman House, n.d.

Frazer, J. G. (ed. and trans.), *Apollodorus: The Library*, 2 vols. London: W. Heinemann and New York: G. P. Putnam's Sons 1921.

French, A. L., *Shakespeare and the Critics*. Cambridge: Cambridge University Press, 1972.

Frye, Northrop, *Anatomy of Criticism: Four Essays*. Princeton, NJ: Princeton University Press, 1957.

Gál, István, *Magyarország, Anglia és Amerika különös tekintettel a szláv világra: Vázlatok a nemzetközi vonatkozások köréből*. Budapest: Officina, n. d. [1945.]

Garrick, David, M. S. *Journal of the Journey to France and Italy, 1763–64*. [In the possession of the Folger Shakespeare Library, Washington.]

Garrick, David, *The Private Correspondence of David Garrick with the most Celebrated Persons of his Time*, 2 vols, ed. Boaden, James. London: H. Colborn and R. Bentley, 1831–2.

Gentleman, Francis, *The Dramatic Censor; or, Critical Companion*, 2 vols. London: J. Bell, 1770.

Gibbon, Edward, *Memoirs of My Life*, ed. Radice, Betty. Harmondsworth: Penguin Books, 1984.

Gibbon, Edward, *The Decline and Fall of the Roman Empire*, 3 vols. New York: Random House, n. d.

Gilley, Sheridan and Sheils, W. J. (eds), *A History of Religion in Britain: Practice and Belief from Pre-Roman Times to the Present*. Oxford, UK and Cambridge, Mass.: Blackwell, 1994.

Grebanier, Bernard, *The Great Shakespeare Forgery: A New Look at the Career of William Henry Ireland*. London: Heinemann, 1966.

Greg, Walter Wilson, 'The Rationale of Copy-Text'. In Greg, *Collected Papers*, ed. Maxwell, J. C. Oxford: Clarendon, 1966, pp. 374–91.

Greguss, Ágost, *Greguss Ágost tanulmányai*, 2 vols. Pest: Ráth Mór, 1872.

Greguss, Ágost, *Shakespeare pályája*. Budapest: Ráth Mór, 1880.

Grinfield, C. V. [Charles Vaughan], *A Pilgrimage to Stratford-upon-Avon, the Birthplace of Shakespeare*. London: Longman, Brown, & Co.; Coventry: John Merridew, 1850.

Gyulai, Pál, *Emlékbeszédek*, 2 vols. Budapest: Franklin-Társulat, 1902.

Gyulai, Pál, *Kritikai dolgozatok 1854–1861*. Budapest: Magyar Tudományos Akadémia, 1908a.

Gyulai, Pál, *Dramaturgiai dolgozatok*, 2 vols. Budapest: Franklin-Társulat, 1908b.

Gyulai, Pál, *Bírálatok, Cikkek, Tanulmányok*, eds Bisztray, Gyula and Komlós, Aladár. Budapest: Akadémiai, 1961a.

Gyulai, Pál, *Gyulai Pál levelezése 1843-tól 1867-ig*, ed. Somogyi, Sándor. Budapest: Akadémiai, 1961b.

Habicht, Werner, *Shakespeare and the German Imagination*. Hertford: Stephen Austin & Sons, 1994.

Halász, Gábor, *Halász Gábor válogatott írásai*, ed. Véber, Károly. Budapest: Magvető, 1959.

Halász, Gábor, *Válogatott írásai*. Budapest: Magvető, 1977.

Halliday, F. E., *The Cult of Shakespeare*. New York: Thomas Yoseloff, 1960.

Harbage, Alfred, *Conceptions of Shakespeare*. Cambridge, Mass.: Harvard University Press, and London: Oxford University Press, 1966.

Helsztyński, Stanisław (ed.), *Poland's Homage to Shakespeare: Commemorating the Fourth Centenary of His Birth 1564–1964*. Warszawa: PWN – Polish Scientific Publishers, 1965.

Hobsbawm, Eric and Ranger, Terence, *The Invention of Tradition*. Cambridge: Cambridge University Press, 1992.

Hume, David, *Dialogues Concerning Natural Religion*, ed. Aiken, Henry D. New York and London: Hafner, 1969.

Hunter, Robert E., *Shakespeare and Stratford-upon-Avon, . . . together With A Full Record of the Tercentenary Celebration*. London: Whittaker & Co.; Stratford-upon-Avon: Edward Adams, 1864.

Husserl, Edmund, *Erfahrung und Urteil: Untersuchungen zur Genealogie der Logik*, 4th ed. Hamburg: F. Meiner, 1972.

Huxley, Thomas Henry, *Science and the Hebrew Tradition, Collected Essays*, Vol. 4. London: Macmillan, 1893.

Ireland, Samuel, *An Investigation of Mr. Malone's Claim to the Character of Scholar, or Critic, Being an Examination of his Inquiry into the Authenticity of the Shakspeare Manuscripts, etc.* New York: Augustus M. Kelley Publishers, 1970, (reprint of the London 1796 or 1797 edition).

Ireland, William Henry, *An Authentic Account of the Shaksperian Manuscripts, etc.* New York: Augustus M. Kelley Publishers, 1971 (reprint of the 1796 edition).

Irving, Washington, *Washington Irving's Sketch Book*. New York: Crown Publishers, 1985.

Jarvis, Simon, *Scholars and Gentlemen: Shakespearian Textual Criticism and Representations of Scholarly Labour, 1725–1765*. Oxford: Clarendon Press, 1995.

Jánosi, Béla, *Szerdahely György aesthetikája*. Budapest: Akadémiai, 1914.

Jephson, J. M., *Shakespeare: His Birthplace, Home, and Grave, a Pilgrimage to Stratford-on-Avon in the Autumn of 1863*. London: Lovell Reeve & Co., 1864.

Joachimi-Dege, Marie, *Deutsche Shakespeare-Probleme im XVIII. Jahrhundert und im Zeitalter der Romantik*. Leipzig: H. Haessel Verlag, 1907.

Jones, Cheslyn, Wainwright, Geoffrey and Yarnold, Edward (eds), *The Study of Liturgy*. London: SPCK, 1978.

Jones, Emrys, *The Origins of Shakespeare*. Oxford: Clarendon Press, 1977.

Jones, George, *The Annual Jubilee Oration upon the Life, Character, and Genius of Shakespeare. Delivered at Stratford-upon-Avon, April 23rd, 1836*. London: Edward Churton; Stratford-upon-Avon: J. Ward; Warwick and Leamington: James Sharpe, 1836.

Jonson, Ben, *Timber: or, Discoveries*, in Jonson, Ben, *Workes. The second volume*. London: John Lane, The Bodley Head, 1641.

Jusserand, J. J., *English Wayfaring Life in the Middle Ages: XIV Century*, trans. Toulmin Smith, Lucy. London: T. Fisher Unwin, 1891.

Kádár, Jolán, 'Shakespeare drámái a magyarországi német színpadokon 1812-ig', *Magyar Shakespeare-Tár*, Vol. IX (1916), pp. 65–111.

Kádár, Jolán, 'Német Shakespeare-előadások Pesten és Budán 1812–1847', *Magyar Shakespeare-Tár*, Vol. X (1918), pp. 21-87.

Kádár, Jolán, 'A budai és pesti német színház Shakespeare-súgókönyvei', *Magyar Shakespeare-Tár*, Vol. XI (1919), pp. 180–231; Vol. XII (1922), pp. 23–53.

Kazinczy, Ferenc, 'Pályám emlékezete', in Kazinczy (1960), Vol. 1, pp. 1–209.

Kazinczy, Ferenc, *Kazinczy Ferenc válogatott művei*, 2 vols, eds Szauder, József and Szauder, Mária. Budapest: Szépirodalmi, 1960.

Kemény, Zsigmond, *Élet és irodalom*, ed. Tóth, Gyula. Budapest: Szépirodalmi, 1971.

Kermode, Frank, *Shakespeare, Spenser, Donne: Renaissance Essays*. London: Routledge & Kegan Paul, 1971.

Kermode, Frank, *Essays on Fiction 1971–1982*. London, Melbourne, Henley: Routledge & Kegan Paul, 1983.

Kéry, László, Országh, László and Szenczi, Miklós (eds), *Shakespeare-tanulmányok*. Budapest: Akadémiai, 1965.

Kiséry, András, 'Hamletizing the spirit of the nation: political uses of Kazinczy's 1790 translation', in Klein and Dávidházi (1996), pp. 11–35.

Kiss, József, 'Shakespear' Jubileuma', *Felső Magyar Országi Minerva*, Vol. II (1826) 2nd quarter.

Klaniczay, Tibor, *Pallas magyar ivadékai*. Budapest: Szépirodalmi, 1985.

Klein, Holger and Dávidházi, Péter (eds), *Shakespeare and Hungary*. Shakespeare Yearbook Vol. 7, Lewiston, Queenston, Lampeter: The Edwin Mellen Press, 1996.

Knight, G. Wilson, *Shakespeare and Religion: Essays of Forty Years*, London: Routledge & Kegan Paul, 1967.

Knight, G. Wilson, *Shakespearean Production: With Especial Reference to the Tragedies*. Washington, DC: University Press of America, 1981.

Leopold, Lajos, *A presztízs*. Budapest: Magvető, 1987.

Le Tourneur, Pierre, *Shakespeare. Traduit de l'anglois*, 20 vols, Paris: Vve Duchesne, etc. 1776–83.

Levin, Yu D. 1988 – Левин, Ю. Д., Шекспир и русская литература XIX. века. Ленин„ рад: Наука, 1988.

Levin, Yu. D., 'Shakespeare and Russian literature: nineteenth-century attitudes', *Oxford Slavonic Papers*, New Series Vol. XXII (1989), pp. 115–32.

Levine, Lawrence W., *Highbrow/Lowbrow: The Emergence of Cultural Hierarchy in America*. Cambridge, Mass. and London: Harvard University Press, 1988.

Lichtenberg, Georg Christoph, *Briefwechsel*, 3 vols, eds Joost, Ulrich and Schöne, Albrecht. München: Verlag C. H. Beck, 1983.

Lodge, David (ed.), *20th Century Literary Criticism: A Reader*. London: Longman, 1972.

Lukács, György, *Világirodalom*, 2 vols, ed. Fehér, Ferenc. Budapest: Gondolat, 1970.

Maller, Sándor, 'Shakespeare-örökségünk', in Maller and Ruttkay (1984), pp. 11–54.

Maller, Sándor and Ruttkay, Kálmán (eds), *Magyar Shakespeare-tükör: Esszék, tanulmányok, kritikák.* Budapest: Gondolat, 1984.

Malone, Edmond, *An Inquiry into the Authenticity of Certain Miscellaneous Papers and Legal Instruments.* New York: Augustus M. Kelley Publishers, 1970, (reprint of the London 1796 edition).

Marder, Louis, *His Exits and His Entrances: The Story of Shakespeare's Reputation.* Philadelphia and New York: J. B. Lippincott, 1963.

Marsden, Jean I. (ed.), *The Appropriation of Shakespeare: Post-Renaissance Reconstructions of the Works and the Myth.* New York, London, Toronto, Sydney, Tokyo, Singapore: Harvester Wheatsheaf, 1991.

Marsden, Jean I., *The Re-Imagined Text: Shakespeare, Adaptation, & Eighteenth-Century Literary Theory.* Lexington: The University Press of Kentucky, 1995.

Mészöly, Dezső, *Shakespeare új tükörben: Esszék és fordítások.* Budapest: Magvető, 1972.

Montagu, Elizabeth, *An Essay on the Writings and Genius of Shakespear, Compared with the Greek and French Dramatic Poets. With Some Remarks Upon the Misrepresentations of Mons. de Voltaire.* New York: Augustus M. Kelley Publishers, 1970.

Móricz, Zsigmond, *Móricz Zsigmond levelei*, 2 vols, ed. Csanak, Dóra F., intro. Vargha, Kálmán. Budapest: Akadémiai, 1963.

Móricz, Zsigmond, *Tanulmányok*, 3 vols, eds Szabó, Ferenc and Nagy, Péter. Budapest: Szépirodalmi, 1978–84.

Muir, Kenneth, *The Singularity of Shakespeare and Other Essays.* Liverpool: Barnes & Noble, 1977.

Nagy, Lajos, *Író, könyv, olvasó*, 2 vols, ed. Gordon, Etel. Budapest: Szépirodalmi, 1959.

Németh, László, *Európai utas: Tanulmányok.* Budapest: Magvető és Szépirodalmi, 1973.

Paley, William, *The Works of William Paley, D. D. with a life, by Alexander Chalmers, esq.*, 5 vols. London: F. C. & J. Rivington, and others, 1819.

Péczeli, József, [Untitled article], *Magyar Musa*, Vol. II, 14 July 1787.

Péczeli, József (trans. and intro.), *Henriás.* 2nd edn. Győr: Strejbig Jósef, 1792.

Péterfy, Jenő, *Péterfy Jenő válogatott művei*, ed. Sőtér, István. Budapest: Szépirodalmi, 1983.

Petersen, Richard S., *Imitation and Praise in the Poems of Ben Jonson.* New Haven, Conn. and London: Yale University Press, 1981.

Petőfi, Sándor, 'III. Richárd király', *Életképek*, Vol. IV, 20 February 1847.

Petőfi, Sándor, *Petőfi az egykorú sajtóban és egyéb nyomtatott forrásokban.* (*Petőfi-adattár*, vol. 1), ed. Kiss, József. Budapest: Akadémiai, 1987.

Pocock, J. G. A., *Virtue, Commerce, and History: Essays on Political Thought and History, Chiefly in the Eighteenth Century.* Cambridge: Cambridge University Press, 1985

Pósa, Péter, *Shakespeare-kultusz hazánkban a századfordulótól Trianonig (1900–1920).* Debrecen: Nagy K., 1942.

Price, Lawrence Marsden, *The Reception of English Literature in Germany.* Berkeley: University of California Press, 1932.

Prickett, Stephen, *Romanticism and Religion: The Tradition of Coleridge and*

Wordsworth in the Victorian Church. Cambridge, New York, Melbourne: Cambridge University Press, 1976.

Radnai, Rezső, *Aesthetikai törekvések Magyarországon 1772–1817*. Budapest: Franklin, 1889.

Rahv, Philip, *Essays on Literature and Politics 1932–1972*, eds Porter, Arabel J. and Dvosin, Andrew J. Boston: Houghton Mifflin, 1978.

Raleigh, Walter, *Shakespeare*. London: Macmillan, 1965.

Richards, I. A., *Practical Criticism: A Study of Literary Judgment*. London and Henley: Routledge & Kegan Paul, 1976.

Ricks, Christopher (ed.), *Selected Criticism of Matthew Arnold*. New York, Scarborough (Ontario), London: The New American Library, 1972.

Riedl, Frigyes, *Shakespeare és a magyar irodalom*, Budapest: Lampel, 1916.

Ritson, Joseph, *Remarks, Critical and Illustrative, on the Text and Notes of the last Edition of Shakespeare*. London: J. Johnson, 1783.

Rónay, Jácint, *Napló-töredék. Hetven év reményei és csalódásai*. N. d., n. p.

Rümelin, Gustav, *Shakespearestudien*. Stuttgart: Verlag der J. G. Cotta'schen Buchhandlung, 1866.

Ruthven, K. K., *Myth*. London: Methuen, 1976.

Salamon, Ferenc, *Irodalmi tanulmányok*, 2 vols. Budapest: Franklin-Társulat, 1889.

Salamon, Ferenc, *Dramaturgiai dolgozatok*, 2 vols. Budapest: Franklin-Társulat, 1907.

Schabert, Ina (ed.), *Shakespeare-Handbuch: Die Zeit, der Mensch, das Werk, die Nachwelt*. Stuttgart: Alfred Kröner Verlag, 1978.

Schelling, Friedrich Wilhelm Joseph, *Philosophie der Mythologie*. Stuttgart and Augsburg: Cotta, 1857.

Schlegel, Friedrich, *Friedrich Schlegel 1794–1802: Seine Prosaischen Jugendschriften*, 2 vols, ed. Minor, J. Wien: C. Konegen, 1906.

Schoenbaum, Samuel, *Shakespeare's Lives*, (new edition). Oxford: Clarendon Press, 1991.

Seary, Peter, *Lewis Theobald and the Editing of Shakespeare*. Oxford: Clarendon Press, 1990.

Shakespeare, William, *Shakespeare's garland, being a collection of new songs, ballads, roundelays, cetches, glees, comic serenatas, etc., performed at the jubilee at Stratford upon Avon*. Dublin: John Mitchell, 1769.

Shakespeare, William, *A Descriptive Account of the Late Gala Festival, at Stratford-upon-Avon, by Commemoration of The Natal Day of Shakespeare; the King's Adopted Birthday, and The Festival of St. George, On the 23rd, 24th, and 25th Days of April, 1827. Transcribed from the notes of a gentleman connected with the newspaper press*. Stratford-upon-Avon: R. Lapworth, 1827.

Shakespeare, William, *A Concise Account of Garrick's Jubilee, held at Stratford-upon-Avon, in honour of Shakespeare, In 1769. And of the Commemorative Festivals In 1827 and 1830*. Stratford-upon-Avon: J. Ward. 1830.

Shakespeare, William, *The Official Programme of The Tercentenary Festival of the Birth of Shakespeare, To be held at Stratford-upon-Avon*. London: Cassell, Petter, & Galpin, 1864.

Simson, Otto von, *The Gothic Cathedral: Origins of Gothic Architecture and the Medieval Concept of Order*, New York: Harper, 1967.

Smidt, Kristian, *Unconformities in Shakespeare's History Plays*. London: Macmillan, 1982.

Smidt, Kristian, *Unconformities in Shakespeare's Early Comedies*. London: Macmillan, 1986.

Smidt, Kristian, *Unconformities in Shakespeare's Tragedies*. London: Macmillan, 1989.

Smidt, Kristian, *Unconformities in Shakespeare's Later Comedies*. London: Macmillan, 1993.

Smith, David Nicol, *Shakespeare in the Eighteenth Century*. Oxford: Clarendon Press, 1928.

Solt, Andor, 'A magyar Shakespeare-kép kialakulása a felvilágosodás és a romantika korában', in Kéry, Országh and Szenczi (eds) (1965), pp. 9–25.

Sőtér, István, *Nemzet és haladás*. Budapest: Akadémiai, 1963.

Spencer, T. J. B. (ed.), *Shakespeare: A Celebration 1564–1964*. Harmondsworth: Penguin Books, 1964.

Spingarn, J. E. (ed.), *Critical Essays of the Seventeenth Century, Vol. 1*. Bloomington: Indiana University Press, 1957.

Stark, Rodney and Bainbridge, William Sims, *The Future of Religion: Secularization, Revival and Cult Formation*. Berkeley, Los Angeles, London: University of California Press, 1985.

Stochholm, Johanne M., *Garrick's Folly: The Shakespeare Jubilee of 1769 at Stratford and Drury Lane*. London: Methuen, 1964.

Szabó, Magda, *Hullámok kergetése: Utijegyzetek*. Budapest: Szépirodalmi, 1965.

Szemere, Bertalan, *Utazás külföldön*, 2 vols, 2nd edn. Pest: Geibel, 1845.

Szemere, Pál, *Szemerei Szemere Pál munkái*, 3 vols, ed. Szvorényi, József. Budapest, 1890.

Szerdahely, György Alajos, *Poesis Dramatica ad Aestheticam seu Doctrinam Boni Gustus Conformata*. Buda: Typis Universitatis, 1784.

Szigethy, Gábor, *Shakespeare-t olvasó Petőfi*. Budapest: Magvető, 1979.

Taylor, Edward, *Cursory Remarks on Tragedy, on Shakespear and on certain French and Italian Poets, principally Tragedians*. London: W. Owen, 1774.

Taylor, Gary, *Reinventing Shakespeare: A Cultural History, From the Restoration to the Present*. New York: Weidenfeld & Nicolson, 1989.

Theobald, Lewis, *Shakespeare Restored: or, a Specimen of the Many Errors, As well Committed, as Unamended, by Mr. Pope in his late Edition of this Poet*. New York: Augustus M. Kelley Publishers, 1970.

Toldy, Ferenc, *A magyar nemzeti irodalom története a legrégibb időktől a jelenkorig rövid előadásban*, 2 vols. Pest: Athenaeum, 1872–3.

Toldy, Ferenc, *Toldy Ferenc kritikai berke. Első kötet. 1826–1836*. Budapest: Ráth Mór, 1874.

Turner, Victor, *Dramas, Fields, and Metaphors: Symbolic Action in Human Society*. Ithaca, NY and London: Cornell University Press, 1974.

Turner, Victor and Turner, Edith, *Image and Pilgrimage in Christian Culture. Anthropological Perspectives*. New York: Columbia University Press, 1978.

Turner, Victor, *The Ritual Process: Structure and Anti-Structure*. Ithaca, NY: Cornell University Press, 1985 (first published 1969).

Vachott, Sándor, Költeményei. Pest: Beimel, n.d. [1847].

Vahot, Imre (ed.), *Magyar Thalia: Játékszini almanach 1853-ra*. Pest: Müller, 1852.

Vajda, János, *Vajda János összes művei, Vol. 6, Politikai röpiratok*, ed. Miklóssy, János. Budapest: Akadémiai, 1970.

Várdai, Béla, 'Egressy Gábor mint Shakespeare-színész', *Magyar Shakespeare-Tár*, Vol. II, No. 3 (1909).

Vickers, Brian (ed.), *Shakespeare: The Critical Heritage*, 6 vols. London, Henley, Boston: Routledge & Kegan Paul, 1974–9.

Victor, Benjamin, *The History of the Theatres of London and Dublin, From the Year 1730 to the present Time*, 3 vols. London: T. Davies, 1761–71.

Walpole, Horace, *The Castle of Otranto*. New York: Holt, Rinehart & Winston, 1963.

Weber, Max, *The Sociology of Religion*, trans. Fischoff, Ephraim, intro. Parsons, Talcott. Boston: Beacon Press, 1964.

Wellek, René, *A History of Modern Criticism: 1750–1950*, 8 vols., New Haven, Conn. and London: Yale University Press, 1955–91.

Wellek, René, *Essays on Czech Literature*. The Hague: Mouton, 1963.

Wellek, René and Warren, Austin, *Theory of Literature*. London: Jonathan Cape, 1954.

Wesselényi, Báró Miklós, *Útinaplója 1821–1822*. Cluj-Kolozsvár: Concordia, 1925.

Wheler, Robert, *History and Antiquities of Stratford-upon-Avon*. Stratford-upon-Avon: J. Ward, [1806].

Wheler, Robert, *A Guide to Stratford-upon-Avon*. Stratford-upon-Avon: J. Ward, 1814.

Whitehead, Alfred North, *Dialogues of Alfred North Whitehead: As Recorded By Lucien Price*. Boston: Little, Brown, 1954.

Willems, Michèle, *La genèse du mythe Shakespearien 1660–1780*. Paris: Presses Universitaires de France, 1979.

Wilson, John (ed.), *Shakespeareana: Catalogue of all the books, pamphlets, etc. relating to Shakespeare*. London, 1827.

Wittgenstein, Ludwig, *Philosophische Untersuchungen (Philosophical Investigations)*, trans. Anscombe, G. E. M. Oxford: Blackwell, 1953.

Wittgenstein, Ludwig, *Philosophical Occasions 1912–1951*, eds Klagge, James C. and Nordmann, Alfred. Indianapolis and Cambridge: Hackett, 1993.

Wordsworth, Charles, *Shakespeare's Knowledge and Use of the Bible: With Appendix Containing Additional Illustration and Tercentenary Sermon Preached at Stratford-on-Avon*. London: Spottiswoode, 1864.

Zerffi, Gusztáv, 'Egressy mint III. Richard', *Honderű*, Vol. V (1847), first period, p. 258.

Index